CREATING
GLAMOROUS
JEWELRY

with

SWAROVSKI ELEMENTS

◆

Dedication
To all those beautiful West Coast muses
who kept me company while I was creating this book.

Creative Publishing international

Copyright © 2010 Creative Publishing international, Inc.

First published in the United States of America by
Creative Publishing international, Inc., a member of
Quayside Publishing Group
400 First Avenue North
Suite 300
Minneapolis, MN 55401
1-800-328-3895
www.creativepub.com
Visit www.Craftside.Typepad.com for a behind-the-scenes peek at our crafty world!

ISBN-13: 978-1-58923-541-0
ISBN-10: 1-58923-541-X

10 9 8 7 6 5 4 3 2 1

Library of Congress Cataloging-in-Publication Data available

Technical Editor: Judith Durant
Copy Editor: Terri Autieri
Proofreader: Karen Levy
Book Design: Sandra Salamony
Cover Design: Sandra Salamony
Illustrations: Julia Pretl
Photographs: Luciana Pampalone, unless otherwise indicated
Fashion Styling: Robin Zachary
Clothing Supplier: Kleinfeld Manhattan

Printed in China

CREATING
GLAMOROUS
JEWELRY

with

SWAROVSKI ELEMENTS

*Classic Hollywood Designs
with Crystal Beads and Stones*

JEAN CAMPBELL

Contents

Introduction

...The designer swept into her atelier, thrust open the drawers of her extensive stash, and settled in to inspect her collection of sparkling beads. She waved her hands over the trays and uttered, "Now which of you will star in the most glamorous designs of all?" The beads called back, like chirpy hopefuls at a Hollywood studio casting call: "Me! Pick me!" But it was the quietly glistening crystals that caught the artist's eye today. "These," she thought, "will be the leading ladies in my latest and greatest production...."

STEP AWAY FROM THE COMPUTER, set down your cell phone, and leave the dirty dishes for later. Come with me as we travel back in time, placing ourselves firmly within the glamour and glitz of Old Hollywood. Imagine streamlined cars zooming over the twisted canyon roads into the valley, dark palm trees against a beautiful sunset, the elegant fabric and cut of a torch singer's dress, mile-high stiletto heels, the clinking of martini glasses, and the swooning sounds of a big band. Let yourself go, feel the romantic intrigue of 1930 to 1960 Hollywood, and allow the atmosphere to slake your inner diva.

I've set the scene for our time travel with studio photographs of some of the most captivating women that have ever graced the silver screen. Marilyn. Elizabeth.

Sophia. See? You know exactly who I'm talking about. In each photo I've chosen, the superstar is wearing a piece of jewelry that I've used as inspiration to create my own design. In the Hollywood tradition, most of these photos were done in soft focus to romanticize the woman within it. But slightly blurring the face means the jewelry is slightly blurred, too. Rather than lament this, I took this as a gift, because it left so much to my imagination. To further the mystery, I made no attempt to find crisp photos of the original pieces or to find out who the original jewelry designers were. Instead, I used the subtle visual suggestion of the piece and paired it with the overall spirit of the woman wearing it to guide me in creating the resulting twenty pieces— earrings, bracelets, and necklaces all worthy of the red carpet.

In the spirit of Hollywood elegance, I've featured crystals in each and every design. Why crystals? As most of you know, crystals make jewelry dance, producing a razzle-dazzle light show unlike any other material. The effect is oh, so Hollywood! I also challenged myself to use crystal shapes that we beaders don't see every day. We see round and bicone beads all the time, but there are so many other shape choices: polygons, navettes, triangles, chatons. The list goes on and on. Opening up our stashes to these other shapes can only help us open up with our designs, too.

If you know your way around a bead shop and have a knack for needle and thread, you'll be able to tackle the projects in this book by following the step-by-step instructions and clear illustrations. I've used standard beadweaving techniques like peyote stitch, right-angle weave, and square stitch to construct the pieces, plus there's a little wirework mixed in, too. Not familiar with, or maybe a little rusty with, these techniques? Just check out the Basics section near the end of the book, and I think you'll get up to speed quite quickly.

I hope you enjoy the romance and elegance of these projects as much as I did while designing them. After you finish your first piece, you'll want to make another. And before you know it, you'll have a whole jewelry box full of glamorous baubles to proudly wear as you star in your own real-life drama.

Swarovski's Early Influence on Haute Couture

WIKIMEDIA COMMONS

Daniel Swarovski I in his laboratory.

SWAROVSKI, the leading provider of high-quality crystals to the fashion industry, had its beginnings in the late 1800s in a small mountain village near the city of Gablonz in Northern Bohemia. There, Daniel Swarovski I (1862–1956) was a crystal-cutting apprentice to his father. He continued to look for ways to innovate the technology, and, by 1892, he had invented the first electrical crystal-cutting device. In 1895, Daniel moved to the village of Wattens, Tyrol, in Austria, with his newly invented machine. Using the machine, his craftsmen could create the most crisp, sparkling crystal cuts the world had ever seen.

Swarovski's revolutionary inventions in crystal-cutting technology not only made it possible for everyday women to afford sparkling costume jewelry that resembled precious stones, but it also revealed a realm of possibilities to high-fashion designers looking to add luxury and glitz to their collections. This was perfect timing for Swarovski as the lust-for-opulence Jazz Age of the 1920s and 1930s was just being ushered in, and crystals became an integral ingredient in fashion. During this time, Swarovski worked closely with Cristóbal Balenciaga, Coco Chanel, and Elsa Schiaparelli, all of whom used crystals to design glittering costumes for entertainers such as France's Mistinguette (Jeanne Borgeois) and America's Josephine Baker. Swarovski innovations, such as crystal trimmings that could be easily sewn right onto fabric, enabled these designers to add thousands of crystals to a dress. The excess dazzle and light created a shimmery aura around the performers, providing perhaps the first "superstar" looks.

Fashion icons around the world caught on to this larger-than-life look, and, by the mid-1950s, Hollywood starlets like those featured in this book counted on crystals not only to dazzle the

Examples of Swarovski's Aurora Borealis crystal finish inspired by Christian Dior.

Coco Chanel (1883–1971), a French fashion icon who worked closely with Swarovski for decades, embraced the use of crystals to enhance her designs. This photograph of the designer was taken in about 1930.

contents of their closets but also to wear as a sensible form of jewelry. No need to pull the multicarat diamonds out of the vault for red carpet soirees when you could wear a crystal version that was just as attention getting. Chanel embraced this concept with gusto, working with jewelry designers like Robert Goossens to make magnificent costume jewelry. The use of crystals in these sophisticated pieces aligned perfectly with Chanel's first fashion tenet—that a woman should always look fabulous—but also underscored her philosophy that tasteful fashion was possible without being too precious or risking wearability.

Another designer who had strong ties with Swarovski's history was Frenchman Christian Dior (1905–1957). His voluptuous, flared designs brought a curvy, excessive femininity back to fashion after the somewhat severe silhouettes of World War II. In his desire to bring the richness of Versailles back to fashion, Dior collaborated with Manfred Swarovski, grandson of the founder, to ask for none other than the Northern Lights. Swarovski responded with a special coating called Aurora Borealis—a multicolor

finish that lends truly dazzling sparkle. The "AB" finish took off like wildfire for designers who created for stage, screen, and runway, and its popularity is just as strong today.

Swarovski continues to work closely with haute couture houses. Crystal-encrusted designs from houses like Yves Saint Laurent, Armani, Versace, Gucci, Prada, Alexander McQueen, and Viktor and Rolf grace the red carpet, catwalk, and jewelry shop windows. Swarovski has also collaborated on movies such as *Moulin Rouge, Ocean's Twelve, NINE, Sex and the City, James Bond,* and more. Today, Swarovski provides the same affordable glitz and glamour that made the material as popular 100 years ago.

Chanel brooch featuring semiprecious stones and Swarovski crystal stone settings, c. 1930.

Balenciaga necklace with Swarovski crystal navettes and pearls, c. 1960.

Audrey

*...The nymph swept her shining locks into an elegant updo,
all the better to show off her wild and brilliant bezelled rivoli earrings.
But what's this? A cigarette? Yes, even spirits of nature need a vice or two....*

PHOTO BY BUD FRAKER, COURTESY OF MPTVIMAGES.COM.

Audrey Hepburn in Breakfast at Tiffany's, *1961.*

Belgium native **Audrey Hepburn** (1929–1993) had a London-based modeling career before being spotted by film producers. In Hollywood, she was usually cast as the youthful, classy ingénue opposite much older leading men. Her first big success was *Roman Holiday* (1953), for which she received an Academy Award for best actress.

Other notable films include *Sabrina* (1954), *Funny Face* (1957), *Love in the Afternoon* (1957), *Breakfast at Tiffany's* (1961), and *My Fair Lady* (1964). Hepburn mostly retired from her film career in her late thirties and acted as an ambassador for UNICEF until the end of her life.

FINISHED LENGTH:
2" (5.1 cm)

TECHNIQUES:
peyote stitch, fringe

MATERIALS AND TOOLS

1 gram silver size 11° seed beads **(A)**

1 gram silver size 15° seed beads **(B)**

1 gram navy iris size 11° seed beads **(C)**

2 Montana blue 14mm foiled
crystal rivolis (#1122)

74 khaki 3mm crystal round beads
(#5000)

36 Montana blue 3mm crystal
round beads (#5000)

2 silver 8mm flat-face earring posts with
wide earring backings

smoke 6 lb (2.7 kg) braided
beading thread

beading wax

clear jeweler's adhesive

scissors

size 12 beading needle

thread burner

1) **DISK.** Use tight thread tension and A to circular peyote
stitch a disk, forming the bezel's back:

Round 1: Place a needle at the end of 1' (30.5 cm) of
doubled and waxed thread. Leaving a 1" (2.5 cm) tail, pick
up six A, and tie a knot to form a tight circle. Pass through
the beads again to pull the knot and tail into the beads.

Round 2: Pick up two A, skip one A from Round 1, and pass
through the next A; repeat around to add a total of six A.
Step up for the next round by passing through the first A
added in this round (*fig. 1*).

Round 3: Pick up one A, pass through the next A from
Round 2, and then pick up two A and pass through the
following A from Round 2; repeat around to add a total of
nine A (*fig. 2, black thread path*). Step up through the first A
added in this round.

Round 4: Pick up one A and pass through the next A of
Round 3; repeat around to add a total of nine A (*fig. 2,
green thread path*). Step up through the first bead added in
this round.

Round 5: Pick up two A and pass through the next A from
Round 4; repeat around to add a total of eighteen A (*fig. 2,
blue thread path*). Step up through the first and second A
added in this round.

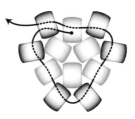

Figure 1. Disk, Round 2.

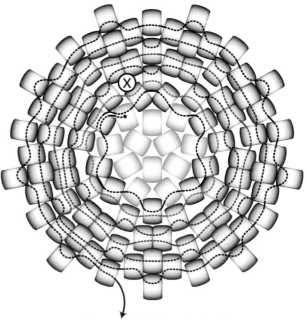

Figure 2. Disk, Rounds 3 to 8.

Round 6: Pick up one A and pass through the next two A from Round 5; repeat around to add a total of nine A *(fig. 2, pink thread path)*. Step up through the first A added in this round.

Round 7: Pick up three A and pass through the next A from Round 6; repeat around to add a total of twenty-seven A *(fig. 2, brown thread path)*. Step up through the first three A added in this round.

Round 8: Pick up one A and pass through the next A from Round 7; then pick up one A, skip one A from Round 7, and pass through the next one; repeat around to add a total of eighteen A *(fig. 2, red thread path)*. Secure the thread and trim.

Post: Place a bit of glue on the back of the earring post finding. Slide the post through the earring back beadwork between Rounds 2 and 3 (marked with an X in fig. 2), gently pressing the glue to the beadwork without allowing the glue to ooze through to the other side or get into bead holes. Set aside to dry thoroughly.

2) **RING.** Use very tight tension and seed beads to circular peyote stitch a flat ring, forming the bezel's front:

Rounds 1 and 2: Use 6' (1.8 m) of waxed single thread to pick up thirty-six A, leaving a 1" (2.5 cm) tail. Tie the beads into a tight circle, and pass through them again to hide the knot and tail.

Round 3: Work circular peyote stitch using one A in each stitch for a total of eighteen A. Weave through the beads to exit an A in Round 1.

Rounds 4 and 5: Work circular peyote stitch using one B in each stitch for a total of eighteen B. Step up by passing through the first B added, and then work another round using one B in each stitch. Weave through the beadwork to exit an A in Round 3 *(fig. 3)*.

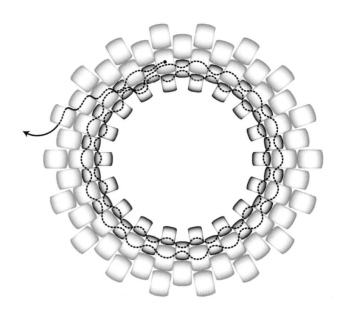

Figure 3. Ring, Rounds 4 and 5.

Zip: Pair the bezel's ring and disk so that the edge beads interlock like a zipper. Use the working thread of the ring to pass through the closest edge bead of the disk and then through the closest edge bead of the ring, zipping the edges together. After the bezel is zipped halfway, slip a rivoli between the layers so that the stone's colored side shows through the ring. Continue zipping the edges to completely encase the rivoli. Weave through the beads to exit a B in Round 5 *(fig. 4)*.

Round 6: Pick up one C and pass through the next two B in Round 5, pulling very tight to form a decrease; repeat around to add a total of nine B. **Note:** This round is done last in order to pull the rivoli tightly into place, so be sure to use tight thread tension. Pull the thread end toward the beadwork to double the working thread; rewax it. Weave through the beadwork to exit an A in the ring's Round 2 *(fig. 5)*.

3) **FRINGE.** Add circles and strands of fringe to the bezel:

Inner circle: Pick up one B, one khaki 3mm crystal, and one C; pass back through the crystal, B, and the next A in ring Round 2. Pull tightly to firmly seat the fringe. Repeat around to add a total of eighteen fringes. Exit from an A in ring Round 3 *(fig. 6)*.

Outer circle: Pick up one A, one blue 3mm crystal, and one C; pass back through the crystal, A, and the next A in ring Round 3. Pull tightly to firmly seat the fringe. Repeat around to add a total of eighteen fringes.

Strands: Exit from the A in disk Round 8 as shown in figure 7. To form the first fringe, pick up one B, one khaki 3mm crystal, one C, one khaki 3mm crystal, one C, one khaki 3mm crystal, and one C. Pass back through the last crystal/C/crystal/C/crystal added. Pick up one B, and pass through the next A in disk Round 8, pulling firmly to seat the fringe.

Continue forming fringe in this way using this bead sequence:

Fringe 2: one B, one khaki crystal, (one C and one khaki crystal) three times, and one C; pass back through the crystals and C, and pick up one B.

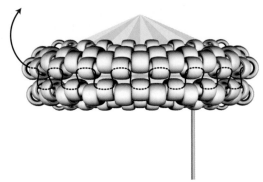

Figure 4. Zipping the bezel.

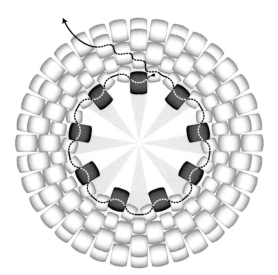

Figure 5. Ring, Round 6.

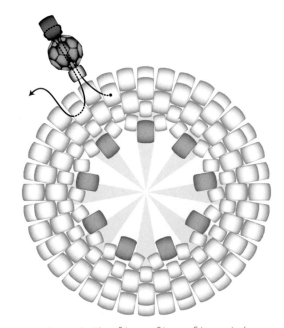

Figure 6. First fringe of inner fringe circle.

Fringe 3: one B, one khaki crystal, (one C and one khaki crystal) four times, and one C; pass back through the crystals and C, and pick up one B.

Fringes 4 and 5: Repeat Fringes 2 and 1 *(fig. 7)*.

Secure the thread and trim.

Repeat all steps to form the second earring.

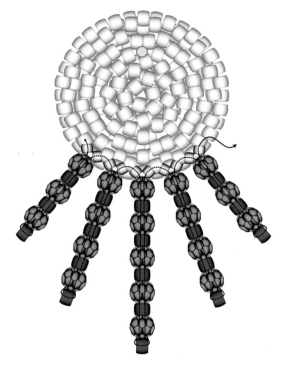

Figure 7. Fringe strands.

Variations

- Make a plain earring by simply forgoing the fringe and securing the thread after Step 2.

- Achieve a double-drop earring by working one bezelled rivoli with an earring post and another without. After you've completed Step 2, securely stitch the two bezels together at their edges. Add fringe as desired or leave plain for a very modern look.

- Instead of including the long, straight fringe, why not try adding a single drop, such as a teardrop or briolette?

#5500
Teardrop bead

#6010
Briolette

Greta

*...The music was as fanciful and delicate as her Bohemian-influenced earrings
but so beautiful and haunting that she just couldn't
get it out of her head....*

Greta Garbo in Romance, *1930.*

Swedish-born film superstar **Greta Garbo** (1905–1990) was one of the few actresses of Hollywood's Golden Age who made a successful transition from silent movies to "talkies." She was nominated for Academy Awards for best actress for a number of films, including *Anna Christie* (1930), *Romance* (1930), *Camille* (1936), and *Ninotchka* (1939). One of the most enigmatic figures in Hollywood, Garbo had many affairs with both men and women but rigorously protected her privacy, spurning any communication with her fans. Garbo is often linked with her line in the film *Grand Hotel* (1932), "I want to be alone."

FINISHED LENGTH:
2 ¹/₂" (6.4 cm)

TECHNIQUES: right-angle weave, peyote stitch, square stitch, fringe

MATERIALS AND TOOLS

4 grams gold-lined clear size 15° cylinder beads **(A)**

6 gold-lined clear size 11° cylinder beads **(B)**

6 topaz 3mm crystal round beads (#5000)

2 topaz 6mm crystal round beads (#5000)

4 topaz 9 x 6mm crystal teardrop beads (#5500)

4 crystal 6mm foiled crystal triangular fancy stones (#4722)

2 crystal foiled 12mm (SS50) foiled crystal round chaton stones (#1028)

2 gold-filled ear wires

crystal 6 lb (2.7 kg) braided beading thread

scissors

size 12 beading needle

thread burner

chain-nose pliers

1) **TRIANGLE BEZELS.** Use tight thread tension and size 15°s to peyote stitch bezels around a triangular stone:

Rounds 1 and 2: Place a needle on the end of 2' (61 cm) of thread. Leaving a 6" (15.2 cm) tail, pick up five A, pass back through the second-to-last A strung, and pull tightly; holding tightly onto the tail to maintain tension, repeat twice. Pass through the first five A added in this round to form a triangle *(fig. 1)*.

Round 3: Pick up one A, skip one A from Round 2, and pass through the next A; repeat around to add a total of nine A. Step up for the next round by exiting through the last bead exited in Round 2 *(fig. 2)*.

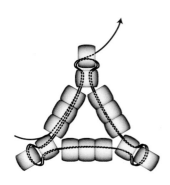

Figure 1. Triangle bezel, Rounds 1 and 2.

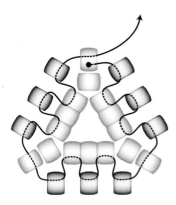

Figure 2. Triangle bezel, Round 3.

Round 4: Pick up one A and pass through the next A of Round 2 (the bead will sit between a Round 2 and a Round 3 bead). Pick up one A, and pass through the next A from Round 3; repeat once. Pick up one A, and pass through the corner A from Round 2. Repeat from the beginning of this round to add four A to each side of the triangle for a total of twelve A. Step up through the first bead added in this round (fig. 3).

Round 5: Pick up one A and pass through the next A from Round 4; repeat around to add a total of twelve A. Step up through the first bead added in this round.

Round 6: Pick up one A and pass through the next A from Round 5; repeat once. Pick up one A, skip the next A (a corner) added in Round 5, pass through the next A, and pull very tightly so that the beadwork cups. Repeat once from the beginning of this round. Place one triangle stone into the beadwork face-up. Hold the stone in place while you pick up one A and pass through the next A from Round 5; repeat once. Pick up one A, skip the next corner A added in Round 5, and pass through the next A from Round 5 (fig. 4).

Repeat the thread path one or more times to tighten and secure the stone in place. **Note:** It is very important to pull the thread very tightly here or your bezel won't hold the stone.

Loop: Exit from a corner A from Round 5. Pick up five A and pass through the last Round 5 A exited; repeat the thread path several times to reinforce. Weave through the beads to exit from the final A stitched in Round 4 on the opposite edge of the triangle (near the corner). Don't trim the thread; set the bezeled triangle aside.

Repeat this entire step to form a second bezeled triangle, this time creating the loop with three B. For this triangle, secure the thread and trim.

2) **TRIANGLE COMPONENT.** Use the working thread of the first bezeled triangle to pick up one A, pass through the mirror A on the second triangle (making sure both stones are face-up and the two loops are opposite), pass back through the A just added, and through the last A exited on the first triangle. Weave through the Round 4 edge beads to exit the center A. Pick up one 3mm bead, pass through the mirror A on the second triangle, pass back through the 3mm bead just added, and through the last A exited on the first triangle. Weave through the Round 4 edge beads to exit the final A, and pick up one A; pass through the mirror A on the second triangle, pass back through the A just added and through the last A exited on the first triangle (fig. 5).

Secure the thread and trim. Set the component aside.

Figure 3. Triangle bezel, Round 4.

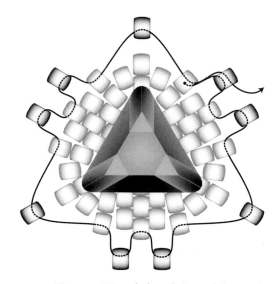

Figure 4. Triangle bezel, Round 6.

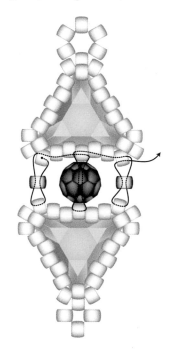

Figure 5. Assembling the triangular component.

3) **ROUND BEZEL.** Use tight thread tension and size 15°s to peyote stitch a bezel around a round stone:

Round 1: Place a needle on the end of 2' (61 cm) of thread. Use A to work a right-angle weave strip seventeen units long. Fold the strip in half. Exiting up through the end bead of the final unit, pick up one A, and pass down through the end A of the first unit. Pick up one A, and pass up through the end A of the final unit, turning the strip into a ring. Repeat the thread path to reinforce. Exit from an edge bead *(fig. 6)*.

Rounds 2 and 3: Pick up one A and pass through the next edge A from Round 1; repeat around to add a total of eighteen beads. Step up for the next round by passing through the first bead added in this round. Repeat to add a third round.

Round 4: Pick up one A and pass through the next two A in Round 3; repeat around to add a total of nine beads. Step up for the next round by passing through the first bead added in this round.

Rounds 5 and 6: Pick up one A and pass through the next A in Round 4; repeat around to add a total of nine beads, using very tight tension. Step up through the first bead added in the round. Repeat to add a sixth round. Weave through the last rounds again to tighten and cup the beadwork. Weave through the beads to exit from an A on the other edge of Round 1 *(fig. 7)*.

Round 7: Place a 12mm crystal round chaton in the bezel. Pick up one A, and pass through the next edge A; repeat around to add a total of eighteen beads. Step up for the next round by passing through the first bead added in this round.

Round 8: Repeat Round 4. Secure the thread and trim. Set the bezelled round aside.

4) **CENTER.** Use size 15°s to add teardrops and rounds to the center of the earring:

Teardrop beads: Start a new 1' (30.5 cm) thread that exits up through the right-side B at the bottom of the triangle component. Pick up one A, and square-stitch it to the last B exited; exit the A. Pick up eleven A and one teardrop from the wide end to the narrow end. Pass through the A square-stitched to the B and back through the teardrop just added *(fig. 8)*.

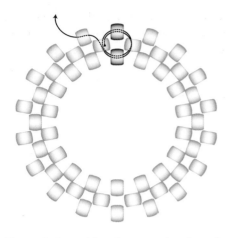

Figure 6. Round bezel, connecting Round 1.

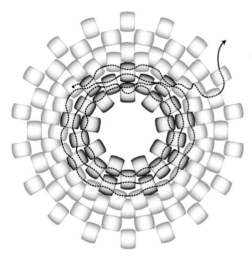

Figure 7. Round bezel, Rounds 4 to 6.

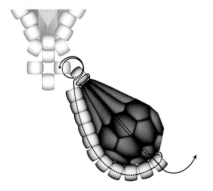

Figure 8. Center, outlining the lower side of the right teardrop.

Pick up eleven A; pass through the A square-stitched to the B and the next eleven A surrounding the teardrop. Pick up one A, one 3mm bead, and one A; skip the final A, and pass back through the 3mm bead and first A to form a fringe; continue through the second set of eleven A to tightly encircle the teardrop with beads *(fig. 9)*.

Weave through beads at the bottom of the triangle component to add a second teardrop to the left-side B. Exit up through the sixth inside A from the bottom fringe of the left teardrop.

Round bead: Pick up two A, one 6mm bead, and six A; pass up through the last A exited on the teardrop, the nearest two A, and down through the 6mm bead. Pick up six A; pass up through the sixth inside A from the bottom fringe of the right teardrop. Weave through the beads to exit two A at the top of the 6mm bead *(fig. 10)*.

Pick up one A and pass through the beads along the edge of the round to exit six A at the bottom of the round bead. Pick up one A and pass through the bead along the other edge of the round bead. Continue weaving through the edge beads to exit from the last A added at the bottom of the round bead.

Assembly: Pick up one A and pass through an A at the edge of Round 1 on the round bezel, near the front. Pick up one A and pass through the last A exited at the bottom of the round bead *(fig. 11)*.

Repeat the thread path to reinforce. Secure the thread and trim. Connect an ear wire to the top loop of the earring.

Repeat all steps to form the second earring.

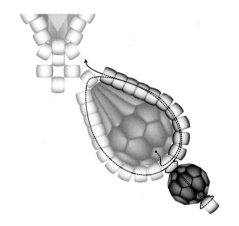

Figure 9. Center, outlining the upper side of the right teardrop.

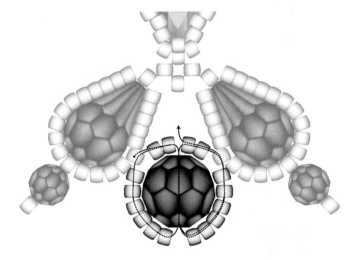

Figure 10. Center, adding the center round bead.

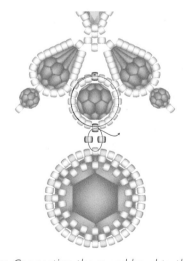

Figure 11. Connecting the round bezel to the center.

Ann

*...Sunday mornings were meant for relaxing, but so were Tuesday mornings, for that matter.
A nice cup of coffee, a bonbon or two, hair up in a jeweled turban,
and a glamorous crystal flower necklace. That's how every day should begin....*

Ann Sheridan, 1940s.

Ann Sheridan (1915–1967) was hurtled to Hollywood fame when she won a beauty contest that included a screen test for Paramount Pictures. She was nicknamed the "Oomph Girl" for her earthy sexiness and was a favorite pinup girl along with Betty Grable during World War II. She appeared in dozens of films, including *Torrid Zone* (1940), *They Drive by Night* (1940), and *I Was a Male War Bride* (1949). She also starred in the television soap opera *Another World* (1964) and *Pistols 'n' Petticoats* (1966).

FINISHED LENGTH:
16" (40.6 cm)

TECHNIQUES: fringe, ladder stitch, herringbone stitch, picot edging

MATERIALS AND TOOLS

1 gram shiny black size 11° seed beads **(A)**

10 grams permanent galvanized silver size 11° seed beads **(B)**

16 aquamarine 13 x 6.5mm crystal briolettes (#6010)

24 Montana AB 2X 4mm crystal bicone beads (#5301)

176 air blue opal 2mm crystal round beads (#5000)

1 silver 22mm beading dome and backing

1 silver 18mm dress clasp

crystal and smoke 6 lb (2.7 kg) braided beading thread

scissors

size 11 beading needle

beading wax

thread burner

chain-nose pliers

white glue

1) **FLOWER.** Stitch beaded fringe to the dome to form a flower:

Petals: Slide a needle to the center of 8' (2.4 m) of thread. Double the thread, wax it thoroughly, and tie the ends into a strong overhand knot. Sew up through an edge hole in the dome and down through the nearest edge hole; pass through the thread loop between the working thread and the knot and pull tightly to secure the thread to the finding. Pass up through the nearest edge hole.

Pick up one A, one briolette, and one A; pass down through the last hole exited and up through the next edge hole, pulling tightly so that the beads sit against the top edge of the dome; repeat to add eight briolettes around the dome's edge. Exit through the first briolette added *(fig. 1)*.

Pick up one A, one briolette, and one A; pass through the next briolette already placed at the edge of the dome; repeat around to add eight briolettes. Repeat the thread path to reinforce. Exit up through a non-edge hole in the dome *(fig. 2)*.

Figure 1. Petals, Layer 1.

Figure 2. Petals, Layer 2.

Center: Pick up one A, one bicone, and one A; pass back through the bicone, the first A just added, the last hole exited, and up through the nearest hole on the dome; repeat to add at least one bicone fringe to each open hole of the dome *(fig. 3)*. Secure the thread and trim.

Back: Rub a small dab of glue on the back of the dome to strengthen and secure the threads; let dry. Place the backing against the dome, and use chain-nose pliers to bend the tabs into place.

2) STRAPS. Use seed beads and crystals to herringbone stitch the necklace straps:

Row 1: Slide a needle to the center of 10' (3.1 m) of thread, leaving a 1' (30.5 cm) tail. Double the thread, and wax it thoroughly. Ladder stitch a strip eight B long.

Row 2: Pick up eight B, pass down through the next B in Row 1 and up through the following B; repeat to form three additional four-stack herringbone stitches (there will be eight stacks of four beads in each row). Step up for the next row by passing the thread under the loop between the last two B in Row 1 and passing up through the last B in Row 1 and the final four B added in Row 2 *(fig. 4)*.

Row 3: Pick up eight B, pass down through the top bead of the seventh Row 2 stack and up through the top bead of the sixth Row 2 stack. Pick up eight B, pass down through the top bead of the fifth Row 2 stack and up through the top bead of the fourth Row 2 stack. Repeat to add two more stacks and pass down through the top two beads of the first Row 1 stack. Loop the thread between beads of the first Row 1 stack so that the thread catches, and pass back through the beads to exit the fifth-to-last B added.

Row 4: Pick up eight B, pass down through the top bead of the second Row 3 stack and up through the top bead of the third Row 3 stack. Pick up five B, two crystal rounds, and one B; pass down through the top bead of the fourth Row 3 stack and up through the top bead of the fifth Row 3 stack. Pick up one B, two crystal rounds, and five A; pass down through the top bead of the sixth Row 3 stack and up through the top bead of the seventh Row 3 stack. Pick up eight B, and pass down through the top two beads of the last Row 2 stack. Loop the thread between beads of the last Row 2 stack so that the thread catches, and pass back through the beads to exit the fifth-to-last B added.

Figure 3. Flower Center, first fringe.

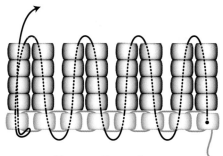

Figure 4. Strap, Row 2.

Row 5: Work four-stack herringbone stitch as in Row 4, this time using all B.

Row 6: Work four-stack herringbone stitch as in Row 4, this time forming the first stack with five B, two crystal rounds, and one B; form the second stack with one B, two crystal rounds, and five B; form the third stack with five B, two crystal rounds, and one B; and the fourth stack with one B, two crystal rounds, and five B *(fig. 5)*.

Rows 7 and on: Repeat Rows 3 to 5 to form a strap 8" (20.3 cm) long. Exit up through the final stack. Don't trim the thread; set aside.

Repeat this step to form a second strap.

3) ASSEMBLY. Finish the necklace:

Straps: Use the working thread of one strap to pass through a briolette at the edge of the dome. Pass down through the next stack of the strap's final row and up through the following stack and into the next briolette at the edge of the dome; repeat to connect each stack to a briolette *(fig. 6)*. Secure the working thread and trim. Repeat to add the second strap to the next four briolettes at the dome's edge.

End: Place a needle on the tail thread of one strap. Pick up three B, loop under the thread between the next two B at the end of the strap, and pass back through the third B just strung. Pick up two B, loop under the thread between the next two B at the end of the strap, and pass back through the second B just strung; repeat five more times, and then repeat a sixth time, this time looping under the final two B at the end of the strap again *(fig. 7)*. Don't cut the thread. Repeat this step for the other strap end.

Clasp: Use the tail threads to securely sew one-half of the clasp to the last few rows of each strap. Position the clasp halves so that the hook is on the back side at the end of one strap and the loop is on the front side at the end of the other strap. Secure the thread and trim.

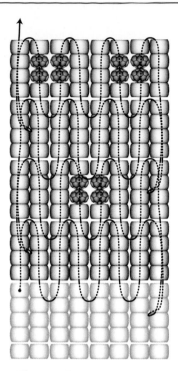

Figure 5. Strap, Rows 3 to 6.

Figure 6. Attaching the straps to the flower.

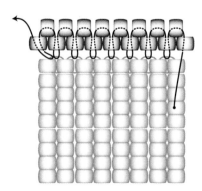

Figure 7. Picot edging.

Working with Thread and Crystals

Although Swarovski crystals tend to have smoother holes than other brands of crystals, you still should be careful about unnecessarily exposing your thread to abrasion. Follow these tips to avoid thread breakage:

♦ Always use braided beading thread for stitching crystals. Nylon thread is great for other beadweaving projects, but once you add crystals, you'll quickly find that the thin fibers that make up nylon thread are just too easily cut. Braided beading thread will hold up to the abrasion much better.

♦ When pulling thread through a crystal, always pull it in line with the bead hole, not at an angle, which will abrade the thread unnecessarily.

♦ Reinforce, reinforce, and then reinforce again.

♦ It's not a bad idea to coat your pieces in clear acrylic floor polish (brand name: Future). If you coat the beads generously, some of the polish will soak into the holes, further strengthening the thread to help avoid breakage. *Note:* I've found that just about any bead can handle the polish, with the exception of after-market coatings on crystals. Check with your vendor to see whether your crystals have an after-market coating; if so, just don't add polish to those beads or stones.

Jamilla

...She was just one of many wives, but not just any woman. She could be described as having an otherworldly aura. It had to do with her mystery, sophistication, elegance, her choice of these exotic drop earrings, and yes, her mad hair-knotting skills....

PHOTO COURTESY OF MPTVIMAGES.COM.

Marlene Dietrich as Jamilla in Kismet, 1944.

Marlene Dietrich (1901–1992) is a cultural icon as well known for her non-Hollywood fame as for her many films. She was a celebrated cabaret singer, recording dozens of singles and albums, and performed often in top clubs and theaters. A bisexual, Dietrich was married to Rudolf Sieber, and they had a daughter together; they lived together for only five years but never formally divorced. Dietrich was one of the first Hollywood fashion icons that the New York and Paris fashion designers embraced as one of their own. She once said of her fashion sense, "I dress for myself. Not for the image, not for the public, not for the fashion, not for men."

FINISHED LENGTH:
2" (5.1 cm)

TECHNIQUES: peyote stitch, fringe

MATERIALS AND TOOLS

1 gram of each size 11° seed beads in olive matte **(A)**, forest green **(B)**, permanent galvanized cranberry **(C)**, and permanent galvanized magenta **(D)**

8 metallic yellow size 8° seed beads **(E)**

0.5 gram olive matte size 15° seed beads **(F)**

2 light rose 5.5mm crystal simplicity beads (#5310)*

8 light green 5mm crystal round pearl beads (#5810)

6 erinite 11 x 5mm crystal briolettes (#6010)

6" (15.2 cm) of 20-gauge gold-filled or gold craft wire

smoke 6 lb (2.7 kg) braided beading thread

scissors

size 11 beading needle

thread burner

round-nose pliers

chain-nose pliers

metal file

wire cutters

1) **BODY.** Peyote stitch the earring body:

Rows 1 and 2: Place the needle on 3' (0.9 m) of thread. Pick up one A, one B, one C, one B, and one A, leaving a 4" (10.2 cm) tail.

Row 3: Peyote stitch one A, one C, and one A. Tie a knot with the working and tail threads to hold the beads in place (*fig. 1, black thread path*).

Row 4: Pass back through the last A added, and peyote stitch one B/one C in each stitch (*fig. 1, red thread path*).

Row 5: Peyote stitch one A, one C, one D, one C, and one A. **Note:** Make the step up to the next and subsequent even rows by looping the thread under the exposed thread at the edge of the beadwork; pass back through the last bead strung (*fig. 2*).

Figure 1. Rows 3 and 4.

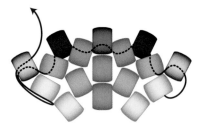

Figure 2. Row 5.

Row 6: Peyote stitch one B, one D, one D, and one B *(fig. 3, black thread path)*.

Row 7: Peyote stitch one A and one C. Weave through the next stitch from the previous row. Peyote stitch one C and one A *(fig. 3, red thread path)*.

Row 8: Peyote stitch one B. Square stitch one D to the next one D from Row 6. Pick up one simplicity bead. Square stitch one D to the next D from Row 6. Pass through the next C from Row 7. Peyote stitch one B *(fig. 4)*.

Row 9: Peyote stitch one A. Pick up one C; pass through the next D/simplicity bead/D. Peyote stitch one C and one A.

Row 10: Peyote stitch one B. Pick up one D; pass through the simplicity bead. Peyote stitch one D and one B *(fig. 5)*.

Row 11: Peyote stitch one A. Pick up one C; pass through the nearest D from Row 10, the simplicity bead, and the next D from Row 10. Peyote stitch one C and one A.

Row 12: Peyote stitch one B. Pick up one D; pass through the simplicity bead. Peyote stitch one D and one B *(fig. 6)*.

Figure 3. Rows 6 and 7.

Figure 4. Row 8.

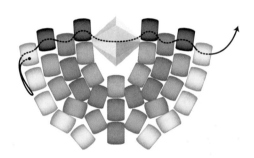

Figure 5. Row 10.

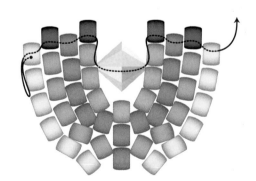

Figure 6. Row 12.

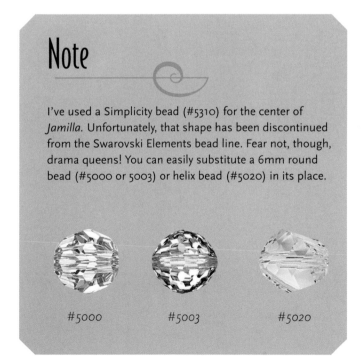

Note

I've used a Simplicity bead (#5310) for the center of *Jamilla*. Unfortunately, that shape has been discontinued from the Swarovski Elements bead line. Fear not, though, drama queens! You can easily substitute a 6mm round bead (#5000 or 5003) or helix bead (#5020) in its place.

#5000   #5003   #5020

Row 13: Peyote stitch one E, one C, two D, one C, and one E *(fig. 7, black thread path)*.

Row 14: Peyote stitch one A. Pick up one C; pass through two D from Row 13. Peyote stitch one C and one A *(fig. 7, green thread path)*.

Row 15: Work a hidden decrease at the beginning of the row. Peyote stitch one A, two C, and one A *(fig. 7, orange thread path)*.

Row 16: Work a hidden decrease at the beginning of the row. Pick up one A; pass through two C from Row 15. Peyote stitch one A *(fig. 7, purple thread path)*.

Row 17: Work a hidden decrease at the beginning of the row. Peyote stitch two A *(fig. 7, blue thread path)*.

Row 18: Work a hidden decrease at the beginning of the row. Pass through the nearest A from Row 17. Pick up one E; pass through the next A of the previous row *(fig. 7, red thread path)*.

Row 19: Weave through the beadwork to exit the A on the right side of Row 1, toward the center. Pick up one A, and pass through the next Row 1 bead; repeat. Step up through the last A added *(fig. 8, blue thread path)*.

Row 20: Pick up one E, and pass through the next A from Row 19 *(fig. 8, red thread path)*.

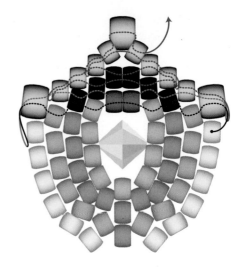

Figure 7. Rows 13 to 18.

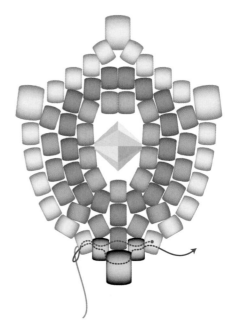

Figure 8. Rows 19 and 20.

2) **FRINGE.** Weave through the beadwork to exit from the A on the right side of Row 7. Double the thread and pick up three F, one B, one pearl, one B, two F, one briolette, and two F; pass back through the last B/pearl/B. Pick up one F; pass through the A on the right side of Row 5. Pull tightly to firm the fringe. Weave through the beadwork to exit from the E in Row 20. Pick up three F, one B, one pearl, one B, two F, one briolette, and two F; pass back through the last B/pearl/B. Pick up three F; pass through the E in Row 20, and weave through the beadwork to exit the A on the left side of Row 5. Pick up one F, one B, one pearl, one B, two F, one briolette, and two F; pass back through the last B/pearl/B. Pick up three F; pass through the A on the left side of Row 7. Secure the thread and trim *(fig. 9)*.

3) **EAR WIRES.** Flush cut 3" (7.6 cm) of gold wire. Use round-nose pliers to form a simple loop at the end of one wire. Open the loop and connect it to the E in Row 17. String one pearl onto the wire and push it down to the loop. Use the widest part of the round-nose pliers to form a U-shaped bend next to the pearl just strung so that the tail wire lies behind the earring. Use chain-nose pliers to form a slight bend at the end of the wire. File the wire end smooth.

Repeat all steps to form the second earring.

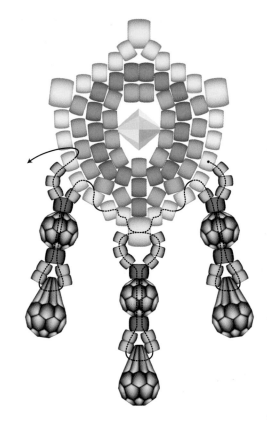

Figure 9. Fringe.

Elizabeth

*...The graceful pixie emerged from her verdant glen, pausing to eye
her beautiful apple-blossom bracelet. She was the only one who knew
about the beautifully detailed leaves at its closure. Being a soul full of delicious secrets,
one more to relish sat fine with her....*

Elizabeth Taylor, c. 1954.

London-born actress **Elizabeth Taylor** gained fame with 1943's *Lassie Come Home,* but it was just the start of an award-winning career in Hollywood that includes classic movies such as *National Velvet* (1944), *Father of the Bride* (1950), *Giant* (1956), *Cat on a Hot Tin Roof* (1958), and *Cleopatra* (1963). Outside the Hollywood scene, Taylor is known for her work on behalf of charity, her many marriages, her recognition by the British Empire as "Dame Commander," and her absolute love of jewelry. Taylor has left a permanent stamp in cinema and has created an unequalled mystique.

See page 39 for
Apple Blossom Earrings.

FINISHED LENGTH:
6 ¹/₄" (15.9 cm)

TECHNIQUES: circular and flat two-drop peyote stitch, double simple loop, square stitch

MATERIALS AND TOOLS

2 grams size 15° ivory cylinder beads

8 grams permanent galvanized mauve size 11° seed beads

2 grams permanent galvanized light green size 11° seed beads

3 peridot 3mm crystal rounds (#5000)

135 creamrose light 6mm crystal pearl beads (#5810)

54 powder rose 6mm crystal pearl beads (#5810)

27 silver 2" (5.1 cm) head pins

2 clear ³/₈ " (1 cm) snap fasteners

crystal and smoke 6 lb (2.7 kg) braided beading thread

scissors

size 11 beading needle

thread burner

wire cutters

round-nose pliers

1) **PETALS.** Use crystal pearls and seed beads to form a petal ring:

Round 1: Place the needle on 2' (61 cm) of thread. Pick up five creamrose light crystal pearls. Tie a square knot, leaving a 1" (2.5 cm) tail. Pass through the first pearl strung.

Round 2: Pick up one size 15° seed bead and pass through the next Round 1 pearl; repeat around. Pass through the first size 15° seed bead added in this round *(fig. 1)*.

Knots: Tie an overhand knot around the thread between the size 15° seed bead just exited and the next pearl, and then pass through the pearl; repeat around *(fig. 2)*. Use the thread burner to trim the working and tail threads close to the beads. Set the petal ring aside.

Repeat this entire step to form a total of twenty-seven petal rings.

2) **FLOWERS.** Slide one powder rose crystal pearl, one petal ring, and one powder rose crystal pearl onto a head pin. With wire cutters, trim the head pin to ¹/₂" (1.3 cm) from the top of the last pearl strung. Use round-nose pliers to form a double simple loop *(fig. 3)*. Set the flower aside. Repeat this entire step to form a total of twenty-seven flowers.

Figure 1. Stitching Petals, Round 2.

Figure 2. Securing Petals, Round 2, with knots.

Figure 3. Constructing the Flower.

3) **BASE.** Use mauve size 11° seed beads and the flowers to peyote stitch the bracelet base:

Rows 1 and 2: Place a needle on 6' (1.8 m) of thread. Slide the needle to the center of the thread to double it. Pick up twenty mauve size 11° seed beads, leaving a 4" (10.2 cm) tail.

Row 3: Pick up two mauve size 11° seed beads, skip two beads previously strung, and pass through the following two beads. Repeat across to work two-drop peyote stitch.

Row 4: Work two two-drop peyote stitches with mauve size 11° seed beads. Work one two-drop peyote stitch using one mauve size 11° seed bead and one flower strung through the double loop. Work two two-drop peyote stitches with mauve size 11° seed beads *(fig. 4)*.

Rows 5 to 9: Work five two-drop peyote stitches using mauve size 11° seed beads.

Rows 10 to 105: Continue with two-drop peyote, adding the remaining twenty-six flowers randomly and working a varied number of plain rows between.

Rows 106 to 138: Work five two-drop peyote stitches using mauve size 11° seed beads.

Rows 139 to 143 (decrease rows): Loop the thread between beads at the edge of the strip. Pass back through the last two beads added. Work across in peyote stitch as before. Repeat. Loop the thread between beads to make the turnaround, pass back through the last two beads added, and work across in two-drop peyote stitch. Continue forming decreases at each end of the strip until you add only two beads at the tip *(fig. 5)*. Don't cut the working thread. **Note:** The last two beads placed will be off-center because of the nature of even peyote stitch.

Tab: Start a new doubled thread that exits Row 1. Work thirty-three rows of two-drop peyote stitch using mauve size 11° seed beads to extend the base to 7" (17.8 cm), or 1 3/4" (4.5 cm) longer than your desired bracelet length. Repeat Rows 139 to 143 to decrease the tab end. Don't cut the thread; set the base aside.

 4) **LEAVES.** Use green size 11° seed beads and a 3mm round crystal to form a square-stitched leaf:

Round 1: Place a needle on 3' (0.9 m) of thread. Pick up one peridot 3mm round crystal and three green size 11° seed beads, leaving a 3" (7.6 cm) tail. Tie a knot to form a tight circle, and pass through the crystal again. Pick up three green size 11° seed beads; pass through the crystal and the three beads just added *(fig. 6)*.

Pick up two green size 11° seed beads and pass through the next three green size 11° seed beads; repeat. Pass through the next green size 11° seed bead *(fig. 7)*.

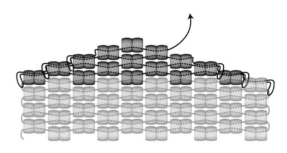
Figure 4. Peyote stitching the base.

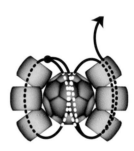
Figure 5. Decreasing the base end.

*Figure 6.
Adding the first beads to Leaf, Round 1.*

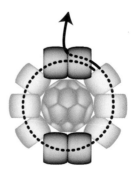
*Figure 7.
Adding the final beads to Leaf, Round 1.*

Round 1 connectors: Pick up one green size 11° seed bead; pass through the following six green size 11° seed beads. Pick up two green size 11° seed beads; pass through the last two beads exited and the two just added to form a square stitch (*fig. 8*).

Round 2: Pick up eight green size 11° seed beads; pass through the top Round 1 connector bead. Pick up one green size 11° seed bead; pass through the bead last exited. Pick up eight green size 11° seed beads; pass through the bottom Round 1 connector beads. Pick up two green size 11° seed beads; pass through the two beads last exited and the two just added (*fig. 9*).

Round 3: Pick up twelve green size 11° seed beads; pass through the top Round 2 connector bead. Pick up one green size 11° seed bead; pass through the bead last exited. Pick up twelve green size 11° seed beads; pass through the bottom Round 2 connector beads. Pick up two green size 11° seed beads; pass through the two beads last exited and the two just added (*fig. 10*).

Point and stem: Pass through the bottom Round 2 connector beads and the next eleven green size 11° seed beads from Round 3. Pick up one green size 11° seed bead; pass through the top Round 3 connector bead. Pick up one green size 11° seed bead; skip the next Round 3 bead, and pass through the following eleven green size 11° seed beads, the bottom Round 2 connector beads, and the bottom Round 3 connector beads. Pick up two green size 11° seed beads, and then pass through the two beads last exited and the two just added; repeat to form a square-stitched strip seven stacks long (*fig. 11*).

Weave through the beads to exit from Round 1. Use a circular square-stitch thread path to connect the beads of Rounds 1 and 2, and then repeat to connect Rounds 2 and 3. Set the leaf aside.

Repeat the entire step to form two more leaves, one with a three-stack stem, one with a four-stack stem.

Figure 8. Adding the Round 1 connector beads.

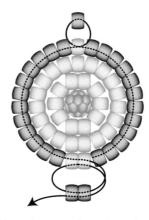

Figure 9. Adding the Round 2 side and connector beads.

Figure 10. Adding the Round 3 side and connector beads.

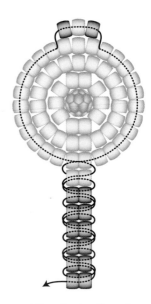

Figure 11. Adding the Leaf's point and stem.

5) **ASSEMBLY.** Stitch the final components of the bracelet onto the base:

Leaves: Position the seven-stack stem leaf on the longer, plain end of the bracelet base so that it sits toward the left side with the stem slightly tucked under the first flowers. Use the working thread to tack the leaf to the base, sewing it on by looping around threads between base beads. Sew the three-stack stem leaf toward the right side of the base and the four-stack stem leaf in the middle, but swooping to the right.

Snaps: Stitch the studded side of one snap to the back of the bracelet at one corner on the leaf end. Repeat to stitch the studded side of the other snap to the other corner on the leaf end. Sew the socket sides of the snaps onto the front of the non-leaf end of the bracelet so they correspond with the studded side of the snaps. Secure all threads and trim.

Apple Blossom Earrings

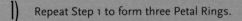

Whip up these flowery earrings to match this bracelet in just a few steps.

1) Repeat Step 1 to form three Petal Rings.

2) Repeat Step 2 to form three Flowers, this time using Powder Rose 6mm crystal pearls for the front flower centers and creamrose 6mm crystal pearls for the backs. Set aside.

3) Use silver 4mm jump rings to connect one flower to each end of ³/₄" (1.9 cm) of 3 x 4mm silver cable chain. Attach the chain at one-third of its length to one ear wire; before closing the ear wire's loop, attach the remaining flower. Close the loop.

4) Use a silver 2" (5.1 cm) 22-gauge head pin to string one powder rose 6mm crystal pearl, the remaining ring, the second chain link, and one crimp tube. Snug the beads and chain; crimp the tube.

5) Use the wide end of round-nose pliers to form a U-shaped bend near the tube. Use your fingers to form a gentle 30° bend ¹/₂" (1.3 cm) from the wire end.

Repeat all steps to form the second earring.

Marilyn

...In a word, she seethed glamour. The hair, the makeup, the jewelry—it was all part of a very orchestrated look that came naturally to her now. But as the blonde beauty toyed with her beautiful crystal bracelet, she realized that deep down she was pining for those bright days on the farm, riding the horses and feeding the chickens....

PHOTO COURTESY OF MPTVIMAGES.COM.

Marilyn Monroe, 1955.

Marilyn Monroe was born Norma Jeane Mortenson in 1926. Growing up in foster homes and an orphanage, Monroe eventually made her way to Hollywood, exploding with sensuality in films like *Niagra* (1953), *Gentlemen Prefer Blondes* (1953), and *How to Marry a Millionaire* (1953). She started her own film company in 1956, producing movies where her Strasberg-trained acting talents could be featured, such as *Bus Stop* (1956), *The Prince and the Showgirl* (1957), and *Some Like It Hot* (1959), for which she won a Golden Globe. Monroe's consummate glamour, voluptuous shape, and steamy sexuality catapulted her to cultural icon status, where she remains today.

FINISHED LENGTH:
6 ¹/₂" (16.5 cm)

TECHNIQUES: netting, square stitch,
peyote stitch

MATERIALS AND TOOLS

7 grams metallic navy AB size 11°
seed beads

1 gram metallic navy AB size 15°
seed beads

34 crystal AB 4mm crystal round beads
(#5000)

34 crystal foiled 10 x 5mm (X7M) bezeled
2-hole closed navettes (#13 304)

7 silver 4 x 10mm two-holed
almond spacers

crystal 6 lb (2.7 kg) braided
beading thread

beeswax or microcrystalline wax

scissors

size 11 beading needle

thread burner

2 gold 6mm magnetic clasps

1) **BAND.** Use seed beads, crystal beads, and navettes to net
the band:

Row 1: Place the needle on the end of 3' (0.9 m) of doubled
waxed thread. Pick up one size 11° seed bead, one crystal
round, and one size 11° seed bead, leaving a 4" (10.2 cm)
tail; pass back through the crystal and the first seed bead
just strung. Pass through the top hole of one navette, and
pick up one size 11° seed bead, one crystal round, and one
size 11° seed bead; repeat thirteen more times. Pass back
through the last crystal round and the second-to-last seed
bead just added. Pass back through the top hole of the last
navette added, but exit out through the bottom hole, toward
the beadwork.

Row 2: Pick up two size 11° seed beads, the top hole of
a spacer, and two size 11° seed beads; pass through the
bottom hole of the next Row 1 navette. Pick up two size
11° seed beads, the top hole of a navette, and two size
11° seed beads; pass through the bottom hole of the next
Row 1 navette. Repeat from the beginning of the row five
more times. Pick up two size 11° seed beads, the top hole
of a spacer, and two size 11° seed beads; pass through the
bottom hole of the final Row 1 navette. Pick up one size 11°
seed bead, one crystal round, and one size 11° seed bead;

pass back through the last crystal round and second-to-last
seed bead added. Weave through this row again to exit out
through the bottom hole of the final Row 1 navette. Pick
up one size 11° seed bead, one crystal round, and one size
11° seed bead; pass back through the last crystal round
and second-to-last seed bead just added *(fig. 1, blue thread
path)*. Secure the thread and trim.

Row 3: Place the needle on the end of 3' (0.9 m) of doubled
waxed thread. Pick up one size 11° seed bead, one crystal
round, and one size 11° seed bead, leaving a 4" (10.2 cm)
tail; pass back through the crystal and the first seed bead
just strung. Pick up the top hole of one navette and two size
11° seed beads; pass through the bottom hole of the final
Row 2 spacer. ✷Pick up two size 11° seed beads, the top hole
of one navette, and two size 11° seed beads; pass through
the bottom hole of the next Row 2 navette. Pick up two size
11° seed beads, the top hole of one navette, and two size 11°
seed beads; pass through the bottom hole of the next Row 1
spacer. Repeat from ✷ five more times. Pick up two size 11°
seed beads, the top hole of one navette, one size 11° seed
bead, one crystal round, and one size 11° seed bead; pass
back through the crystal round and second-to-last seed bead.
Pass back through the top hole of the last navette added, but
exit out through the bottom hole, toward the beadwork.

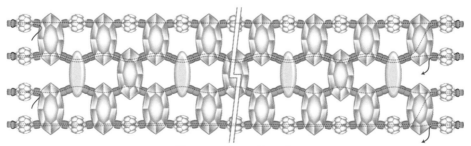

Figure 1. Netted band.

Row 4: Pick up one size 11° seed bead, one crystal round, and one size 11° seed bead; pass through the bottom hole of the next Row 3 navette; repeat twelve more times. Pick up one size 11° seed bead, one crystal round, and one size 11° seed bead; pass back through the crystal round and the second-to-last seed bead just added. Weave through this row again to exit out through the bottom hole of the final Row 3 navette. Pick up one size 11° seed bead, one crystal round, and one size 11° seed bead; pass back through the last crystal round and second-to-last seed bead just added (*fig. 1, red thread path*). Secure the thread and trim.

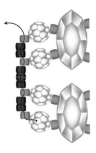

Figure 2. Square-stitched tab, Row 1.

2) CLASP. Square stitch tabs, and attach a clasp to the netted band:

Row 1: Place a needle on the end of 2' (61 cm) of thread. Secure the thread to the band beadwork so that it exits from a seed bead at the end of Row 1. Pick up two size 11° seed beads; pass through the seed bead at the end of the band's Row 2. Pick up three size 11° seed beads; pass through the seed bead at the end of the band's Row 3. Pick up two size 11° seed beads; pass through the seed bead at the end of the band's Row 4 (*fig. 2*).

Rows 2 and 3: Use size 11° seed beads to work two rows of square stitch eleven beads wide.

Clasp: Securely sew half of one clasp to the third bead in Row 3, passing through the connection many times to reinforce; repeat to add one-half of the other clasp to the ninth bead in Row 3 (*fig. 3*). Secure the thread and trim.

Repeat this step at the other end of the band.

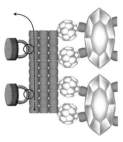

Figure 3. Stitching the clasps to the square-stitched tab.

3) CLASP COVER. Peyote stitch a ring to cover the clasp assembly:

Rounds 1 and 2: Place a needle on the end of 2' (61 cm) of single thread. Pick up thirty size 11° seed beads, leaving an 8" (20.3 cm) tail. Tie a knot to form a tight circle; pass through the first bead strung to hide the knot.

Rounds 3 to 9: Work tubular peyote stitch with one size 11° seed bead in each stitch for a total of nine rounds.

Round 10: Work tubular peyote stitch with two size 15° seed beads in each stitch; secure the working thread and trim.

Attachment: Place the needle on the tail thread. Slide the ring over one end of the bracelet so that the ring's Row 1 meets the clasp assembly's Row 1. Stitch each up bead in the ring's Row 1 to the clasp assembly's Row 1 (*fig. 4*). Secure the thread and trim. Repeat this step at the other end of the band.

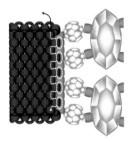

Figure 4. Attaching the clasp cover.

Natalie

*...The perky teen idol had to stop herself from releasing an audible giggle.
She was young, but experienced enough in the world to know when someone was feeding her a fantas
Instead, she rested her head on her whimsical, yet sophisticated new vinyl and crystal bracelet and
enjoyed the tall tale for what it was—an entertaining piece of fiction....*

Natalie Wood, c. 1956.

Academy Award–winning actress **Natalie Wood** was born in San Francisco in 1938 to Russian émigré parents. She was coddled by her stage mother and became a much sought-after child performer, appearing in films such as *Miracle on 34th Street* (1947). Her film career blossomed when she was 16, playing opposite James Dean in *Rebel Without a Cause* (1955), and it continued with films like *West Side Story* (1960), *Splendor in the Grass* (1961), and *Gypsy* (1962).

FINISHED LENGTH:
6 ½" (16.5 cm)

TECHNIQUES: riveting, whipstitch, fringe

MATERIALS AND TOOLS

6 x 10" (15.2 x 25.4 cm) piece of bronze metallic vinyl fabric

4 x 10" (10.2 x 25.4 cm) piece of stiff black felt

14 to 20 crystal and silver 3mm crystal rivets (#53 008) (no backing required)

220 to 250 bright gold 3mm crystal round pearl beads (#5810)

1 silver 22mm beading dome with flat backing

1 gram gold-lined clear size 15° seed beads

smoke 6 lb (2.7 kg) braided beading thread

1 black 8mm metal snap

1 size 6° seed bead, any color

clear industrial-strength jeweler's adhesive or two-part epoxy

white glue

scissors

paper and pencil

ball-point pen

beading awl

jeweler's hammer

2 mm-wide nail

eyelet setter

beading mat, thick towel, or other cushioned surface

size 11 beading needle

thread burner

chain-nose pliers

1) **FABRIC.** Copy or trace the templates at right onto a piece of paper. Trim each template to the line. Lay Template A *(fig. 1)* on the back of the vinyl, along one side. Use a pen to trace the template. Turn Template A over, and lay it along the front side of the vinyl; trace it. Trim out both templates and set aside. Use Template B *(fig. 2)* to cut a shape out of the stiff felt. Trace the dome backing onto the remaining felt; trim out. Set all the fabric pieces aside.

2) **RIVETS.** Set rivets into one piece of vinyl:

Mark: Use the pen to lightly mark fourteen or more spots down the front of one of the vinyl pieces where the rivets will go. **Note:** The bracelet shown has rivets set in a diagonal pattern approximately every ³/₄" (1.9 cm).

Holes: Use the beading awl to poke thick holes through the vinyl at each of the marks.

Set: Place one rivet through one of the holes, from front to back. Keeping the rivet in the hole, set the rivet face on a soft, firm surface. Place the nail into the back of the rivet, and gently tap it with the hammer to separate the prongs. Remove the nail. Place the eyelet setter into the center of the prongs *(fig. 3)*; gently tap the hammer to fully separate the prongs flat against the back of the vinyl. **Note:** Be very careful as you tap so that you don't shatter the crystal. Repeat this section to set a rivet in each of the holes in the vinyl. If desired, add a tiny dab of jeweler's adhesive to the back of each rivet, securing it to the back of the vinyl.

Figure 1. Template A.

Figure 2. Template B.
✳Note: Photocopy the above templates at 200 percent.

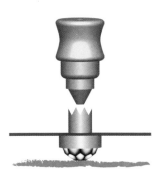

Figure 3. Setting the rivet.

EDGING. Use pearls to form a whipstitched edging, assembling the bracelet at the same time:

Knot: Slide a needle to the center of 6' (1.8 m) of thread. Double the thread and tie the ends into a strong overhand knot. Sandwich the stiff felt piece between the riveted and unriveted vinyl pieces. Stitch into the unriveted vinyl from back to front about 2 mm from the edge so that the knot is hidden between the fabric layers.

Edging: Pick up one pearl and stitch into the riveted vinyl from front to back about 2 mm from the edge and 3 mm down from where the thread last exited; sew through the unriveted vinyl from back to front and pull tightly to form a whipstitch *(fig. 4)*. Repeat this section around the edge of the vinyl pieces to form a pearl edging.

Reinforce: Pass through all the pearls again to reinforce, and slightly pull the bracelet into a curved shape with the rivets on the outside of the curve.

BUTTON. Form a beaded clasp cover:

Knot: Slide a needle to the center of 6' (1.8 m) of thread. Double the thread, and tie the ends into a strong overhand knot. Sew up through one of the holes in the dome and down through the nearest one; pass through the loop between the working thread and the knot, and pull tightly to secure the thread to the finding. Pass up through the nearest hole.

Fringe: Pick up one pearl and one seed bead; pass back through the pearl, down through the last hole exited, and up through the next nearest hole *(fig. 5)*. Repeat to add at least two fringes to each hole of the dome. Secure the thread and trim. Smear a generous amount of white glue onto the back of the beadwork; let dry. Set the dome aside.

SNAP. Sew the snap to the band ends.

Socket: Sew the socket side of the snap to the riveted side of the vinyl about ¹/₂" (1.3 cm) from one end of the band on the curving downward edge *(fig. 6)*.

Stud: Firmly stitch the studded side of the snap to the felt circle so that its edge touches the edge of the felt circle. Place the felt circle at the other end of the band on the curving downward edge so that only one-third of the circle overlaps and the snap faces toward the band's back *(fig. 7)*. Stitch the circle in place, carefully making the stitches so that they don't show on the back of the band. ***Note:*** The socket and snap will be on opposite edges of the band.

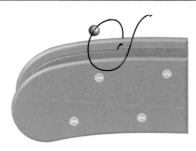

Figure 4. Whipstitched edging.

Figure 5. Adding fringe to the dome.

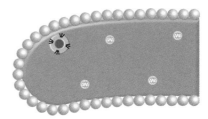

Figure 6. Socket placement.

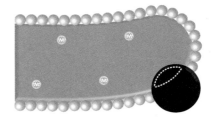

Figure 7. Stud placement.

Figure 8. Attaching the dome backing to the felt circle.

Apply jeweler's adhesive to the dome backing, keeping clear of the center hole. Place the backing on the non-snap side of the felt circle. Pass through the backing's center hole, pick up the size 6° seed bead, and pass back through the felt *(fig. 8)*; repeat the thread path several times to reinforce, connecting the backing to the felt circle. Secure the thread and trim; let dry.

Dome: Place the dome over the backing. Use chain-nose pliers to clamp the backing's prongs over the dome.

Olivia

*...Her neatly coifed hair rolled and undulated like the river in the Japanese print on the wall.
But this powerful and captivating woman could never just blend into the woodwork,
especially while wearing her favorite sparkling fringed necklace with the toggle up front....*

PHOTO BY PAUL HESSE, COURTESY OF MPTVIMAGES.COM.

Olivia de Havilland, c. 1950.

Olivia de Havilland was born in Tokyo in 1916 and moved to California as a child with her mother and younger sister, who would become the famous actress Joan Fontaine. In her twenties, De Havilland landed a seven-year contract with Warner Brothers and starred in numerous films, including *Robin Hood* (1938) and *Gone with the Wind* (1939). De Havilland tired of the swooning woman stereotype, so she started refusing these types of roles, causing friction with the studio contract. Her actions played a critical role in helping shape actors' contract rights. De Havilland won the Academy Award for best actress for *To Each His Own* (1946) and *The Heiress* (1949). She has lived in Paris since the 1950s.

FINISHED LENGTH:
17" (43.2 cm)

TECHNIQUES: peyote stitch, fringe, picot, stringing, crimping

MATERIALS AND TOOLS

2 grams permanent galvanized silver size 15° seed beads **(A)**

3 grams permanent galvanized silver size 11° seed beads **(B)**

3 grams permanent galvanized silver size 8° seed beads **(C)**

3 grams permanent galvanized light blue green size 11° seed beads **(D)**

80 crystal AB 4mm crystal bicone beads (#5301)

3 amethyst 12 x 8mm crystal polygon beads (#5203)

7 peridot AB 8mm crystal round beads (#5000)

29 light azore 9 x 6mm crystal teardrop beads (#5500)

24 aquamarine 9 x 6mm crystal teardrop beads (#5500)

29 indicolite 9 x 6mm crystal teardrop beads (#5500)

6 sterling silver 2mm crimp tubes

54" (1.4 m) of medium sterling silver flexible beading wire

crystal 6 lb (2.7 kg) braided beading thread

scissors

size 12 beading needle

thread burner

wire cutters

crimping pliers

RING. Peyote stitch a sculptural toggle ring:

Disk 1, Rounds 1 and 2: Place a needle on the end of 4' (1.2 m) of thread. Pick up twelve A, twelve B, twelve C, and twelve B, leaving a 1" (2.5 cm) tail. Tie a knot to form a tight circle and pass through all the beads again, pulling tight to hide the entire tail within the beads. Exit from the first A.

Disk 1, Round 3: Pick up one A, skip one A from the previous round, and pass through the next A; repeat five times to add a total of six A. Pick up one B, skip one B from the previous round, and pass through the next B; repeat five times to add a total of six B. Pick up one C, skip one C from the previous round, and pass through the next C; repeat five times to add a total of six C. Pick up one B, skip one B from the previous round, and pass through the next B; repeat five times to add a total of six more B. Step up for the next round by passing through the first A added in this round (*fig. 1, blue thread path*).

Note: For each stitch in each subsequent round, add the bead size that will match the down bead from two previous rounds (same size beads will always touch sides).

Figure 1. Disk 1, Rounds 3 and 4.

Disk 1, Round 4: Pick up two beads and pass through the next bead of the previous round; then pick up one bead and pass through the following bead of the previous round; repeat around to add a total of thirty-six beads. Step up for the next round by passing through the first two beads added in this round (*fig. 1, red thread path*).

Disk 1, Round 5: Pick up one bead and pass through the next bead of the previous round, then pick up one bead and pass through the following two beads of the previous round; repeat to add a total of twenty-four beads. Step up through the first bead added in this round.

Disk 1, Round 6: Pick up one bead and pass through the next bead of the previous round; then pick up two beads and pass through the following bead of the previous round; repeat around to add a total of thirty-six beads. Pull tightly so that the beadwork slightly curves. Step up through the first bead added in this round (*fig. 2, blue thread path*).

Disk 1, Round 7: Repeat Round 5 (*fig. 2, red thread path*). Don't cut the thread; set the disk aside.

Disk 2: Repeat Disk 1, Rounds 1 to 6. Weave through the beadwork to exit Round 1. Pick up one bead, and pass through the next Round 1 bead; repeat around to add a total of twenty-four beads.

Ring assembly: Pair the disks so their edges touch. Use Disk 2's working thread to zip together the beads of Disk 2's outer edge to the beads of Disk 1's outer edge (*fig. 3*). Repeat the thread path to reinforce. Secure the thread and trim. Use Disk 1's working thread to zip together the inner edge of Disk 1 to the inner edge of Disk 2. Repeat the thread path to reinforce; secure the thread and trim. Set the toggle ring aside.

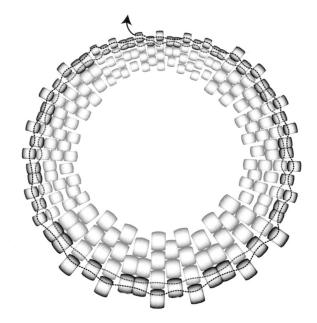

Figure 2. Disk 1, Rounds 6 and 7.

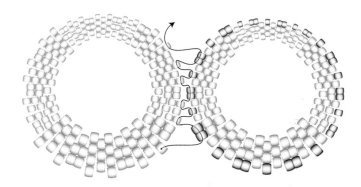

Figure 3. Zipping the disks together.

2) **BAR.** Peyote stitch a tube, and embellish it to form a toggle bar:

Tube: Place a needle on the end of 4' (1.2 m) of thread. Use D to peyote stitch a strip twenty-four beads wide and ten rows long, leaving a 1' (30.5 cm) tail. Fold the strip in half lengthwise; zip the first and last rows together to form a tube; weave back through the zipped beads to reinforce. Exit from an edge bead.

End: Pick up one A, one bicone, and one D; pass back through the bicone. Pick up one A; pass down through an edge bead on the other side of the same tube end; then pass up through the nearest edge bead D.

Pick up one A, pass through the bicone and D, pass back through the bicone, pick up one A, pass down through an open edge bead at the end of the tube, and up through the nearest unembellished D *(fig. 4)*. Repeat to connect each edge D to the bicone. Exit up through an edge D.

Picots: Pick up three A; pass down through the next edge D and up through the following edge D *(fig. 5)*. Repeat around until there are five picots. Secure the working thread and trim.

Use the tail thread to repeat the end and picot portions of this step to the other end of the tube.

Loop: Weave the tail thread through the tube beads to exit from the sixth bead in any row. Pick up seven D, and pass through the eighth bead in the same row to form a loop *(fig. 6)*. Repeat the thread path several times to reinforce. Secure the thread and trim. Set the toggle bar aside.

Figure 4. Embellishing the toggle end.

Figure 5. Adding picots.

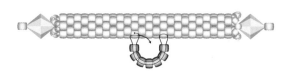

Figure 6. Forming a loop on the toggle bar.

3) **FRINGE.** Attach fringe to the toggle ring:

Fringe 1: Place a needle on the end of 1' (30.5 cm) of thread. Pick up thirty D; pass through the toggle ring, and tie a knot to form a tight circle around the ring's edge, leaving a 1" (2.5 cm) tail. Pass through all the beads again, pulling tightly to hide the tail within the beads *(fig. 7, blue thread path)*. Pick up one D, one bicone, one D, one light azore teardrop, one D, one 8mm round, one D, one indicolite teardrop, and one D; skip the last D, and pass back through the rest of the beads *(fig. 7, red thread path)*. Repeat the thread path several times to reinforce. Secure the thread and trim.

Fringe 2: Repeat the Fringe 1 loop, then form a fringe using this stringing sequence: (one D and one bicone) twice, one D, one light azore teardrop, one D, one polygon, one D, one 8mm round, one D, one indicolite teardrop, and one D. Secure the thread and trim. ***Note:*** Be sure to place the fringes in number order along the toggle ring's edge.

Fringe 3: Repeat the Fringe 1 loop, then form a fringe using this stringing sequence: (one D and one bicone) three times, one D, one light azore teardrop, one D, one aquamarine teardrop, one D, one 8mm round, one D, one indicolite teardrop, and one D. Secure the thread and trim.

Fringe 4: Repeat the Fringe 1 loop, then form a fringe using this stringing sequence: one D, one bicone, one D, one aquamarine teardrop, one D, one bicone, one D, one light azore teardrop, one D, one polygon, one D, one 8mm round, one D, one indicolite teardrop, and one D. Secure the thread and trim.

Fringe 5: Repeat Fringe 3.

Fringe 6: Repeat Fringe 2.

Fringe 7: Repeat Fringe 1.

4) **ASSEMBLY.** Form the necklace:

Cut the beading wire into three 18" (45.7 cm) pieces.

Strand 1: Use one piece of beading wire to string one crimp tube, fifteen D, and the toggle ring at its thinnest portion; pass back through the tube, snug the beads, and crimp. String one D, then (one light azore, two D, one bicone, and two D) twenty-one times. String one light azore, one D, one crimp tube, ten D, and the toggle bar loop; pass back through the tube, snug the beads, and crimp.

Figure 7. Adding fringe to the toggle ring.

Strand 2: Use one piece of beading wire to string one crimp tube, fifteen D, and the toggle ring at its thinnest portion; pass back through the tube, snug the beads, and crimp. String two D, then (one bicone, two D, and one aquamarine teardrop) twenty-one times. String two D, one bicone, two D, one crimp tube, ten D, and the toggle bar loop; pass back through the tube, snug the beads, and crimp.

Strand 3: Repeat Strand 1, replacing the light azore teardrops with indicolite teardrops.

Carmen

...It was stunning how many times she had to answer the question,
"What's under that turban?" She gazed at her sparkling beaded ring and smirked
at the simple answer: It was a mind full of dreams and desires...

Carmen Miranda, c. 1945.

Portugal native **Carmen Miranda** (1909–1955) grew up in Rio de Janeiro, where as a young woman she entertained her hat shop coworkers with her performances of Brazilian hits. She was soon performing in local nightclubs, on albums, and in films. Miranda hit New York by storm on Broadway's *The Streets of Paris* in 1939, and performed as herself in the film *Down Argentine Way* (1940). She continued to perform in Hollywood films through 1953, and was a regular at the Copacabana in New York. Miranda's signature style, which included fruit-topped turbans, bright shiny fabrics, loads of jewelry, platform shoes, and salsa-style dancing, became all the rage in the United States during WWII, and her persona was elevated to Latin bombshell icon status.

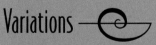

FINISHED SIZE:
1 ³/₈" (3cm) (ring top)

TECHNIQUES: tubular peyote stitch, fringe, flat peyote stitch, whipstitch

MATERIALS AND TOOLS

5 grams permanent galvanized gold size 11° seed beads **(A)**

1 gram olive size 15° seed beads **(B)**

12 crystal copper 2mm crystal round beads (#5000)

12 khaki 3mm crystal round beads (#5000)

6 tanzanite 4mm crystal round beads (#5000)

1 Siam 6mm top-drilled bicone bead (#6301)

6 bright gold 4mm crystal pearl round beads (#5810)

12 bright gold 3mm crystal pearl round beads (#5810)

smoke 6 lb (2.7 kg) braided beading thread

beading wax

scissors

size 12 beading needle

thread burner

1) **TOP.** Use tight thread tension to peyote stitch, fringe, and embellish the top of the ring:

Rounds 1 and 2: Place a needle at the end of 4' (1.2 m) of waxed thread. Leaving a 1" (2.5 cm) tail, pick up forty-eight A, and tie a knot to form a tight circle. Pass through the beads again to pull the knot and tail into the beads.

Rounds 3 and 4: Work tubular peyote stitch around the circle, using one A in each stitch, for a total of two rounds with twenty-four A in each round. Step up for each round by passing through the first bead added in the current round.

Round 5: Pull the thread end down to the beadwork to double it. Work tubular peyote stitch around the circle, using one A in the first stitch and one 2mm crystal bead in the second stitch; repeat, alternating around to add a total of twelve A and twelve 2mm crystal beads (*fig. 1, black thread path*). Step up through the first bead added in this round.

Round 6: Work tubular peyote stitch using one A in each stitch (*fig. 1, blue thread path*). Step up through the first bead added in this round.

Round 7: Pass through the next Round 6 A to form a decrease, then peyote stitch one khaki 3mm crystal round; repeat around to form a total of twelve decreases and add twelve crystal rounds (*fig. 1, red thread path*). Step up through the first crystal round added in this round.

Round 8: Work tubular peyote stitch using one A in each stitch. Step up through the first bead added in this round.

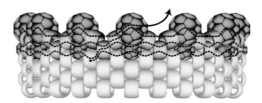

Figure 1. Ring Top, Rounds 5 to 7.

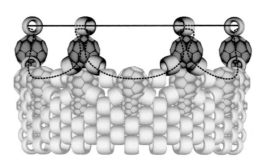

Figure 2. Ring Top, Rounds 9 and 10.

Round 9: Pick up one A, one 4mm tanzanite crystal round, and one A; pass back through the crystal round. Pick up one A; pass through the next A/khaki 3mm crystal round/A from the previous round. Repeat to add a total of six fringes. Weave through beads to exit through an A at the end of a fringe (*fig. 2, blue thread path*).

Round 10: Without adding any beads, pass through all the A fringe tips one time to connect them into a tight circle (*fig. 2, red thread path*). Exit from the first A fringe tip exited.

Center: Pick up the 6mm bicone bead. *Loop around the thread between the fringe tips, up through the center of Round 10, and pass back through the 6mm bicone bead. Repeat from * until the bead is securely seated in the center of the ring top. Weave through the beads to exit up through the third A added in one of the Round 9 fringes *(fig. 3)*.

Embellishment Round 1: Pick up one B, one 4mm pearl, and one B, then pass down through the first A added in the following fringe and up through the adjacent A; repeat to add a total of six pearls. Weave through the beads to exit a 2mm crystal bead in Round 5 *(fig. 4, blue thread path)*.

Embellishment Round 2: Pick up one B, one 3mm pearl, and one B, then pass through the next 2mm crystal bead in Round 5; repeat around to add a total of twelve pearls *(fig. 4, red thread path)*.

Reinforce: Weave through the beads to exit from Round 1. Repeat the thread path for Rounds 1 and 2, pulling with each stitch to tighten the rounds. Secure the thread and trim.

2) BAND. Use A to work a flat peyote-stitched ring band:

Row 1: Start a new 3' (0.9 m) length of doubled thread that exits from Round 1 of the ring top underneath a 2mm crystal bead. Pick up one A, and pass through the next Round 1 A; repeat twice.

Row 2: Pick up one A; pass back through the last A added in the previous row; repeat twice.

Continue to work flat peyote stitch for a total of 37 rows or long enough to fit comfortably around your finger.

Zip: Fold the strip in half so the end touches the other side of the ring top's Round 1 and the beads interlock like a zipper. Weave the last beads of the strip and the Round 1 beads together, creating a seamless connection *(fig. 5)*.

Edging: Use the working thread to whipstitch the exposed threads on each edge of the flat peyote-stitched strip, reinforcing the band *(fig. 6)*.

If possible, pass through the band beads again to reinforce. Secure the thread and trim.

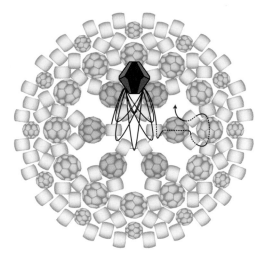

Figure 3. Adding the center bead.

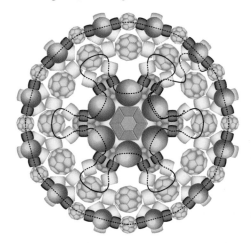

Figure 4. Embellishment, Rounds 1 and 2.

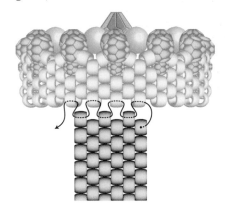

Figure 5. Zipping the band to the ring top.

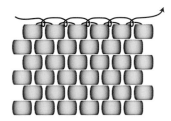

Figure 6. Whipstitching the ring band.

Cleo

*...She was a queen with all the powers of a country at her fingertips,
but she also had a few weaknesses. Powerful men, for one. And earrings.
Long, beautiful, flowing earrings that accentuated her sleek neck and framed the face
over which wars had been fought and won....*

Vivien Leigh in the 1951 theater production of Anthony and Cleopatra *at St. James Theater in London*

Vivien Leigh (1913–1967), an English native, graced the silver screen with her luminous beauty and great acting talent in films such as *Gone with the Wind* (1930) and *A Streetcar Named Desire* (1951), but her first love was the theater. The stage is where her career began and continued throughout her life. She portrayed characters in a wide range of plays, from Thornton Wilder's Sabina in *The Skin of Our Teeth* (1946) to a host of William Shakespeare leading ladies, including Cleopatra in *Anthony and Cleopatra* (1951), opposite husband Laurence Olivier. Though plagued with mental health problems, Leigh is remembered for her perfectionism and brilliance as an actress.

See page 61 for Easy Cleo Earrings.

FINISHED LENGTH:
3" (7.6 cm)

TECHNIQUES:
fringe, wirework

MATERIALS AND TOOLS

2 grams permanent galvanized gold size 11° seed beads

2 brass size 6° metal seed beads

20 Pacific opal 8mm crystal round beads (#5000)

12 metallic blue 2X 4mm crystal bicone beads (#5301)

2 brass 3mm metal melon beads

6 brass 9 x 8mm Deco bead caps

2 brass or gold-plated 1" (2.5 cm) head pins

4 brass or gold-plated 1" (2.5 cm) eye pins

2 brass or silver 8mm flat-face earring posts with wide earring backings

smoke 6 lb (2.7 kg) braided beading thread

clear watchmaker's cement

scissors

size 11 beading needle

thread burner

wire cutters

chain-nose pliers

round-nose pliers

1) COMPONENTS. Form the links that will hang from the earring base:

Simple bead links: Slide one 8mm round bead and one bead cap onto one eye pin, and form a 3mm simple loop to secure the bead; repeat to form one more simple bead link. Set aside.

Connector bead links: Slide one 8mm round bead and one bead cap onto one eye pin, form a 4mm simple loop to secure the bead, and then open the loop and add one size 6° seed bead; close the loop. Repeat to form another connector bead link. Set aside.

Dangle: Slide one 3mm melon bead, one 8mm round bead, and one bead cap onto one head pin, and then form a 3mm simple loop to secure the beads; repeat to form a second dangle. Set aside.

2) EARRING BODY. Use crystals and seed beads to form the body of the earring:

Outer circle: Place a needle on the end of 4' (1.2 m) of thread. Pick up one 8mm round bead and one size 11° seed bead five times, and then pick up one more 8mm round bead, leaving a 1" (2.5 cm) tail. Pass through the size 6° bead attached to one of the connector bead links. Tie a square knot to form a tight circle, and pass through the next 8mm round bead and size 11° bead.

Fringe: Pick up one size 11° bead, one bicone, and one size 11° bead; pass back through the bicone, the first size 11° bead just added, and the last size 11° bead exited on the circle to form a fringe (*fig. 1*). Repeat the thread path to reinforce. Pass through the circle beads to exit from the next size 11° bead.

Figure 1.
Adding the fringe.

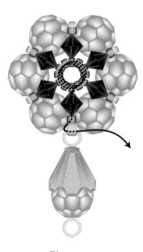

Figure 2.
Establishing the center.

Repeat to add one fringe to each size 11° bead of the circle and to the size 6° bead.

Inner circle: Weave through the beads to exit from a size 11° bead at the tip of a fringe. Pick up one size 11° bead, and pass through the size 11° bead at the tip of the next fringe; repeat around to connect all the fringes. Repeat the thread path several times to tighten the beads into a neat circle. Weave through the beads to exit from the size 6° bead (*fig. 2*).

Post: Place one earring post into the inner circle so that the flat part nestles into the center of the beadwork and the post extends through the inner circle *(fig. 3)*.

Center: Pick up three size 11° beads, one 8mm round bead, and three size 11° beads; pass in front of the earring post and through the size 11° bead at the opposite side of the outer circle. Pass back through the beads just added and the size 6° bead, pulling tight to center the strand. Repeat the thread path to reinforce. Weave through the beads to exit a size 11° bead of the outer circle *(fig. 4)*. **Note:** The 8mm round bead should temporarily keep the post in place.

Repeat the Fringe section. Repeat the Inner Circle section so that the fringes connect on the other side of the earring body. Secure the thread and trim.

3) **ASSEMBLY.** Connect one simple link to the bottom of the connector link already placed. Connect one dangle to the bottom of the simple link just placed. Add a liberal amount of watchmaker's cement to the back of the post, securing it to the inner circle of beads; let dry.

Repeat steps 2 and 3 to form the second earring.

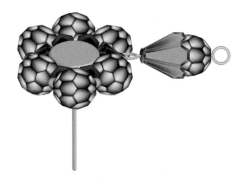

Figure 3. Placing the earring post.

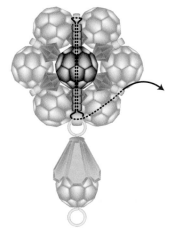

Figure 4. Adding the center bead.

Easy Cleo Earrings

Inspired by the same photo, you can make this variation of Cleopatra's earrings in minutes.

MATERIALS AND TOOLS

2 crystal 16mm (SS29 inclusions) metal flower buttons (#60 408)

2 crystal AB 8mm crystal bicone beads (#5301)

2 brass 9 x 8mm Deco bead caps

2 brass or gold-plated 1" (2.5 cm) head pins

2 brass or silver 8mm flat face earring posts with wide earring backings

clear watchmaker's cement

sandpaper

wire cutters

round-nose pliers

1) Lightly sand the face of an earring post and the back of one metal button. Set aside.

2) Slide one bicone bead and one bead cap onto one head pin. Form a 3mm simple loop to secure the bead.

3) Attach the bicone bead dangle to a loop at the back of one metal button.

4) Use the watchmaker's cement to glue the flat part of the sanded earring post to the back of the metal button; let dry.

Repeat all steps to form the second earring.

Vivien

...Her beauty was legendary. It was said that one look could melt a heart of stone. Yes, she knew her outer appearance was fetching, but the luminosity of her spirit, captured within the warm and sparkling rose stone that always dangled from her neck, was what really drew people to her....

Vivien Leigh, c. 1952

English actress **Vivien Leigh**, born Vivian Hartley in 1913, is best known for her award-winning performances as Scarlett O'Hara in *Gone with the Wind* (1930) and Blanche DuBois in *A Streetcar Named Desire* (1951). She was married to Laurence Olivier for twenty years, and they performed together on both stage and screen. Leigh's great beauty was only rivaled by her tenacity as an actress, as she always strove to perfect her roles.

FINISHED LENGTH:
16" (40.6 cm), extends to 18" (45.7 cm)

TECHNIQUES: right-angle weave, peyote stitch, fringe, wirework

MATERIALS AND TOOLS

5 grams permanent galvanized golden pear size 11° seed beads **(A)**

28 permanent galvanized dark rose size 11° seed beads **(B)**

2 grams gold-lined olive luster size 15° seed beads **(C)**

1 light rose 30 x 22mm crystal oval fancy stone (#4127)

28 crystal silver shade 4mm crystal round beads (#5000)

31 tanzanite 4mm crystal round beads (#5000)

45 khaki 3mm crystal round beads (#5000)

8 amethyst 6mm crystal round beads (#5000)

8 padparadscha 12 x 8mm polygon beads (#5203)

2" (5.1 cm) of sterling silver 4 x 5mm extender chain

1 sterling silver 6 x 10mm lobster clasp with jump ring

1 sterling silver 2" (5.1 cm) head pin

2 sterling silver 5mm jump rings

crystal 6 lb (2.7 kg) braided beading thread

40" (1 m) of silver 22- or 24-gauge wire

scissors

size 11 beading needle

thread burner

wire cutters

chain-nose pliers

round-nose pliers

BEZEL. Use tight thread tension to stitch a bezel around the fancy stone:

Round 1: Place a needle on the end of 3' (0.9 m) of thread. Use A to form a strip of right-angle weave twenty-seven units long. Fold the strip in half. Exiting up through the end bead of the final unit, pick up one A and pass down through the end bead of the first unit. Pick up one A and pass up through the end bead of the final unit, turning the strip into a ring *(fig. 1)*. Repeat the thread path to reinforce. Exit from an edge bead.

Round 2: Pick up one A and pass through the next edge A from Round 1; repeat around to add a total of twenty-eight A. Step up for this and subsequent rounds by passing through the first bead added in the current round.

Rounds 3 and 4: Pick up one C and pass through the next A of the previous round; repeat around to add a total of twenty-eight C in each of two rounds. Weave through the beadwork to exit from an A on the other edge of Round 1.

Round 5: Pick up one A and pass through the next edge A from Round 1; repeat around to add a total of twenty-eight A.

Round 6: Place the fancy stone into the beadwork face-side up. Pick up one C and pass through the next edge A from Round 1; repeat around to add a total of twenty-eight A. Exit down through a horizontal A in Round 1 *(fig. 2)*.

Figure 1. Connecting Round 1 into a ring.

Figure 2. Round 6 and the step-up for embellishment rounds.

2) **BEZEL EMBELLISHMENT.** Add crystal embellishments to the bezel to form a focal piece:

Fringe: Pick up one A, one crystal silver shade 4mm crystal round bead, and one A; pass back through the crystal, the first A just added, and the last Round 1 A exited. Weave through the beadwork to exit down through the next horizontal Round 1 A. Repeat this section to add a total of twenty-eight fringes around the bezel. Weave through the beads to exit up through the first horizontal A exited in Round 1 *(fig. 3)*.

Picots: Pick up one B, one tanzanite 4mm crystal bead, and one B; skip one fringe, pass down through the next A/crystal shade 4mm bead/A fringe to form a picot, then pass back through the crystal shade 4mm bead and A; repeat to add a total of fourteen picots. Exit through an A at the bottom of one fringe *(fig. 4)*.

Fringe connection: Pick up one khaki 3mm crystal bead and pass through the A at the bottom of the next fringe *(fig. 5)*; repeat around to add a total of twenty-eight khaki crystals. Repeat the thread path several times to reinforce. Secure the thread and trim; set the focal piece aside.

3) **LINKS.** Form beaded-wire components:

Short links: Cut 1" (2.5 cm) of wire and form a simple loop at one end. Slide on one amethyst 6mm crystal bead and form another simple loop to secure it. Set the link aside. Repeat to form a total of eight short links.

Long links: Cut 4" (10.2 cm) of wire and form a wrapped loop at one end. Slide on one khaki 3mm bead, one tanzanite 4mm bead, one polygon bead, one tanzanite 4mm bead, and one khaki 3mm bead; form a wrapped loop to secure the beads. Set the link aside. Repeat to form a total of eight long links.

Extender: Slide one polygon bead, one tanzanite 4mm bead, and one khaki 3mm bead onto a head pin. Form a wrapped loop that attaches to one end of the extender chain. Set aside.

4) **ASSEMBLY.** Connect components in this order: the extender and one short link and one long link four times. Use a jump ring to connect the final long link to the upper right side of the focal piece, making the connection in the space between the fringe and fringe connection.

Repeat to form another chain, this time beginning with the clasp and connecting to the upper left side of the focal piece *(fig. 6)*. **Note:** The chain placement works well with seven khaki 3mm beads between the jump rings.

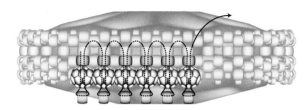

Figure 3. Fringe.

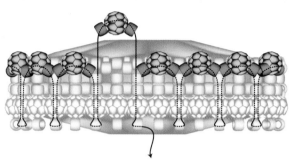

Figure 4. Picots.

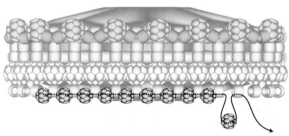

Figure 5. Fringe connection.

Figure 6. Using jump rings to connect the chains to the focal piece.

Maggie

*..."Yes, I have my own race car," the ravishing bouffanted beauty
explained as she showed off her uniquely curved and subtly sparkling cuff.
"And yes, I can light my own cigars, thank you very much..."*

PHOTO COURTESY OF MPTVIMAGES.COM.

Natalie Wood as Maggie DuBois opposite Tony Curtis in The Great Race, 1965.

Actress **Natalie Wood** (1938–1981) appeared in fifty-six film and television productions throughout her lifetime, and was nominated several times for Academy and Golden Globe awards, winning a Golden Globe in 1979 for her role in the television drama series, *From Here to Eternity*. Wood had three marriages—two to actor Robert Wagner and one to producer Richard Gregson. "Almost every girl falls in love with the wrong man," Wood once said. "I suppose it's part of growing up."

FINISHED LENGTH:
7" (17.8 cm)

TECHNIQUES:
right-angle weave, circular peyote stitch, stringing, crimping

MATERIALS AND TOOLS

176 mocca 4mm crystal round beads (#5000)

155 crystal Dorado 2X 4mm crystal round beads (#5000)

68 crystal copper 2mm crystal round beads (#5000)

5 grams silver-lined brown size 15° seed beads **(A)**

2 grams permanent galvanized gold size 11° seed beads **(B)**

20 gold size 6° metal seed beads **(C)**

4 gold 2 x 2mm crimp beads

1 black 8mm metal snap

smoke 6 lb (2.7 kg) braided beading thread

20" (51 cm) of gold heavy flexible beading wire

beading wax

size 12 beading needle

thread burner

crimping pliers

round-nose pliers

chain-nose pliers

1) CURVE. Embellish a right-angle weave strip to form a curved component:

Base: Slide a needle to the center of 6' (1.8 m) of thread. Double the thread and wax it well. Pick up one mocca round and one A four times, leaving a 1" (2.5 cm) tail. Tie a knot with the working and tail thread to form a tight circle then pass through several beads to hide the knot, exiting through one mocca round. Pick up one A and one mocca round three times, pick up one A, and then pass through the last mocca round exited and the first A/mocca round and second A/mocca round just added, pulling tightly to form a circle; repeat to form three more right-angle weave units. Exit through the final A added.

Shaping: Pick up one copper round and pass through the nearest A of the previous right-angle weave unit; repeat to add a total of four A. Weave through the beads to exit from the first side bead of the base's first unit. Pass through the nearest A/mocca round/A of the next unit, gently pulling tightly; repeat three times to curve the base. Exit through the mocca round at the end of the base *(fig. 1)*.

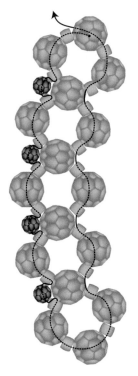

Figure 1. Shaping the base.

Embellishment: Pick up one A, one crystal Dorado round, and one A, then pass through the top mocca round of the next base unit, taking care to pass the thread through the bead in the same direction as the previous mocca round (*fig. 2*); repeat to add a diagonal strand of beads to the front of each right-angle weave unit. The base will spiral.

Repeat the embellishment on the other side of the base. Exit through the first mocca round added on the opposite side of the base.

Curve: Bend the spiral between your fingers so the copper beads lay across the front of the curve. Pick up one A and pass through the nearest mocca round at the back of the bend, pulling tightly to secure the curve; repeat twice. Pick up one A and pass through the nearest crystal Dorado round. Weave through the beads at the end of the beadwork to exit from the first mocca round on the back of the curve. Pick up one A and pass through the nearest crystal Dorado round. Pick up one A and pass through the nearest mocca round. Pick up one A and pass through the nearest crystal Dorado round. Pick up one A and pass through the nearest mocca round (*fig. 3*). Secure the thread and trim. Set aside.

Repeat this entire step ten more times to form a total of eleven curved components. ***Note:*** Each curved component adds about 1/2" (1.3 cm) to the bracelet length, so you may plan accordingly to size.

2) **CLASP.** Peyote stitch a disk to use for the clasp:

Round 1: Slide a needle to the center of 6' (1.8 m) of thread. Double the thread and wax it well. Pick up six B, leaving a 1" (2.5 cm) tail. Tie a square knot to form a tight circle; pass through the beads again to hide the knot.

Round 2: Pick up one B and pass through the next B in the previous round; repeat around to add a total of six B. Step up through the first B added in this round.

Round 3: Pick up two B and pass through the next B in the previous round; repeat around to add a total of twelve B. Step up through the first two B added in this round.

Round 4: Pick up one A and pass through the next B added in the previous round, then pick up one B and pass through the next B added in the previous round; repeat around to add a total of six A and six B. Step up through the first A added in this round (*fig. 4*).

Round 5: Pick up one B and pass through the next B added

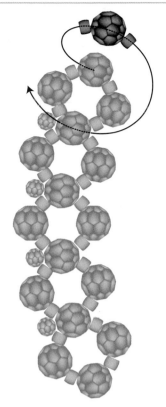

Figure 2. Embellishing the base.

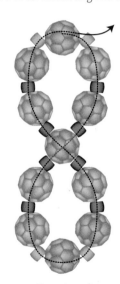

Figure 3. Securing the curve.

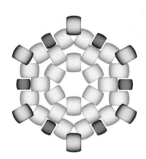

Figure 4. Disk, Round 4.

in the previous round, then pick up one B and pass through the next A added in the previous round; repeat around to add a total of twelve B. Step up through the first B added in this round *(fig. 5)*.

Round 6: Pick up one B and pass through the next B added in the previous round, then pick up one C and pass through the next B added in the previous round; repeat around to add a total of six B and six C. Step up through the first B added in this round.

Round 7: Pick up one A and one B and pass through the next C in the previous round, then pick up one B and one A and pass through the next B in the previous round; repeat around to add a total of twelve A and twelve B. Step up through the first A/B added in this round *(fig. 6)*.

Round 8: Pick up two B and pass through the next B/A added in the previous round, then pick up one B and pass through the next A/B added in the previous round; repeat around to add a total of eighteen B. Step up through the first B added in this round *(fig. 7)*.

Round 9: Pick up one B and pass through the next B added in the previous round, pick up one copper round and one A and pass through the next B added in the previous round, then pick up A and one copper round and pass through the next B added in the previous round; repeat five more times, except using C instead of B on the third and fifth repeats *(fig. 8)*.

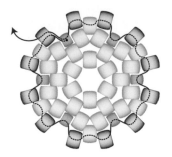

Figure 5. Disk, Round 5.

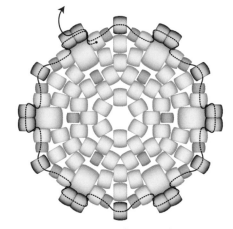

Figure 6. Disk, Rounds 6 and 7.

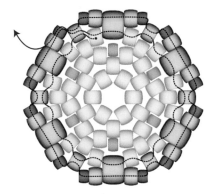

Figure 7. Disk, Round 8.

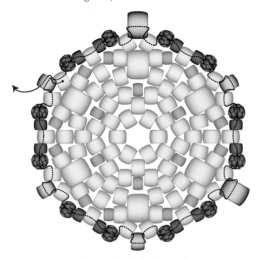

Figure 8. Disk, Round 9.

Reinforce: Weave through the Round 9 beads again until you exit the B after the first C. Pick up one B, pass back through the C, then pick up one B and pass through the B before the first C; repeat the thread path to reinforce. Continue to weave through the Round 9 beads, adding the extra reinforcement to the second C in the round. **Note:** Be careful to avoid stitching near the seam on the C. Weave through the beadwork to exit from Round 3 *(fig. 9)*.

Snap: Place the socket side of the snap on the beadwork so the back of the socket sits in the disk's center hole. Securely stitch the snap in place. Secure the thread and trim; set the disk aside.

Repeat this entire step to form a second disk, but before adding the other side of the snap, exit Round 2 and pick up one A, one crystal Dorado round, and one A; lay the strand across the disk's hole and pass through a B on the other side of Round 2. Pick up one A, pass back through the crystal dorado round, pick up one A, and pass through the Round 2 B originally exited *(fig. 10)*. Repeat the thread path to reinforce. Sew the studded half of the snap to the reverse side of the disk. Secure the thread and trim; set aside.

3) **ASSEMBLY.** Use 10" (25.4 cm) of beading wire to string one crimp bead, pass through a C in Round 9 of the disk with the socket side of the snap, pass back through the crimp bead, and crimp; repeat to add the second wire to the other Round 9 C on the same disk.

String two crystal Dorado rounds on each wire, pass one wire through the end base unit of one curved component, then pass the other wire through the unit at the other end of the same component so the component's curve points up toward the same side as the socket side of the snap; repeat to add all the curved components. String two crystal Dorado rounds and one crimp bead on one wire, pass through the corresponding Round 9 C on the second disk so the studded side of the snap points down, pass back through the crimp bead, snug the beads and components, and crimp; repeat for the second wire. Trim any excess wire.

Use round- and chain-nose pliers to pry open a C at the seam. Put the bead around a crimped tube and gently close the C around the tube. Repeat to cover each crimp.

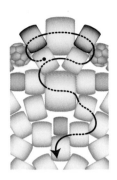

Figure 9. Reinforcing the size 6° beads in Round 9.

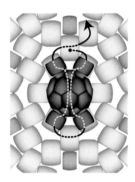

Figure 10. Placing the embellishment at the center of Disk 2.

Mae

...Did she really pull out this opulent reversible necklace for a schlub like this?
Oh, the steaks were good and the martinis dry, but the conversation about hedge funds
was droll and she could just tell he had two left feet. "I wonder," she thought,
"if there's a taxi parked in the alley outside the fire escape"...

PHOTO COURTESY OF MPTVIMAGES.COM.

Mae West as Lady Lou in She Done Him Wrong *(1933).*

Mae West's (1893–1980) illustrious and often controversial career included stage, screen, and radio acting, but she was also an accomplished playwright, producer, director, and singer. Her Broadway play *Diamond Lil* (1928) and the films *I'm No Angel* (1933) and *Klondike Annie* (1936) propelled her to the top of the entertainment charts, but censors and moralists dogged her constantly for her portrayals of loose women and open sexuality. In 1927 she was jailed on morals charges for producing, directing, and starring in the Broadway show *Sex.* The constant pressure by vice-watchers brought out what is perhaps West's most famous quality, her use of blistering double entendres such as the line, "Is that a pistol in your pocket, or are you just glad to see me?"

See page 82 for
Lucky Strike Earrings.

FINISHED LENGTH:
19" (48.3 cm)

TECHNIQUES:
peyote stitch, right-angle weave, wirework

MATERIALS AND TOOLS

7 grams permanent galvanized silver size 11° seed beads **(A)**

7 grams permanent galvanized gold size 11° seed beads **(B)**

5 grams permanent galvanized light green size 11° seed beads **(C)**

5 grams permanent galvanized light blue size 11° seed beads **(D)**

5 grams permanent galvanized mauve size 11° seed beads **(E)**

2 grams permanent galvanized silver size 15° silver seed beads **(F)**

8 permanent galvanized light rose size 8° seed beads **(G)**

60 creamrose 3mm crystal pearl rounds (#5810)

26 light blue 6mm crystal pearl rounds (#5810)

14 bright gold 8mm crystal pearl rounds (#5810)

6 crystal AB 8mm foiled crystal chaton stones (SS39; #1028)

10 crystal copper 2mm crystal rounds (#5000)

4 crystal AB 16 x 11mm crystal baroque pendants (#6090)

1 cystal AB 22 x 15mm crystal baroque pendant (#6090)

20 sterling silver 5mm jump rings

5 sterling silver 6mm jump rings

1 silver or black 3/8" (9mm) hook and eye dress clasp

crystal 6 lb (2.7 kg) braided beading thread

2' (61 cm) of silver 24-gauge wire

scissors

size 11 beading needle

thread burner

wire cutters

round-nose pliers

FLOWERS. Use pearls and seed beads to peyote stitch individual flowers:

Round 1: Place the needle on 2' (61 cm) of thread. Pick up five A and tie the tail and working thread into a square knot to form a tight circle, leaving a 6" (15.2 cm) tail. Pass through the first A strung.

Round 2: Pick up one A and pass through the next bead of the previous round; repeat around to add a total of five A. Step up for the next round by passing through the first A added in this round.

Round 3: String two A and pass through the next bead of the previous round; repeat around to add a total of ten A. Step up through the first A added in this round.

Round 4: String one A and pass through the next bead of the previous round; repeat around to add a total of ten A. Step up through the first A added in this round *(fig. 1)*.

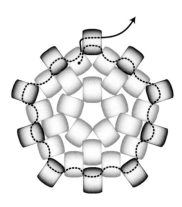

Figure 1. Flowers, Rounds 1 to 4.

Rounds 5 and 6: Repeat Round 4, this time using B, to form two more rounds. Pull tightly with each stitch so that the beadwork cups. Repeat the Round 6 thread path only (don't add any beads) to secure the tension.

Round 7: Pick up two B and pass through the next bead of the previous round; repeat around to add a total of twenty B. Step up through the first B added in this round.

Round 8: Pick up one B and pass through the next bead of the previous round, then pick up one C and pass through the following bead of the previous round; repeat around to add a total of ten B and ten C. Step up through the first B added in this round.

Round 9: Pick up one C and pass through the next bead of the previous round; repeat around to add a total of twenty C. Step up through the first C added in this round.

Round 10: Pick up one D and pass through the next bead of the previous round, then pick up one B and pass through the following bead of the previous round; repeat around to add a total of ten D and ten B. Step up through the first D added in this round.

Round 11: Pick up two D and pass through the next bead of the previous round; repeat around to add a total of forty D. Step up through the first two D added in this round.

Round 12: Pick up one E and pass through the next two beads of the previous round; repeat around to add a total of twenty E. Step up through the first E added in this round.

Round 13: Pick up two E and pass through the next bead of the previous round; repeat around to add a total of forty E *(fig. 2)*. Repeat the thread path to reinforce the round. Secure the working thread, but leave the tail thread.

Center: Pass the tail thread through the center of the flower from back to front. Pick up one blue 6mm pearl and one F; pass back through the pearl and the flower center. Pick up one G and pass through the center of the flower, the pearl, and the F *(fig. 3)*. Repeat the thread path several times to reinforce. Secure the thread and trim. Set the flower aside.

Repeat this entire step seven times to form a total of eight flowers.

Figure 2. Flowers, Rounds 5 to 13.

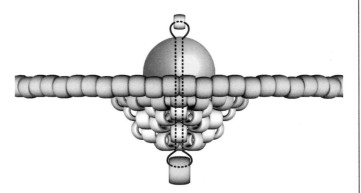

Figure 3. Adding the flower center.

2) SMALL BEZELS.

Work two circular peyote-stitched disks and attach them together to form a bezelled chaton component:

DISK 1

Round 1: Thread the needle with 1' (30.5 cm) of thread. Pick up five A and tie a tight knot to form a tight circle, leaving a 1" (2.5 cm) tail. Pass through the beads again to hide the knot.

Round 2: Pick up one A and pass through the next A from the previous round; repeat around to add a total of five A. Step up for the next and subsequent rounds by passing through the first bead added in the current round.

Round 3: Pick up two A and pass through the next A from the previous round; repeat around to add a total of ten A.

Rounds 4 and 5: Pick up one A and pass through the next A from the previous round; repeat around to add a total of ten A for two rounds.

Round 6: Pick up one creamrose 3mm pearl and pass through the next A from the previous round; repeat around to add a total of ten pearls *(fig. 4)*. Repeat the thread path with no beads; secure the thread and trim. Set aside.

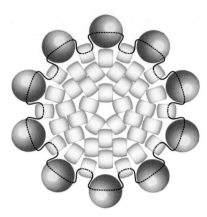

Figure 4. Small Bezel, Disk 1.

DISK 2

Rounds 1 and 2: Thread the needle with 1' (30.5 cm) of thread. Pick up twenty A and tie a tight knot to form a tight circle, leaving a 1" (2.5 cm) tail. Pass through all the beads again, and pull tightly to pull the tail inside the beads.

Rounds 3 and 4: Pick up one A, skip an A on the initial circle, and pass through the following A; repeat around to add a total of twenty A. Step up through the first bead added in the round, and repeat to stitch a fourth round.

Round 5: Set a chaton, pointed side down, on top of Disk 1. Set Disk 2 on top of the chaton. Keep the elements pinched between the thumb and forefinger of your nondominant hand as you pass through one pearl from Disk 1 and the next A from the previous round of Disk 2; repeat around to zip the edges of the disks together, encasing the chaton *(fig. 5)*.

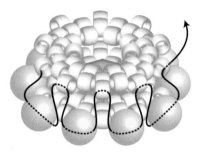

Figure 5. Zipping the Small Bezel.

Loop: Weave through the beads to exit a Round 3 A. Pick up six F; pass through the next Round 3 A to form a loop. Repeat the thread path to reinforce.

Round 5: Weave through the beads of Disk 2 to exit Round 1. Pick up one F and pass through the next two A from Round 4; repeat around to add a total of ten F. Repeat the thread path to reinforce. Secure the thread but don't trim. Set aside.

Repeat this entire step three more times to form a total of four small bezels. Repeat again, this time omitting the loop (this bezel will be used for the clasp).

3) **SMALL BEZEL COMPONENT.** Weave the working thread of one small bezel through the beads to exit from the creamrose 3mm pearl opposite the loop. String one F; pass down through the creamrose 3mm pearl of a second small bezel that's opposite its loop. String one F; pass up through the creamrose 3mm pearl last exited on the first small bezel to form a right-angle weave unit *(fig. 6)*. Repeat the thread path to reinforce. Secure all working and tail threads and trim. Attach one 5mm jump ring to each loop; set aside. Repeat this entire step to form a second small bezel component.

4) **LARGE BEZEL.** Form a large bezel similar to the small ones:

DISK 1

Rounds 1 to 5: Repeat Rounds 1 to 5 for the Small Bezel, Disk 1.

Round 6: Pick up two A and pass through the next A from the previous round; repeat around to add a total of twenty A. Step up through the first two A added in this round.

Round 7: Pick up one A and pass through the next two A from the previous round; repeat around to add a total of ten A. Step up through the first A added in this round.

Round 8: Pick up three A and pass through the next A from the previous round; repeat around to add a total of thirty A. Step up through the first A added in this round.

Round 9: Pick up one A, skip one A from the previous round, and pass through the following A, then pick up one A and pass through the next A from the previous round; repeat around to add a total of thirty A. Step up through the first A added in this round.

Round 10: Pick up one creamrose 3mm pearl and pass through the next A from the previous round, then pick up one copper 2mm crystal round and pass through the following A from the previous round; repeat around. Secure the thread and trim. Set aside.

DISK 2

Rounds 1 to 3: Repeat Rounds 1 to 3 of the Small Bezel, Disk 2.

Rounds 4 to 8: Repeat Rounds 6 to 10 of the Large Bezel, Disk 1.

Round 9: Repeat Round 4 of the Small Bezel, Disk 2 to zip together the bezel, incorporating both the creamrose pearls and the copper crystals.

Round 10: Repeat Round 5 of the Small Bezel, Disk 2.

Loops: Weave through the beads to add loops as with

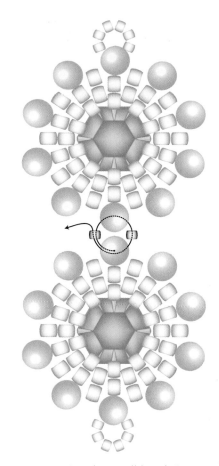

Figure 6. Connecting the small bezels into a component.

the Small Bezel, this time so the loops surround the first, fourth, and seventh edge pearls.

Sew in and out of Disks 1 and 2, capturing the thread between beads around the chaton to secure the crystal in place *(fig. 7)*. Secure the thread and trim.

Dangle: Attach one 5mm jump ring to each loop of the large bezel. Attach one 6mm jump ring to the 22 x 15mm baroque pendant. Use one 5mm jump ring to connect the 6mm jump ring just placed to a 5mm jump ring attached to one of the loops. Set the large bezel aside.

5) LEAF. Use seed beads to form a sculptural peyote-stitched leaf:

BASE

Round 1: Thread the needle with 1' (30.5 cm) of thread. Pick up six A and tie a tight knot to form a tight circle, leaving a 1" (2.5 cm) tail. Pass through the beads again to hide the tail.

Rounds 2 and 3: Pick up one A and pass through the next A from the previous round; repeat around to add a total of six A. Step up through the first A added in this round. Repeat to form another round.

Round 4: Pick up two A and pass through the next A from the previous round; repeat around to add a total of twelve A. Step up through the first two A added in this round.

Round 5: Pick up one B and pass through the next two A from the previous round; repeat once. Pick up one G; pass through the next two A from the previous round. Repeat from the beginning of this round to add four B and two G. Repeat the thread path to reinforce. Step up through one G *(fig. 8)*.

Round 6: Pick up one A and two B; pass through the next B from the previous round. Pick up three B; pass through the following B from the previous round. Pick up two B and one A; pass through the next B from the previous round. Repeat from the beginning of the round to form the other side. Step up through the first A of this round.

Round 7: Pick up one A; pass through the next two B from the previous round and pull tightly so the A clicks into place. Pick up one B; pass through the next three B from the previous round. Pick up one B; pass through the next two B from the previous round. Pick up one A; pass through the next A from the previous round and continue through the G from Round 5 and the following A from Round 6. Repeat from the beginning of the round to form the other side of the round. Step up through the first A added in this round *(fig. 9)*.

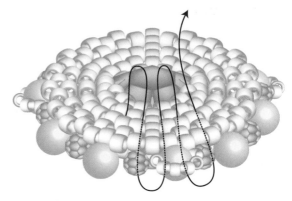

Figure 7. Stitching the Large Bezel's disks together around the chaton.

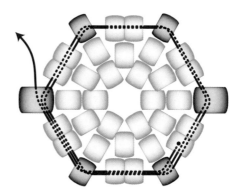

Figure 8. Leaf Base, Round 5.

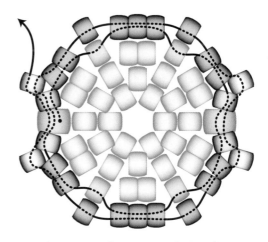

Figure 9. Leaf Base, Rounds 6 and 7.

LEAF POINTS

Row 1: Pick up one A and two B; pass through the next B from the previous round. Pick up one B, skip one B from the previous round, and pass through the next B. Pick up one B; pass through the next B from the previous round. Pick up two B and one A; pass through the next A from the previous round. Turn the thread path around by looping around the thread between the next two beads and exit back through the final A *(fig. 10)*. You will need to do this type of hidden turnaround for this and subsequent rounds. **Note:** You will be working back and forth now.

Row 2: Pick up one A; pass through two B from the previous row. Pick up one B; pass through one B. Pick up two B; pass through one B. Pick up one B; pass through two B. Pick up one A; pass through one A. Form a hidden turnaround as before.

Row 3: Pick up one A and one B; pass through one B. Pick up one B; pass through two B. Pick up one B; pass through one B. Pick up one B and one A; pass through one A. Form a hidden turnaround *(fig. 11)*.

Row 4: Pick up one A; pass through the next B. Pick up one B; pass through the next B. Pick up two B; pass through the next B. Pick up one B; pass through the next B. Pick up one A; pass through the next A. Form a hidden turnaround.

Row 5: Pick up one A; pass through one B. Pick up one B; pass through two B. Pick up one B; pass through one B. Pick up one A; pass through one A. Form a hidden turnaround.

Row 6: Work across in this stitch sequence: one A; two B; one A. Form a hidden turnaround.

Row 7: Pick up one A; pass through two B. Pick up one A; pass through one A. Form a hidden turnaround. Pull very tightly so that the beadwork curves.

Row 8: Pick up one A, one G, and one A; pass through one A *(fig. 12)*.

Weave through the beads to exit from the opposite side of the base. Repeat Rows 1 to 8 to form a leaf on the other side of the base. Secure the thread and trim. Set aside.

Repeat the entire step to form a second leaf.

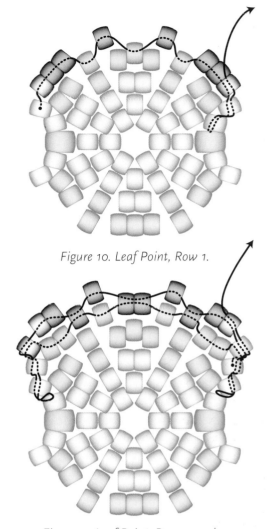

Figure 10. Leaf Point, Row 1.

Figure 11. Leaf Point, Rows 2 and 3.

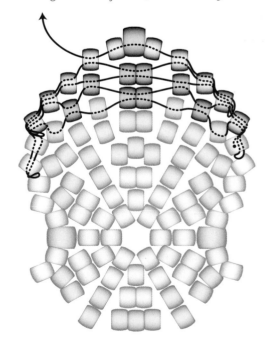

Figure 12. Leaf Point, Rows 4 to 8.

6) LEAF TOP.
Thread a needle on 1' (30.5 cm) of doubled thread. Start the thread so that it exits the final G added on a leaf. Pick up three A, one 6mm pearl, and three A; pass through the last G exited and continue through the next three A and the pearl. Pick up nine A; pass back through the fourth A just added to form a loop. Pick up three A; pass through the pearl, down through the bottom three A, through the G, and up through the bottom three A on the other side of the pearl *(fig. 13)*.

Pick up one A; pass up through the top three A on the side of the pearl, through the loop, and down through the top three A on the other side of the pearl. Pick up one A; pass down through the bottom three A on the side of the pearl *(fig. 14)*. Secure the thread and trim. Attach a 5mm jump ring to the leaf's loop; set the leaf aside.

Repeat this step to add a loop to the other leaf.

7) FLOWER CHAIN.
Stitch the flowers together to form the necklace straps:

Loop: Secure a new 3' (0.9 m) thread that exits from two Round 13 E on one of the flowers. Pick up six F and pass through the two E last exited to form a loop; repeat the thread path to reinforce. Weave through twenty-four Round 12 and Round 13 E.

Connecting unit: Pick up one A and pass through two Round 13 E of a second flower, then pick up one A and pass through the two E originally exited to form a right-angle weave unit, similar to the way you connected the small bezel component. Repeat the thread path to reinforce and exit the first A added in this step.

Pick up one 3mm pearl; pass through the second A added in this step, back through the pearl just added, and through the first A added in this step to center the pearl over the right-angle weave unit. Repeat the thread path to secure. Weave through twenty-four Round 12 and 13 E of the second flower *(fig. 15)*.

Repeat the Connecting Unit to attach four flowers into a curving chain, taking care that all the flowers face up. Don't cut the working thread; set the chain aside.

Repeat this entire step again to form a second chain, taking care to place the connections so that this chain mirrors the first one.

Figure 13. Leaf Point, adding the pearl and loop.

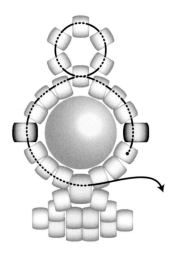

Figure 14. Leaf Point, adding the sides.

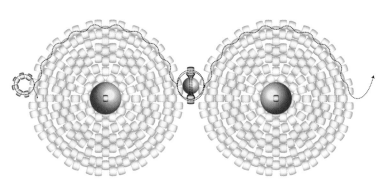

Figure 15. Flower chain loop and connecting unit.

8) CLASP. Add a hidden dress-hook clasp:

Hook: Use the working thread that's exiting two E at one end of a flower chain to pick up one A; pass through a pearl at the edge of the remaining small bezel, taking care that the chaton faces up. Pick up one A; pass through the two E originally exited on the flower. Repeat the thread path to reinforce. Securely stitch the hook half of the clasp to the back of the small disk; secure the working thread and trim.

Loop: Use the working thread at the end of the other flower chain to securely stitch the loop half of the clasp to the edge of the flower; secure the working thread and trim.

9) LINKS. Form a series of beaded wire links:

Link 1: Cut a $^3/_4$" (1.9 cm) piece of wire, and form a simple loop at one end. Slide on one blue 6mm pearl, and form another simple loop to secure it. Set aside. Repeat three times to form a total of four links.

Link 2: Cut a $^7/_8$" (2.2 cm) piece of wire and form a simple loop at one end. Slide on one gold 8mm pearl and form another simple loop to secure it. Set aside. Repeat three times to form a total of four links.

Link 3: Attach one 6mm jump ring to a 16 x 11mm baroque pendant. Use one 5mm jump ring to attach the 6mm jump ring just added to another 5mm jump ring. Cut a 1" (2.5 cm) piece of wire, and form a simple loop at one end. Slide on one blue 6mm pearl, the last 5mm jump ring just placed, and one blue 6mm pearl. Form another simple loop to secure the beads. Set aside. Repeat three times to form a total of four links.

Link 4: Cut a 1 $^1/_4$" (3.2 cm) piece of wire, and form a simple loop at one end. Slide on one blue 6mm pearl, one gold 8mm pearl, and one blue 6mm pearl and form another simple loop to secure the beads. Set aside. Repeat once to form a total of two links.

Link 5: Cut a 1 $^3/_8$" (3.4 cm) piece of wire, and form a simple loop at one end. Slide on one gold 8mm pearl, one creamrose 3mm pearl, the jump ring of one leaf, one creamrose 3mm pearl, and one gold 8mm pearl. Form another simple loop to secure the pearls. Repeat once to form a total of two links.

10) ASSEMBLY. Connect components to build the necklace:

Top row, right side: Connect the large bezel's two-o'clock position jump ring to one Link 1, one Link 2, one small disk component, one Link 2, and one Link 1. Use one 5mm jump ring to connect the Link 1 just placed to the loop at the end of one of the flower chains.

Bottom row, right side: Connect components to the jump ring at the large bezel's two-o'clock position in this order: one Link 3, one Link 5, one Link 3, one Link 2, and one Link 4. Connect the final Link 4 placed to the 5mm jump ring connected to the end of the same flower chain.

Repeat this entire step to connect the large bezel's ten-o'clock position jump ring to the remaining flower chain, forming the left side of the necklace.

Lucky Strike Earrings

*Echo the flash and glamour of Ms. West's
necklace with a pair of sparkling earrings.*

FINISHED LENGTH:
2" (5.1 cm)

TECHNIQUES: wirework

MATERIALS AND TOOLS

6 crystal 8mm crystal flower beads (#5744)

2 crystal AB 18mm two-holed sew-on crystal
rivolis (#3200)

2 crystal AB 8mm crystal marguerite
lochroses (#3700)

8 sterling silver 2" (5.1 cm) head pins

8 sterling silver 5mm jump rings

2 silver 6mm button-post earring findings

wire cutters

chain-nose pliers

round-nose pliers

1) Slide one crystal flower bead onto one head pin; form a wrapped loop to secure the
bead and set aside. Repeat twice to form a total of three flower dangles.

2) Slide one marguerite onto a head pin, and trim the pin to $^1/_2$" (1.3 cm) above the
bead. Form a simple loop, leaving $^1/_8$" (3 mm) from the top of the bead. Use chain-
nose pliers to bend the simple loop at a 90° angle. Set the marguerite dangle aside.

3) Open one jump ring and slide on one flower dangle. Close the ring.

4) Open one jump ring and slide on one flower dangle, the jump ring placed in the
previous step, and the final flower dangle. Close the ring.

5) Open one jump ring and slide on the marguerite dangle, the jump ring placed in
the previous step, and the bottom hole of the rivoli. Close the ring.

6) Use one jump ring to connect the top hole of the rivoli to an earring post.

Repeat all steps to form the second earring.

Dorothy

...The beauty-marked siren had a secret, all right: An alluring voice could draw them in by ear, but a wrist decked with mesmerizing glimmer and a scattering of sparkle at the ear made a girl absolutely irresistible....

Dorothy Dandridge in a publicity photo for Carmen Jones *(1954).*

Dorothy Dandridge (1922–1965) was a child entertainer well known for her singing talents who performed extensively throughout the United States, including at the Apollo Theater and the Cotton Club. Although she got her first break in Hollywood doing a bit part in an *Our Gang* (1935) short, she gained popular fame with her performance as the lead in *Carmen Jones* (1954), a musical adaptation of Bizet's opera *Carmen,* that featured an all African-American cast. That same year she was nominated for the Academy Awards for best actress — only the third African-American actress at the time to have achieved the honor.

See page 89 for Super Nova Earrings.

FINISHED LENGTH:
7" (17.8 cm)

TECHNIQUES:
right-angle weave

MATERIALS AND TOOLS

5 grams antique gold-lined size 15°
seed beads **(A)**

238 crystal AB 4mm crystal round beads
(#5000) **(B)**

88 peridot 3mm crystal round beads
(#5000) **(C)**

8 crystal-foiled 10 x 7mm two-holed
sew-on stones (#3210)

1 sterling silver 1" (2.1 cm) four-loop
sliding clasp

2" (5.1 cm) of gold French wire

crystal 6 lb (2.7 kg) braided
beading thread

scissors

size 11 beading needle

thread burner

wire cutters

1) BASE. Work rows of right-angle weave to form the base of
the bracelet:

Row 1, Unit 1: Place a needle on 6' (1.8 m) of thread. Pick
up (one A and one B) four times, leaving a 4" (10.2 cm) tail.
Tie a square knot with the working and tail thread to create
a tight circle of beads. Pass through the beads again to
reinforce; exit from the second B added.

Row 1, Unit 2: Pick up (one A and one B) three times and
then one A; pass through the last B exited from the previous
unit, and continue through the beads just added to exit the
second B *(fig. 1)*.

Row 1, Unit 3: Repeat Row 1, Unit 2.

Row 1, Unit 4: Repeat Row 1, Unit 2, but this time exit from
the third B added *(fig. 2)*.

Row 2, Unit 1: Pick up (one A and one B) three times and
then one A; pass through the last B exited from the previous
row, and continue through the beads just added to exit the
third B.

Figure 1.
Base: Unit 2, Row 1.

Figure 2.
Base: Unit 4, Row 1.

Row 2, Unit 2: Pick up one A; pass through the nearest edge B from the previous row. Pick up (one A and one B) twice and then one A; pass down through the nearest side bead of the previous unit, and continue through the first A added in this unit, the nearest edge B from the previous row, and the next A and B added in this unit *(fig. 3)*.

Row 2, Unit 3: Pick up (one A and one B) twice and then one A; pass through the next edge bead of the previous row. Pick up one A; pass up through the side bead of the previous unit, and continue through the beads just added to exit the second B.

Row 2, Unit 4: Pick up one A; pass through the next edge bead of the previous row. Pick up (one A and one B) twice and then one A; pass down through the side bead of the previous unit, and continue through the beads to exit from the second B added in this unit *(fig. 4)*.

Rows 3 to 26: Repeat Row 2 twenty-four times. Secure the thread and trim.

2) **ZIGZAGS.** Add columns of zigzag embellishments to the base:

Column 1: Turn the base so the short edges are on the left and right. Start a new 6' (1.8 m) thread that exits one horizontal-holed B at the upper-left corner from left to right. Pick up one A, one C, and one A, and pass through the horizontal-holed B directly below the one last exited from left to right; repeat twice.

Column 2: Pass through the nearest two A and the next B on the bottom edge of the bracelet, from left to right. Pick up one A, one C, and one A, and pass through the horizontal-holed B directly above the one last exited from left to right; repeat three times.

Column 3: Pass through the nearest two A and the next B on the upper edge of the bracelet, from left to right. Pick up one A, one C, and one A, and pass through the horizontal-holed B directly below the one last exited from left to right. Weave through the beadwork to exit from one B two below the last one exited from left to right. Pick up one A, one C, and one A; pass through the horizontal-holed B directly below the one last exited *(fig. 5)*. **Note:** You will purposefully skip two unit embellishments in this column to leave a space for the sew-on stone addition.

Continue across, embellishing the units, leaving two units unembellished at the center of every third column. Secure the thread and trim.

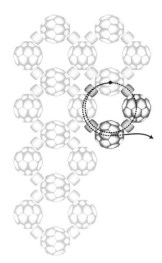

Figure 3. Base: Unit 2, Row 2.

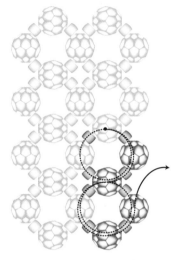

Figure 4. Base: Units 3 and 4, Row 2.

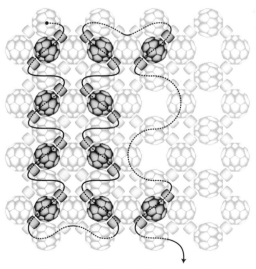

Figure 5. Zigzags, Columns 1 to 3.

3) **STONES.** Add sew-on stones to the unembellished spaces on the base:

Upper connection: Start a new 4' (1.2 m) doubled thread that exits down through the vertical-holed B at the upper left corner of Column 3. *Pick up four A, one hole of a sew-on stone from back to front, and three A; pass back through the same hole to form a picot. Pick up four A; pass up through the vertical-holed B at the upper right corner of the same column. Weave through the beadwork to exit down through the vertical-hole B at the upper right corner of the next partially embellished column. Pick up four A, one hole of a sew-on stone from back to front, and three A; pass back through the same hole to form a picot. Pick up four A; pass up through the vertical-holed B at the upper left corner of the same column. Weave through the beadwork to exit down through the vertical-holed B at the upper left corner of the next partially embellished column. Repeat from * to add one sew-on stone to every third column.

Lower connection: Weave through the beadwork to exit up through the vertical-holed B at the lower right corner of the last column with a sew-on stone. *Pick up four A and pass through the sew-on stone from back to front. Pick up three A and pass back through the same hole to form a picot. Pick up four A and pass down through the vertical-holed B at the lower left corner of the same column. Weave through the beadwork to exit up through the vertical-holed B at the lower left corner of the next column with a sew-on stone. Pick up four A and pass through the sew-on stone in this column from back to front. Pick up three A and pass back through the same hole to form a picot. Pick up four A and pass down through the vertical-holed B at the lower right corner of the same column. Weave through the beadwork to exit up through the vertical-holed B at the lower right corner of the next column with a sew-on stone *(fig. 6)*. Repeat from * to connect the second hole of the sew-on stones to the lower portion of the base. Secure the thread and trim.

CLASP. Start a new doubled 12" (30.5 cm) thread that exits between the first and second B at one end of the bracelet. Pick up a ¼" (6 mm) piece of French wire, pass through the first loop of one clasp half, and pass through the next B; repeat to attach the remaining clasp loops to the end of the bracelet *(fig. 7)*. Secure the thread and trim. Repeat this step at the other end of the bracelet.

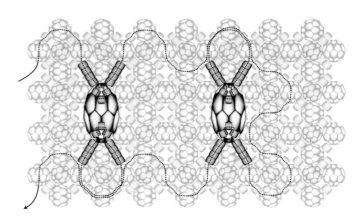

Figure 6. Stones: Upper and lower connections.

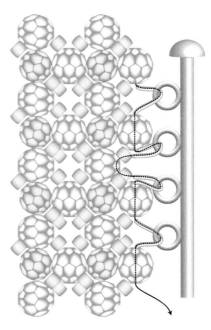

Figure 7. Adding the clasp.

Super Nova Earrings

Make these explosive earrings to complement your new bracelet.

FINISHED SIZE: 1 ¹/₂" (3.8 cm)

TECHNIQUES: netting, tubular peyote stitch, fringe

MATERIALS AND TOOLS

3 grams antique gold-lined size 15° seed beads

2 crystal 9mm (SS39) crystal round with brass settings (#17012)

18 crystal AB 4mm crystal round beads (#5000)

16 peridot 3mm crystal round beads (#5000)

2 silver 11mm flat-back earring findings with prongs

crystal 6 lb (2.7 kg) braided beading thread

clear jeweler's adhesive

acrylic floor polish (optional)

scissors

size 11 beading needle

thread burner

Figure 1. Earrings: Connecting the nets.

Figure 2. Earrings: Adding the bottom rounds.

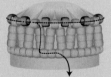

Figure 3. Earrings: Branch fringe.

1) Place a needle on the end of 2' (61 cm) of thread. Pick up twenty-eight seed beads; slide them to 1" (2.5 cm) from the end of the thread, and tie a knot to form a tight circle. Pass through the beads again to hide the knot. Slide one chaton brass setting inside the seed bead circle.

2) Pick up seven seed beads, skip two seed beads of the initial circle, and pass through the next seed bead; repeat around the circle. Step up for the next round by passing through the first four beads of the first net.

3) Pick up one seed bead and pass through the fourth seed bead of the next net; repeat around to connect all the nets over the top of the stone. Repeat the thread path to reinforce, and then weave through the beadwork to exit from two seed beads between nets in the initial circle *(fig. 1)*.

4) Pick up one seed bead, skip one seed bead of the initial circle, and pass through the next two seed beads; repeat around to work tubular peyote stitch with one seed bead in each stitch. Step up through the first bead added in this step.

5) Pick up two seed beads, and pass through the next seed bead added in the previous step; repeat around. Step up through the first two beads added in this step.

6) Pick up one seed bead, and pass through the next two seed beads added in the previous step; repeat around. Weave through the beadwork to exit from one seed bead at the base of a net on the initial circle *(fig. 2)*.

7) Pick up four seed beads, one 4mm crystal, and one seed bead; pass back through the crystal and three seed beads. Pick up one seed bead, one 3mm crystal, and one seed bead; pass back through the crystal and seed bead just added and continue through the first seed beads added in this step. Pass through the last bead exited in the initial circle so the branched fringe sits on top of it. Pass through the next three seed beads of the initial circle to exit one seed bead at the base of a net *(fig. 3)*.

Repeat to form branched fringe around the single seed beads of the initial circle, varying the lengths to create a pleasing design and making the fringes with 4mm crystals and others with 3mm crystals. Secure the thread and trim.

8) Add jeweler's adhesive to the face of the earring finding. Press the bottom of the setting into the adhesive. Fold the prongs over the beadwork.

9) If desired, add a thin coat of acrylic floor polish to the fringe legs to secure and stiffen; let dry.

Repeat all steps to form the second earring.

Hedy

... A woman filled with brains and beauty like this doesn't need stars over the head, on the dress, or at the forehead. No, a simple chain of stars at the neck will do, complementing the glint and sparkle of life in her eyes and reminding anyone who sees her the real meaning behind the term "superstar"...

Hedy Lamarr in Ziegfield Girl, *1941*

Sensuous and stunning, Austrian-born actress **Hedy Lamarr** (1913–2000) was not only called the "Most Beautiful Woman in Films," but also she was a talented mathematician who helped discover frequency hopping, a secret communications system that kept radio-controlled weapons from being jammed by the enemy. Lamarr starred in the Czech *Ekstaste* (1933), an overtly sexual film in which she appeared nude. Her role in that movie caused a sensation worldwide, even causing the U.S. government to ban it. Hollywood welcomed her with open arms, though, and she appeared in several successful films, including *Algiers* (1938), *Lady of the Tropics* (1939), *White Cargo* (1942), and *Samson and Delilah* (1949).

See page 94 for Superstar Earrings.

FINISHED LENGTH:
28" (71.1 cm)

TECHNIQUES:
peyote stitch, fringe, wirework

MATERIALS AND TOOLS

1 gram silver size 15° seed beads

5 grams permanent galvanized silver
size 11° seed beads

14 permanent galvanized gold size 8°
seed beads

15 crystal AB 7mm crystal marguerite
lochrose (#3700)

3 crystal 20mm crystal star pendants
(#6714)

1 sterling silver 1" (2.5 cm) head pin

29 sterling silver 5mm jump rings

5 sterling silver 6mm jump rings

28" (71.1 cm) of sterling silver 3 x 4mm
cable chain

smoke 6 lb (2.7 kg) braided
beading thread

scissors

size 11 beading needle

thread burner

wire cutters

chain-nose pliers

round-nose pliers

1) STAR.

Use tight thread tension to peyote stitch a beaded star:

Round 1: Place a needle on the end of 2' (61 cm) of thread. Pick up five size 11° seed beads and tie the tail and working thread into a square knot to form a tight circle, leaving a 6" (15.2 cm) tail. Pass through the beads again, and pass through the first bead strung.

Round 2: Pick up one size 11° seed bead and pass through the next bead from the previous round; repeat around to add a total of five beads. Step up for the next round by passing through the first bead added in this round.

Round 3: Pick up two size 11° seed beads and pass through the next Round 2 bead; repeat around to add a total of ten beads. Step up for the next round by passing through the first bead added in this round (*fig. 1*).

Round 4: Pick up one size 11° seed bead and pass through the next Round 3 bead; repeat around to add a total of ten beads. Step up for the next round by passing through the first bead added in this round (*fig. 2, black thread path*).

Round 5: Pick up two size 11° seed beads and pass through the next Round 4 bead, the nearest Round 3 bead, and the following Round 4 bead; repeat around to add a total of ten beads. Step up through the first bead added in this round (*fig. 2, red thread path*).

Figure 1. Star, Round 3.

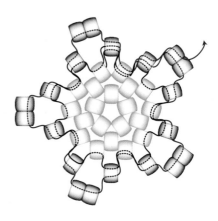

Figure 2. Star, Rounds 4 and 5.

Round 6: Pick up one size 11° seed bead, pass through the next Round 5 bead, and weave through the beads to exit from the following Round 5 bead; repeat three times. For the fourth point, pick up one size 11° seed bead and six size 15° seed beads; pass through the beads again to form a loop, and then pass through once more to reinforce. Pass through the next Round 4 bead, the nearest Round 3 bead, and the following Round 4 bead. Add a loop for the fifth point as for the fourth, then pass through the next Round 5 bead *(fig. 3)*. Secure the thread and trim.

Center: Place a needle on the end of 8" (20.3 cm) of thread. Pick up one size 8° seed bead and pass through the hole at the center of the star. Pick up one marguerite and one size 15° seed bead; pass back through the marguerite and star and tie a square knot with the working and tail threads *(fig. 4)*. Repeat the thread path two more times to reinforce. Secure the thread and trim. Set the star aside.

Repeat this entire step thirteen more times to form a total of fourteen beaded stars.

2) **ASSEMBLY.** Add crystal embellishments to the bezel to form a focal piece:

Crystal stars: Connect one 6mm jump ring to one crystal star. Connect one 6mm jump ring to the jump ring just placed. Use another 6mm jump ring to connect the jump ring last placed to the center link of the chain. Use one 6mm jump ring to connect a second star to the second link to the right of the star just placed; repeat to place the third star to the left.

Dangle: Slide the remaining marguerite onto the head pin. Form a simple loop ¹/₄" (6 mm) from the top of the bead. Bend the head pin at a 90-degree angle so the loop is flush with the back of the bead. Attach the simple loop to the 6mm jump ring that connects the center crystal star to the chain *(fig. 5)*.

Beaded stars: Use 5mm jump rings to connect the loops of each beaded star to the chain, leaving 1 ¹/₄" (3.2 cm) of bare chain between the stars *(fig. 6)*. Add seven stars on each side of the crystal stars, making sure the marguerites face forward.

Use the final 5mm jump ring to connect the end links of the chain.

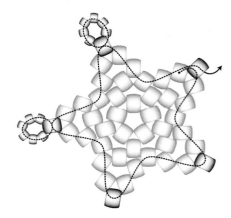

Figure 3. Star, Round 6.

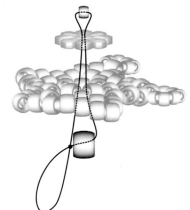

Figure 4. Adding the star's center.

Figure 5. Attaching the crystal stars and dangle.

Figure 6. Attaching the beaded stars.

Superstar Earrings

Make a couple extra stars while you're at it and you've got earrings in a flash.

MATERIALS AND TOOLS

12 silver size 15° seed beads

1 gram permanent galvanized silver size 11° seed beads

2 permanent galvanized gold size 8° seed beads

2 crystal AB 7mm crystal marguerite lochrose (#3700)

2 sterling silver 1" (2.5 cm) head pins

smoke 6 lb (2.7 kg) braided beading thread

scissors

size 11 beading needle

thread burner

wire cutters

round-nose pliers

chain-nose pliers

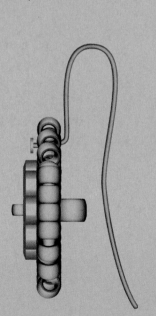

Figure 1. Earring assembly.

1) Repeat Step 1, page 92, to form two beaded stars, except don't add any size 15° seed beads in Round 6 so you end up with no loops. Set the stars aside.

2) Use the tip of round-nose pliers to grasp one head pin right above the stopper disk. Form a 90-degree bend.

3) Slide the head pin through one of the points of the star between Rounds 4 and 5 from front to back so the straight end of the head pin sticks straight up from the star's point.

4) Use the widest point of round-nose pliers to form a wide U-shaped bend ¹/₄" (6 mm) from the tip of the star's point. This is the earring hook.

5) Use chain-nose pliers to form a slight 15-degree bend ³/₄" (1.9 cm) from the top of the hook. Trim the end of the head pin to ¹/₄" (6 mm) from the bend just made *(fig. 1)*.

Repeat all steps to form the second earring.

Grace

*... She was a classic beauty with a regal look, even when she wasn't
wearing a ball gown and a fabulously glamorous crystal necklace. This princess had
loyal subjects everywhere, even the bag boy at the corner grocery store revered her,
playing the part of one of many vassals in her vast fiefdom....*

Grace Kelly in To Catch a Thief *(1955).*

Grace Kelly (1929–1982) was trained as a stage actor and worked as a model and in New York theater until she had her film debut in 1951 in *14 Hours*. Her real success in Hollywood began with her appearance in *High Noon* (1952), and continued with the many Alfred Hitchcock films in which she was featured, including *Dial M for Murder* (1954), *Rear Window* (1954), and *To Catch a Thief* (1955). Kelly gave up her acting career to marry Prince Rainier of Monaco in 1956 and had three children with him.

FINISHED LENGTH:
16 ¹/₂" (41.9 cm)

TECHNIQUES:
stringing

MATERIALS AND TOOLS

2 grams permanent galvanized metallic silver size 11° seed beads **(A)**

38 violet opal 6mm crystal round beads (#5000) **(B)**

53 violet opal 4mm crystal round beads (#5000) **(C)**

1 amethyst 8mm crystal round bead (#5000) **(D)**

2 amethyst 6mm crystal round beads (#5000) **(E)**

6 sterling silver 7mm twisted jump rings

2 sterling silver 5mm jump rings

1 sterling silver 14mm toggle clasp

crystal 6 lb (2.7 kg) braided beading thread

beading wax

scissors

size 11 beading needle

thread burner

1) **CENTERPIECE.** String loops of crystals and seed beads to form the necklace's focal point:

Base strand: Place a needle on the end of 3' (0.9 m) of doubled thread and wax well. Pick up seven A, leaving a 1" (2.5cm) tail; pass through all the beads again to form a tight circle, exiting through the first A. Pick up one B, one A, one C, one A, one D, one A, one C, one A, one B, and seven A, then pass through the seven A again to form a tight circle. Pass back through the last B, A, C, A, and D *(fig. 1)*.

Inner circle: Pick up (one A and one C) three times. Pick up one A, one B, and one A. Pick up (one C and one A) three times. Pass through the base strand D *(fig. 2, black thread path)*. Repeat the thread path to reinforce. Exit through the base strand's C to the left of the D.

Middle circle: Pick up (one A and one C) five times. Pick up one A, one B, and one A. Pick up (one C and one A) five times. Pass through the base strand's C to the right of the D *(fig. 2, blue thread path)*. Pass through the next A/D/A/C and repeat the thread path to reinforce. Exit through the second C added in this circle.

Outer circle: Pick up (one A and one C) five times. Pick up two A, one C, and one A; pass back through the C just strung and the next A, then pull tightly to form a fringe. Pick up (one A and one C) five times, then pick up one A; pass through the second-to-last C added in the middle circle *(fig. 2, red thread path)*. Weave through the beads of the middle circle and base strand. Repeat the thread path to reinforce. Secure the thread and trim. Set the centerpiece aside.

Figure 1. Centerpiece: base strand.

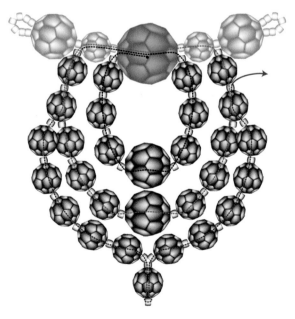

Figure 2. Centerpiece: inner, middle, and outer circles.

2) **SIDE COMPONENT.** String loops of crystals and seed beads to form the side components:

Base strand: Place a needle on the end of 3' (0.9 m) of waxed doubled thread. Pick up seven A, leaving a 1" (2.5 cm) tail; pass through all the beads again to form a tight circle, exiting through the first A. Pick up (one B and one A) six times. Pick up six A; pass through the last seven A again to form a tight circle. Pass back through the nearest B and continue to weave through the beads to exit the second B added.

Inner circle: Pick up (one A and one C) twice. Pick up one A, one E, and one A. Pick up (one C and one A) twice. Pass through the fourth B on the base strand *(fig. 3, blue thread path)*. Repeat the thread path to reinforce. Exit through the base strand's second B.

Outer circle: Pick up (one A and one C) four times. Pick up one A, one B, and one A. Pick up (one C and one A) four times; pass back through the fifth B of the base strand *(fig. 3, red thread path)*. Repeat the thread path to reinforce. Secure the thread and trim. Set aside.

Repeat this entire step to form a second side component.

3) **LINKS.** Place a needle on the end of 2' (61 cm) of waxed doubled thread. Pick up seven A, leaving a 1" (2.5 cm) tail; pass through all the beads again to form a tight circle, exiting through the first A. Pick up (one B and one A) six times. Pick up six A; pass through the last seven A again to form a tight circle. Pass back through the last B added *(fig. 4)*. Repeat the thread path to reinforce. Secure the thread and trim; set the link aside. Repeat this step three more times to form a total of four links.

4) **ASSEMBLY.** Use a plain 5mm jump ring to connect one half of the clasp to one link; use twisted 8mm jump rings to continue connecting components in this order: one link, one side component, the centerpiece, one side component, two links; use a plain 5mm jump ring to connect the final link to the other half of the clasp.

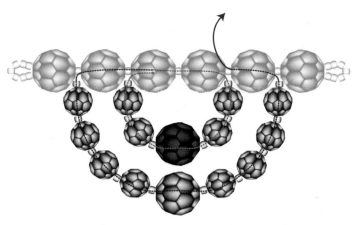

Figure 3. Side component: inner and outer circles.

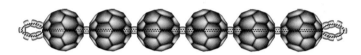

Figure 4. Link.

Sophia

...Once the photo shoot was over, the beauty replaced her mink stole with a lamé jacket, donned her Norum sunglasses, and tied a colorful Hermes chiffon scarf around her perfectly set hair. Then she spun her necklace around to reveal a stunning bezelled cabochon that doubled as a clasp, and fled into the warm Southern California night in her white 1958 Buick Limited convertible....

PHOTO COURTESY OF MPTVIMAGES.COM.

Sophia Loren as Stella in the The Key, *1958.*

Stunning Italian film actress **Sophia Loren's** luminary acting career has spanned sixty years, including not only numerous Hollywood movies such as *Boy on a Dolphin* (1957) and *Houseboat* (1958) but also critically acclaimed Italian films like Vittorio de Sica's *Two Women* (1960).

Loren has commanded international fame as well as the hearts of fellow actors and fans around the world. William Holden, *The Key*'s (1958) leading man, remarked, "She didn't walk into the room, she swept in. I never saw so much woman coming at me in my entire life."

FINISHED LENGTH:
17" (43.2 cm)

TECHNIQUES: stringing, right-angle weave, square stitch, picots, circular peyote stitch, crimping

MATERIALS AND TOOLS

2 grams permanent galvanized lavender size 11° seed beads

23 crystal 4mm (SS18) chaton montées (#53201)

22 crystal 6mm (SS29) roses montées (#53103)

46 air blue opal 3mm crystal round beads (#5000)

272 crystal AB 4mm crystal round beads (#5000)

1 amethyst 18mm (SS75) round rivoli chaton (#1122)

1 sterling silver 5mm crimp cover

2 sterling silver 2 x 3mm crimp tubes

22" (55.9 cm) of medium flexible beading wire

crystal 6 lb (2.7 kg) braided beading thread

clear acrylic floor wax (optional)

2 bead stoppers or other clips

scissors

size 11 beading needle

thread burner

crimping pliers

wire cutters

small plastic paintbrush (optional)

1) **BASE STRAND.** Place a bead stopper on one end of the flexible beading wire. Use the other end of the wire to string one air blue opal 3mm round bead, one chaton montée, one air blue opal 3mm round bead, and one roses montée twenty-two times, followed by one air blue opal 3mm round bead, one chanton montée, and one air blue opal 3mm round bead. Place a bead stopper on the loose wire end.

Figure 1. Inner circle's first stitch.

2) **INNER CIRCLES.** Place a needle on one end of 6' (1.8 cm) of thread. Add the other thread end to one of the bead stoppers. Pass through the base strand's first 3mm round bead/chaton montée/3mm round bead/roses montée sequence.

✳Pick up three seed beads and pass through the vertical hole of the roses montée just exited (*fig. 1*), pulling snugly so that the beads rest against the finding.

Pick up three seed beads and pass through the horizontal hole of the same roses montée. Repeat from ✳ to complete four corners with right-angle weave (*fig. 2*).

Figure 2. Completing the inner circle's four corners.

Weave through the nearest three seed beads and pick up one seed bead; repeat peyote stitching around to complete the circle. Pass through the horizontal hole of the roses montée and into the following 3mm round bead/chaton montée/3mm round bead/roses montée sequence (*fig. 3*).

Repeat to encircle each roses montée with seed beads. Secure the working and tail threads and trim.

3) **OUTER CIRCLES.** Place a needle on one end of 6' (1.8 m) of thread. Add the other thread end to one of the bead stoppers. Pass through the first air blue opal 3mm round and in one end and down through the side of the first chaton montée.

Pick up six crystal AB 4mm round beads, and pass up through the side of the next chaton montée. Pick up five crystal AB 4mm round beads, and pass down through the side of the previous chaton montée, the first six beads added in this section, and the first three beads just added (*fig. 4*).

Pass back through the nearest two seed beads on the inner circle and through the last crystal AB 4mm round bead exited to join with a square stitch. Pass through the next two crystal AB 4mm rounds beads of the outer circle, down through the adjacent chaton montée, through the base strand beads, and exit down through the next chaton montée (*fig. 5*).

Repeat to add an off-center outer circle to each roses montée. Secure the working and tail threads and trim. Set the necklace aside.

4) **BUTTON.** Bezel the rivoli to form a clasp button:

Round 1: Use 3' (0.9 m) of thread to pick up one crystal AB 4mm round bead and one seed bead twelve times. Tie the beads into a circle, leaving a 4" (10.2 cm) tail. Pass through the first seed bead added.

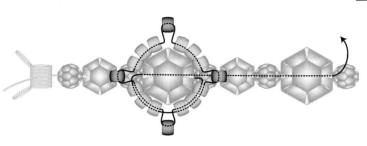

Figure 3. Encircling the inner circle.

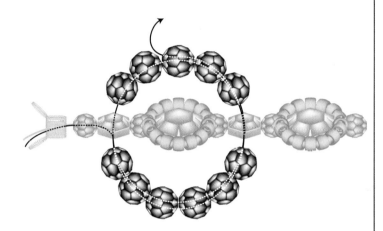

Figure 4. Adding the outer circle.

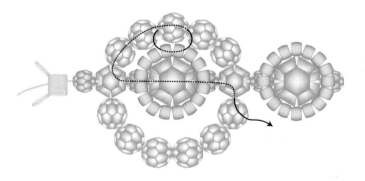

Figure 5. Square stitching the top of the outer circle to the inner circle.

Round 2: Pick up three seed beads; pass through the last Round 1 seed bead exited, and continue through the next crystal AB 4mm round bead and seed bead. Repeat around to add a total of twelve picots. Weave through the beads to exit from the second bead added in this round *(fig. 6)*.

Round 3: Pick up two seed beads, pass through the middle bead of the next picot, and pull tightly; repeat peyote stitching around to connect all the picots. Repeat the thread path to secure. Weave through the beads to exit from a Round 1 seed bead *(fig. 7)*.

Round 4 (back): Repeat Round 2.

Round 5 (back): Place the rivoli into the beadwork so that its face touches Round 3. Pick up one seed bead, and pass through the middle bead of the next Round 4 picot; repeat around to connect all the picots. Pass through the round again to secure. Exit from one bead added in this round.

Shank: Pick up eight seed beads; pass through the seed bead on the opposite side of Round 5, then back through the beads just added *(fig. 8)*. Repeat the thread path several times to reinforce. Secure the thread and trim. Set the button aside.

5) **CLASP.** Finish the base strand ends with a button/loop clasp:

Button: Remove one bead stopper. String one crystal AB 4mm round bead, one crimp tube, and the button through the shank. Pass back through the tube and crimp.

Loop: Remove the remaining bead stopper. Adjust the beadwork along the base strand so that the inner and outer circles move freely, but no beading wire shows. String one crimp tube and seventeen crystal AB 4mm round beads. Pass back through the tube. Adjust the beadwork again, ensuring that the inner and outer circles are snug but aren't bunched up. Crimp the tube. Trim any excess wire. Use the crimping pliers to gently squeeze the crimp cover over the loop-end crimp.

If desired, dab the entire necklace with clear acrylic floor wax to strengthen and firm the beadwork. Let dry thoroughly.

Figure 6. Adding the Button's Round 2 picots.

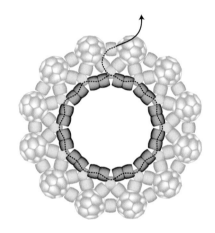

Figure 7. Connecting the Button's picots.

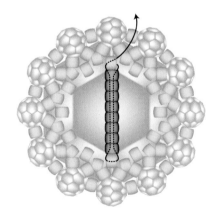

Figure 8. Forming the Button shank.

Variations

- Don't like button/loop clasps? Just crimp half of a commercial clasp to each wire end.

- The strap design for this necklace would work very well for a bracelet design. Simply change the number of 4mm round beads in the outer circles so they are even—five on top and five on the bottom.

- Looking for matching earrings? Encircle a roses montées as in Step 2, then glue the beadwork to the flat face of a post earring finding.

- Another way to make a pair of earrings is to completely bezel the roses montées with seed beads as the earrings described on page 113. For the version shown, you'd just work a couple rounds of peyote stitch to account for the element's thinner profile.

Zsa Zsa

...The feline starlet, whose stunning crystal and chain necklace tumbled down
her décolletage like a colorful dancing brook, purred to the quite dashing photographer,
"Oh, dahling, when will we be done here?" She really didn't have anywhere else to go today
and she wondered if he did either....

PHOTO BY GABI RONA, COURTESY OF MPTVIMAGES.COM.

Zsa Zsa Gabor, 1958.

A native of Budapest, Hungary, **Zsa Zsa Gabor** has a wide range of film, television, and stage credits, including movies such as *Moulin Rouge* (1951), *Lili* (1953), and *Naked Gun 2 ¹/₂: The Smell of Fear* (1991) and TV programs such as *General Electric Theater* (1956–1961), *Gilligan's Island* (1965) and *The Fresh Prince of Bel-Air* (1991). Almost as well known for her many husbands (nine) and sumptuous jewelry and clothing, Gabor has always symbolized the glamour, glitz, and romance of Hollywood.

See page 113 for *Sparkling Stud Earrings.*

FINISHED LENGTH:
16" (40.6 cm), extends to 17" (43.2 cm)

TECHNIQUES:
right-angle weave, peyote stitch, square stitch, fringe, wirework

MATERIALS AND TOOLS

2 grams opaque navy size 15° seed beads

5 grams purple-lined matte light sapphire size 11° seed beads

6 crystal AB 16mm crystal rivoli chatons (#1122)

12 violet 4mm crystal round beads (#5000)

4 amethyst 12 x 8mm crystal polygon beads (#5203)

20 Colorado topaz 9 x 6mm crystal teardrop beads (#5500)

6 Colorado topaz 11 x 5mm crystal briolette pendants (#6010)

5 Colorado topaz 13 x 6mm crystal briolette pendants (#6010)

277 bright gold 3mm crystal round pearl beads (#5810)

2 gold 6mm crystal round pearl beads (#5810)

4 gold 8mm crystal round pearl beads (#5810)

17 bright gold 11 x 8mm crystal pear-shaped pearl beads (#5821)

1 crystal 6mm (SS29) roses montée (#53103)

11 gold 5 x 7mm oval jump rings

13 gold ball-end 2" (5.1 cm) head pins

1 gold 7 x 12mm lobster clasp with jump ring

smoke 6 lb (2.7 kg) braided beading thread

16" (40.6 cm) of gold-plated 7 x 9mm decorative chain

scissors

size 11 beading needle

thread burner

wire cutters

round-nose pliers

1) **BEZEL.** Use tight thread tension to stitch a rivoli bezel:

Round 1: Place a needle on the end of 2' (61 cm) of thread. Use size 11° beads to form a strip of right-angle weave seventeen units long. Fold the strip in half. Exiting up through the end bead of the final unit, pick up one size 11° bead and pass down through the end bead of the first unit. Pick up one size 11° bead and pass up through the end bead of the final unit, turning the strip into a ring. Repeat the thread path to reinforce. Exit from an edge bead (*fig. 1*).

Round 2: Peyote stitch around by picking up one size 11° bead and passing through the next edge bead from Round 1; repeat to add a total of eighteen beads. Step up for this and subsequent rounds by passing through the first bead added in the current round.

Round 3: Pick up one size 11° bead and pass through the next two beads of the previous round to form a decrease; repeat around to add a total of nine beads.

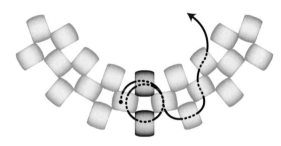

Figure 1. Bezel, Round 1.

Round 4: Pick up two size 11° beads and pass through the next bead of the previous round; repeat around to add a total of eighteen beads.

Round 5: Pick up one size 11° bead and pass through the next two beads of the previous round; repeat around to add a total of nine beads.

Round 6: Pick up one size 11° bead and pass through the next bead of the previous round; repeat around to add a total of nine beads. Weave through the beadwork to exit a size 11° bead at the other side of Round 1 *(fig. 2, black thread path)*.

Round 7: Pick up one size 11° bead and pass through the next edge Bead in Round 1; repeat eight times. Place one rivoli, face-side up, into the beadworked cup; complete the round to add a total of eighteen beads.

Round 8: Pick up one size 15° bead and pass through the next bead of the previous round; repeat around to add a total of eighteen beads. Weave through beads to exit a Round 1 edge bead close to the front of the bezel.

Pearls: Pick up one 3mm pearl, pass through the next Round 1 edge bead, and pull tightly to seat the pearl; repeat around to add a total of eighteen pearls. Exit from the first pearl added *(fig. 3)*. Don't trim the working thread; set aside.

Repeat this entire step five more times to form a total of six bezelled rivolis.

FOCAL PIECE. Connect and embellish the bezelled rivolis:

Rivolis: With the working thread of one rivoli exiting up through a pearl, pick up two size 11° beads and pass down through a pearl at the edge of a second bezelled rivoli. Pick up one size 11° bead and pass down through the next edge pearl of the second bezelled rivoli. Pick up two size 11° beads and pass up through the edge pearl next to the one last exited on the first bezelled rivoli. Pick up one size 11° bead and pass up through the first pearl exited in this step. Repeat the thread path to reinforce. Square stitch the single beads between the pearls together to further reinforce *(fig. 4)*. Secure the thread and trim.

Repeat this entire step to connect all six bezelled rivolis in a formation as shown in *figure 5*.

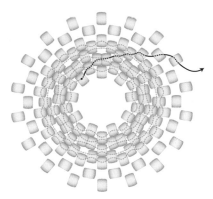

Figure 2. Bezel, Rounds 2 to 6.

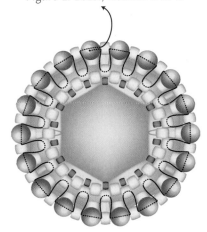

Figure 3. Bezel, adding the pearls.

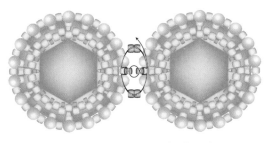

Figure 4. Connecting the bezels.

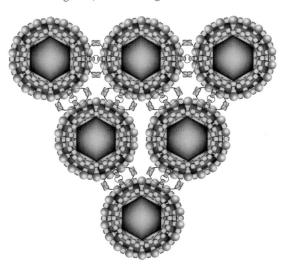

Figure 5. Focal piece connecting points.

Center, bottom layer: Start a new 2' (61 cm) of doubled thread that exits the top two size 11° beads that connect the second and fifth bezels. Pick up one 3mm pearl, one polygon bead, one roses montée, one polygon bead, and one gold 3mm pearl; pass through the bottom two size 11° beads that connect the fourth and sixth bezels. Pass back through the last pearl and polygon just added, and through the roses montée, exiting out through its upper left side hole. Pick up one polygon and one 3mm pearl; pass through the top two size 11° beads that connect the second and fourth bezels. Pass back through the pearl and polygon just added and continue straight through the roses montée. Pick up one polygon and one 3mm pearl; pass through the bottom two size 11° beads that connect the fifth and sixth bezels. Pass back through the pearl and polygon just added. Repeat this entire thread path to reinforce. Exit from the roses montée *(fig. 6)*.

Center, top layer: Pick up two 3mm pearls and pass through the next hole of the roses montée; repeat to add eight pearls around the stone. Pass through all the pearls again to form a tight circle. Exit between two pearls that sit between two polygons *(fig. 7)*.

Spikes: Pick up one size 11° bead, one 8mm pearl, and one size 11° bead; pass back through the 8mm pearl and first size 11° bead and then through the next two 3mm pearls at the center. Pull very tightly so that the spiked fringe isn't loose. Repeat to add a total of four spikes *(fig. 8)*. Repeat the thread path if possible to reinforce. Secure the thread and trim.

Peyote-stitched tab: Start a new 2' (61 cm) of thread that exits from a Round 1 edge bead at the bottom of the sixth bezel as shown. Pick up one size 11° bead and pass through the next Round 1 edge bead; repeat. Pick up one size 11° bead; pass back through the last bead added. Pick up one size 11° bead; pass back through the first bead added in this section. Pick up one size 11° bead; pass through the first bead exited in this section and the final bead added *(fig. 9)*.

Fringe 1: Pick up one 3mm pearl, one size 11° bead, one 11 x 8mm pear-shaped pearl, and one size 11° bead; pass back through the teardrop, seed bead, 3mm pearl, the last bead exited on the tab, and through the next bead on the tab.

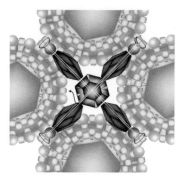

Figure 6. Center, bottom layer.

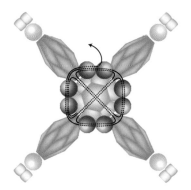

Figure 7. Center, top layer.

Figure 8. Adding the spikes.

Figure 9. Peyote-stitched tab.

Continue forming fringes in a similar manner off each end bead of the tab in this sequence:

Fringe 2: Three 3mm pearls, one size 11° bead, one pear-shaped pearl, and one size 11° bead.

Fringe 3: One 3mm pearl, one 6mm pearl, four 3mm pearls, one pear-shaped pearl, and one size 11° bead.

Fringes 4 and 5: Repeat Fringes 2 and 1 *(fig. 10)*.

3) BEADED CHAIN. Weave an ornate beadworked chain to use as a necklace strap:

Unit 1: Place a needle on the end of 6' (1.8 m) of thread. Pick up one 3mm pearl, one 9 x 6mm crystal teardrop bead from the small end, one size 11° bead, three 3mm pearls, one size 11° bead, one 3mm pearl, one size 11° bead, one 3mm pearl, one size 11° bead, and one 3mm pearl; pass through the fourth pearl added in this unit. Pick up two 3mm pearls, one size 11° bead, and one crystal teardrop from the large end; pass through the first five beads added in this unit *(fig. 11)*.

Pick up one 3mm pearl, skip the nearest pearl, and pass through the next two 3mm pearls, size 11° bead, crystal teardrop, and 3mm pearl. Pick up one 3mm pearl; pass through the pearl last exited and the nearest teardrop, size 11° bead, and 3mm pearl *(fig. 12)*.

Pick up one 3mm pearl; pass through the first 3mm pearl added in the previous section. Pick up one 3mm pearl; pass through the nearest 3mm pearl, size 11° bead, crystal teardrop, 3mm pearl, crystal teardrop, size 11° bead, and nearest two 3mm pearls *(fig. 13, red thread path)*. Pick up one 3mm pearl, and square stitch it to the 3mm pearl attached to the pearl between the teardrops; weave through the beads to exit the pearl at the top of the unit *(fig. 13, black thread path)*.

Units 2 to 5: Repeat Unit 1, substituting the pearl last exited for the first pearl added (the bottom pearl between the teardrops). **Note:** The thread path will switch from moving to the right to moving to the left with every other unit.

Connector loop: Exiting the 3mm pearl at the top of the Unit 5 loop, pick up seven size 11° beads; pass through the pearl and the size 11° beads again two more times to reinforce; secure the thread and trim.

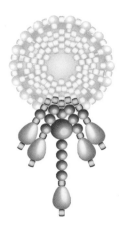

Figure 10. Bezel fringe sequence.

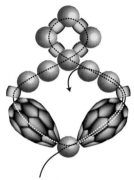

Figure 11. Beaded chain, Unit 1's first stitch.

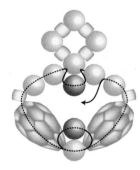

Figure 12. Beaded chain, Unit 1's second and third stitches.

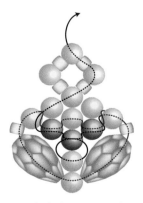

Figure 13. Beaded chain, completing Unit 1.

Unit embellishment: Start a new 3' (0.9 m) of thread that exits from the 3mm pearl at the base of Unit 5's top loop. Pick up one size 15° bead, one 4mm crystal round bead, and one size 15° bead; pass through the pearl at the top of Unit 5's top loop. Pick up one size 15° bead; pass back through the 4mm crystal round bead just placed. Pick up one size 15° bead; pass through the 3mm pearl at the base of Unit 5's top loop, and weave through the beadwork to exit from the 3mm pearl at the base of Unit 4's top loop *(fig. 14)*.

Repeat this section to embellish each loop between the units. Exit from the 3mm pearl at the bottom of Unit 1. Don't cut the thread; set the chain aside.

Repeat this entire step to form a second chain.

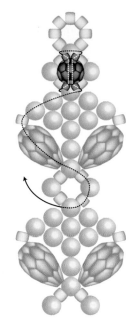

Figure 14. Unit embellishment.

 BEADED CHAIN CONNECTION. Connect the beaded chain to the focal piece:

Connector loop: Use the working thread of one chain to pick up one size 11° bead; pass through a 3mm pearl at the upper left corner of the first bezel on the focal piece. Pick up one size 11° bead; pass through the next 3mm pearl on the bezel. Pick up one size 11° bead; pass through the 3mm pearl at the bottom of the chain *(fig. 15)*. Repeat the thread path to reinforce.

Embellishment: Repeat the Unit Embellishment, using the size 11° bead just added between the bezel on the pearls as the bottom connection point. Repeat the thread path to reinforce; weave through the beads to exit one pearl to the left on the same bezel *(fig. 16)*.

Chain loop: Pick up one size 11° bead, six 3mm pearls, and one size 11° bead; pass down through the left-side crystal teardrop in Unit 1 and through the beadwork to exit the same point first exited in this section *(fig. 17)*. Repeat the thread path as many times as possible to firmly reinforce it. Secure the thread and trim.

Repeat this entire step to connect the second chain to the upper right of the third bezel on the focal piece.

Figure 15. Connector loop.   *Figure 16. Connector embellishment.*

 METAL CHAIN. Add metal chain embellishments to the necklace:

Clasp: Separate out one 2 ³/₄" (7 cm) piece of chain; open an end link and connect it to the open loop at the end of one beaded chain; close the link. Connect the clasp to the open end of this chain.

Extender: Separate out one 3 ¹/₂" (8.9 cm) piece of chain; open an end link, and connect it to the loop at the end of the other beaded chain; close the link. Slide one 6mm pearl onto one head pin; form a wrapped loop that attaches to the open end of this chain.

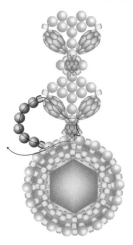

Figure 17. Chain loop.

Charms: Slide a pearl teardrop onto a head pin, form a simple loop, and set aside; repeat to form a total of twelve pearl charms.

Dangles: Remove the end link of the remaining chain and set aside. Use an oval jump ring to connect one 11 x 5mm briolette pendant to the second link of the chain, skip one link, then attach a pearl charm to the next link; repeat to alternate two more 11 x 5mm briolette pendants with pearl charms and then two 13 x 6mm briolette pendants with pearl charms. Add one pearl charm, one 13 x 6mm briolette

pendant, and one pearl charm to the center link, and then repeat the dangle sequence to mirror the first side. Use the link removed at the beginning of this section to connect the chain to itself about 2 ³/₄" (7 cm) from the ends of the chain.

Assembly: Connect one end of the chain to the left loop at the top edge of the focal piece. Connect the other end of the chain to the right loop.

Sparkling Stud Earrings

A simple pair of crystal stud earrings finish off this sparkling ensemble.

FINISHED SIZE: 11 mm

TECHNIQUES: peyote stitch

MATERIALS AND TOOLS

2 grams gold size 15° cylinder beads

2 crystal 9mm (SS39) crystal rounds with brass settings (#17012)

2 gold or silver 8mm flat-face earring posts

crystal 6 lb (2.7 kg) braided beading thread

scissors

size 12 beading needle

thread burner

1) Place a needle on the end of 2' (61 cm) of thread. Work rounds of circular peyote stitch as follows:

Round 1: Pick up six size 15° beads; slide them to 1" (2.5 cm) from the end of the thread, and tie a knot to form a tight circle. Pass through the beads again to hide the knot.

Round 2: Pick up one size 15° bead, and pass through the next bead of the previous round; repeat around to add a total of six beads. Step up for this and subsequent rounds by passing through the first bead added in the current round.

Round 3: Repeat Round 2.

Round 4: Pick up two size 15° beads, and pass through the next bead of the previous round; repeat around to add a total of twelve beads.

Round 5: Pick up one size 15° bead, and pass through the next bead of the previous round; repeat around to add a total of twelve beads. Place an earring post through the hole in the center of the beadwork.

2) Work rounds of tubular peyote stitch as follows:

Rounds 6 and 7: Repeat Round 5 twice, pulling tightly with each stitch so that the beadwork cups around the flat face of the earring finding.

Round 8: Repeat Round 5, placing the back of a crystal setting on top of the flat face of the earring post mid-round. Keep the tension very tight.

Round 9: Pick up one size 15° bead, pass through the next bead of the previous round, wrap the thread around the closest prong on the setting, and pass through the next bead of the previous round *(fig. 1)*; repeat around to seat the setting. Weave through the round again to peyote stitch the beads that were missed from the prong-wrapping.

Rounds 10 to 12: Repeat Round 5 three times. Secure the thread and trim.

Figure 1. Earrings: Round 9, hooking thread around prong setting.

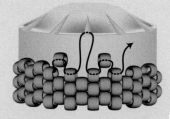

Dinah

...The doe-eyed girl next door donned her ornate bezeled crystal necklace and elegant floor-length Chanel gown and floated onto the smoky nightclub stage. As she opened her mouth to belt out yet another torch song, all she could think was how nice it would be to hit the links....

PHOTO COURTESY OF MPTVIMAGES.COM.

Dinah Shore, c. 1950.

Tennessee native **Dinah Shore** was born Frances Rose Shore in 1916 to Russian-Jewish immigrant parents. Her love of singing started at an early age, and at only fourteen she was singing torch songs in a Nashville night club. She had a recording contract with RCA Victor by the time she was twenty-four, and Eddie Cantor, host of the popular radio show *A Time to Smile*, featured her as a regular.

Shore's popularity grew with her string of number-one hits in the early 1940s, including *You'd Be So Nice to Come Home To* and *I'll Walk Alone,* and she became a wildly popular fixture on the USO tours during World War II. She appeared in several movies, including *Up in Arms* (1944), but gained Emmy Award–winning status with her many network television talk shows that ran from 1956 to 1980.

FINISHED LENGTH:
16 ³/₄" (42.5 cm)

TECHNIQUES: right-angle weave, tubular peyote stitch, stringing

MATERIALS AND TOOLS

6 grams permanent galvanized silver size 11° seed beads **(A)**

3 grams galvanized silver size 15° seed beads **(B)**

213 white 3mm round crystal pearl beads (#5810)

51 crystal AB 6mm round crystal beads (#5000)

44 crystal AB 4mm round crystal beads (#5000)

9 white opal-foiled 8 x 6mm oval fancy stones (#4120)

1 crystal silver shade 30 x 22mm oval fancy stone (#4127)

6 lapis lazuli 15 x 18mm oval cabochons

¹/₂" (1.3 cm) of silver medium French wire (gimp)

1 sterling silver 11mm toggle clasp

crystal 6 lb (2.7 kg) braided beading thread

scissors

2 size 12 beading needles

thread burner

wire cutters

1) **LARGE CRYSTAL BEZEL.** Work right-angle weave and tubular peyote stitch to form a bezel around the large fancy stone:

Round 1: Place a needle at the end of 4' (1.2 m) of thread. Use A to form a strip of right-angle weave twenty-nine units long. Fold the strip in half. Exiting up through the end bead of the final unit, pick up one A and pass down through the end bead of the first unit. Pick up one A and pass up through the end bead of the final unit, turning the strip into a ring. Repeat the thread path to reinforce. Exit from an edge bead *(fig. 1)*.

Round 2: Pick up one A and pass through the next edge A from Round 1; repeat around to add a total of thirty A. Step up for this and subsequent rounds by passing through the first bead added in the current round.

Rounds 3 to 5: Pick up one B and pass through the next A of the previous round; repeat around to add a total of thirty B in each of three rounds. Weave through the beadwork to exit from an A on the other edge of Round 1.

Round 6: Set the large fancy stone inside the beadwork so that the back touches Rounds 2 to 5. Pick up one B, and pass through the next edge A from Round 1; repeat around to add a total of thirty B.

Round 7: Pick up one B and pass through the B from Round 5; repeat around to add a total of thirty B. Exit down through a horizontal A in Round 1 *(fig. 2)*.

Figure 1. Large bezel, connecting Round 1.

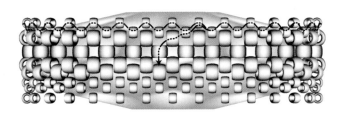

Figure 2. Large bezel, Round 7.

Pearls: Pull the thread end down to the beadwork to double the thread. String one pearl, and pass down through the next horizontal A in Round 1; repeat around to add one pearl to the outside of each right-angle weave unit in Round 1 *(fig. 3)*. Weave through the beads to exit the Round 1 vertical A on the bezel's back that sits directly in the center at one end of the oval.

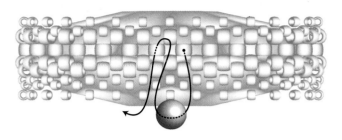

Figure 3. Large bezel, pearls.

 LAPIS LAZULI BEZEL. Work right-angle weave and tubular peyote stitch to form a bezel around a cabochon:

Round 1: Place a needle at the end of 3' (0.9 m) of thread. Use A to form a strip of right-angle weave sixteen units long. Fold the strip in half. Exiting up through the end bead of the final unit, pick up one A and pass down through the end bead of the first unit. Pick up one A and pass up through the end bead of the final unit, turning the strip into a ring. Repeat the thread path to reinforce. Exit from an edge bead.

Round 2: Pick up one A and pass through the next edge A from Round 1; repeat around to add a total of seventeen A. Step up for this and subsequent rounds by passing through the first bead added in the current round.

Rounds 3 and 4: Pick up one B and pass through the next A of the previous round; repeat around to add a total of seventeen B in each of two rounds. Weave through the beadwork to exit from an A on the other edge of Round 1.

Round 5: Set a cabochon inside the beadwork so that the front touches Rounds 2 to 4. Pick up one B and pass through the next edge A from Round 1; repeat around to add a total of seventeen B.

Rounds 6 and 7: Pick up one B and pass through the B from Round 5; repeat around to add a total of seventeen B. Exit down through a horizontal A in Round 1.

Pearls: Pull the thread end down to the beadwork to double the thread. String one pearl and pass down through the next horizontal A in Round 1; repeat around to add one pearl to the outside of each right-angle weave unit in Round 1. Secure the thread and trim. Set aside.

Repeat this entire step to form a total of six lapis lazuli bezels.

3) **SMALL CRYSTAL BEZEL.** Work right-angle weave and tubular peyote stitch to form a bezel around a small fancy stone:

Round 1: Place a needle at the end of 2' (61 cm) of thread. Use A to form a strip of right-angle weave eight units long. Fold the strip in half. Exiting up through the end bead of the final unit, pick up one A and pass down through the end bead of the first unit. Pick up one A and pass up through the end bead of the final unit, turning the strip into a ring. Repeat the thread path to reinforce. Exit from an edge bead.

Round 2: Pick up one B and pass through the next edge A from Round 1; repeat around to add a total of nine B. Repeat the thread path again, pulling very tightly to cup the beadwork. Weave through the beadwork to exit from an A on the other edge of Round 1.

Round 3: Set a small fancy stone into the beadwork with the back against Round 2. Pick up one B and pass through the next edge A from Round 1; repeat around to add a total of nine B. Repeat the thread path again, pulling very tightly to hold the stone in place. Exit down through a horizontal A in Round 1.

Pearls: Pull the thread end down to the beadwork to double the thread. String one pearl and pass down through the next horizontal A in Round 1; repeat around to add one pearl to the outside of each right-angle weave unit in Round 1. Secure the thread and trim. Set aside.

Repeat this entire step to form a total of nine small stone bezels.

 FOCAL PIECE. Use the working thread of the large crystal bezel to pick up one A, one 6mm crystal, and one A; pass through a vertical Round 1 A at one end on the back of a small bezel. Pass back through the A/6mm/A just added and through the last A exited on the large bezel. Weave through the beads to exit through the next Round 1 vertical A on the back of the large bezel, toward the center *(fig. 4, blue thread path)*.

Pick up one A; pass through the A/6mm/A connection beads. Pick up one A; pass through the next vertical Round 1 A on the back of the small bezel. Weave through the beads to exit the mirror Round 1 A on the back of the small bezel, toward the center.

Pick up one A; pass through the A/6mm/A connection beads. Pick up one A; pass through the next vertical Round 1 A on the other side of the center Round 1 A on the back of the large bezel *(fig. 4, red thread path)*. Secure the thread and trim.

 ASSEMBLY. Connect the bezels using strands of crystal beads:

Focal to lapis lazuli bezel: Start a new 1' (31 cm) thread that exits up through the upper left vertical Round 1 A on the back of the small bezel placed in the focal piece. Pick up one A, one 4mm crystal, three 6mm crystals, one 4mm crystal, and one A; pass down through the lower right vertical Round 1 A on the back of a second small bezel. Pick up one A, one 4mm crystal, one 6mm crystal, one 4mm crystal, and one A; pass through the top center vertical Round 5 A on the back of a lapis lazuli bezel. Pick up one A, one 4mm crystal, one 6mm crystal, one 4mm crystal, and one A; pass up through the first A exited in this section to form a triangle.

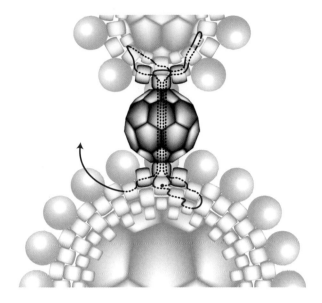

Figure 4. Focal piece connection.

Repeat the thread path at least once to reinforce; secure the thread and trim *(fig. 5)*.

Repeat this section to link three lapis lazuli bezels, always starting in the upper left corner of the last small bezel added.

Strap: Start a new 8" (20.3 cm) of thread that exits up through the upper left vertical Round 1 A on the back of the last small bezel placed. Pick up one A, one 4mm crystal, three 6mm crystals, one 4mm crystal, and one A; pass down through the lower right vertical Round 1 A on the back of another small bezel and back through all the beads just added. Pass up through the last A exited on the previous small bezel *(fig. 6, blue thread path)*. Repeat the thread path to reinforce; secure the thread and trim.

Clasp: Cut the French wire into two ¹/₄" (6 mm) pieces. Set aside. Start a new 1' (31 cm) of thread that exits up through the upper left vertical Round 1 A on the back of the last small bezel placed. Pick up one A, one 4mm crystal, seven 6mm crystals, one 4mm crystal, one A, one piece of French wire, and half of the clasp; pass back through the A/4mm crystal/6mm crystals/A and through the last A exited on the previous small bezel *(fig. 6, red thread path)*. Repeat the thread path to reinforce; secure the thread and trim.

Repeat this entire step in mirror to form the other side of the necklace.

Figure 5. Connecting the focal piece to a lapis bezel.

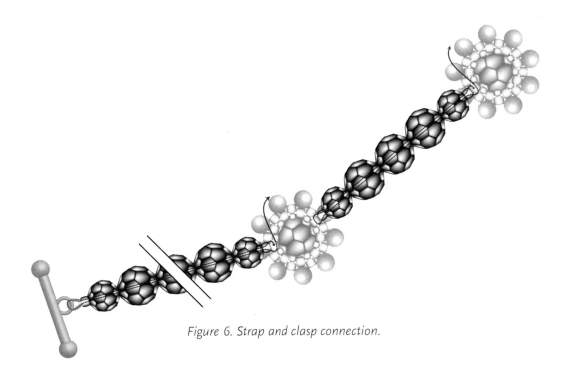

Figure 6. Strap and clasp connection.

Marlene

...A substantial gold bracelet with a jet center was all the smoldering beauty needed for accessorizing. Her porcelain skin, perfectly shaped features, flowing blonde hair, and long, slender fingers took care of the rest....

Marlene Dietrich, 1935.

Born in Berlin, Germany, in 1901, **Marlene Dietrich** rose to Hollywood fame through bit parts in German films and stage work in the 1920s. It was with her character Lola Lola in *The Blue Angel* (1930) that she swept to international fame, singing the song she's most known for, "Falling in Love Again." Dietrich's smoky, sultry looks were featured in dozens of film noir selections, including *Blonde Venus* (1932), *Shanghai Express* (1932), and *Morocco* (1930), the latter for which she received her only Oscar nomination.

FINISHED LENGTH:
6 ³/₄" (17.2 cm)

TECHNIQUES: right-angle weave, peyote stitch, herringbone stitch, square stitch, ladder stitch

MATERIALS AND TOOLS

10 grams metallic light gold permanent galvanized size 11° seed beads **(A)**

1 gram gold-lined clear size 15° seed beads **(B)**

2 grams bronze metallic size 11° cylinder hex beads **(C)**

36 crystal copper 2mm crystal round beads (#5000) **(D)**

12 crystal dorado 4mm crystal round beads (#5000)

1 Jet 30 x 22mm oval fancy stone (#4127)

1 gold 6mm magnet clasp

smoke 6 lb (2.7 kg) braided beading thread

scissors

size 11 beading needle

thread burner

1)

BEZEL. Use tight thread tension to right-angle weave and peyote stitch a seed bead bezel around the fancy stone:

Round 1: Place a needle on the end of 2' (61 cm) of thread. Use A to form a strip of right-angle weave twenty-seven units long. Fold the strip in half. Exiting up through the end bead of the final unit, pick up one A and pass down through the end bead of the first unit. Pick up one A and pass up through the end bead of the final unit, turning the strip into a ring. Repeat the thread path to reinforce. Exit from an edge bead *(fig. 1)*.

Rounds 2 to 4: Pick up one B and pass through the next edge bead from the previous round; repeat around to add a total of twenty-eight beads. Step up for the next round by passing through the first bead added in the current round. Repeat to form a total of three rounds with B. Pass through the final round again to pull the beadwork into a circle. Weave through the beads to exit from the opposite edge of Round 1.

Rounds 5 to 7: Place the fancy stone in the beadwork, flat-side down, ensuring that there is one right-angle weave unit centered at each end of the oval. Pick up one A, and pass through the next Round 1 bead; repeat around to add a total of twenty-eight beads *(fig. 2)*. Step up through the first bead added in this round. Repeat to add two more rounds, this time with B, securing the stone in place. Secure the thread and trim. Set the bezeled stone aside.

Figure 1. Bezel, connecting Round 1.

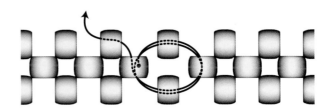

7
6
5

1

2
3
4

Figure 2. Bezel, Rounds 2 to 7.

INNER BAND. Herringbone stitch the core of the bracelet's band:

Row 1: Place a needle on the end of 6' (1.8 m) of thread. Work a ladder-stitched strip six A long, leaving a 2' (61 cm) tail.

Rows 2 to 8: Work herringbone stitch with one A and one C in the first stitch, two A in the second stitch, and one C and one A in the third stitch (*fig. 3*); repeat to form a total of seven rows.

Row 9: Work one herringbone stitch with one A and one C. Pick up one D, and pass up through the next A from the previous row. Herringbone stitch two A. Pick up one D, and pass up through the next C from the previous row. Herringbone stitch one C and one A (*fig. 4*).

Rows 10 to 17: Repeat Row 9.

Strands: Pick up one A, one 4mm crystal bead, and one A; pass down through the next A from the previous row and up through the following A. Pick up one A, one 4mm crystal bead, and one A; pass down through the next A from the previous row (it will be on the outside edge of the band). Weave through the beads to exit up through the last A added (*fig. 5*).

Loops: Pick up five A; pass down through the first A of the second strand just added. Pick up one A; pass up through the second A of the first strand. Pick up five A; pass down through the first A of the first strand (*fig. 6*).

Repeat the thread path to reinforce. Exit between the second and third A just added.

Stem: Use the tail thread to ladder stitch the first and last A of Row 1 together, forming a circle.

Use A to work six-bead tubular herringbone stitch for nineteen rounds. Use a square-stitched thread path to secure the final round. ***Note:*** If you need a larger bracelet, repeat the rounds to lengthen the stem one-half the length necessary to fit.

Clasp: Securely sew half of the clasp to the end of the stem, weaving back and forth through the final round to center the clasp over the stem's end (*fig. 7*).

Repeat this entire step to form a second inner band.

Figure 3. Inner band, Row 2.

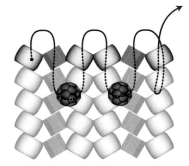

Figure 4. Inner band, Row 9.

Figure 5. Inner band strands.

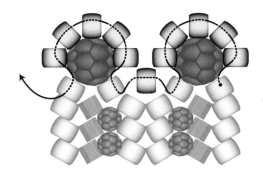

Figure 6. Inner band loops.

Figure 7. Attaching the clasp to the inner band's stem.

3) **INNER ASSEMBLY.** Place the looped end of one of the inner bands against the end of the bezeled stone so that it straddles the centered right-angle weave unit. Make sure that the convex side of the stone faces up. Use the remaining working thread of the band to stitch the bezel to the band, attaching the inner two A of each loop to the corresponding top A on the bezel *(fig. 8)*.

Repeat to connect the other inner band to the opposite side of the bezel.

4) **OUTER BAND.** Work a herringbone-stitched band to sheath and embellish the inner band:

Row 1: Place a needle on the end of 8' (2.4 m) of thread, leaving a 2' (61 cm) tail. Work a ladder-stitched strip six A long.

Rows 2 to 20: Work herringbone stitch with two A in each stitch to form a strip twenty rows long (or long enough to match the inner band's stem, plus one row).

Row 21: Work one herringbone stitch with two A; one herringbone stitch with one A, one C, one A; and one herringbone stitch with two A.

Row 22: Pass down through the second-to-last A added in the previous row. Pick up one A and pass down through the second-to-last A added in the previous row and up through the A just added. Continue ladder stitch to form a strip six A long. Wrap the strip behind the first row of one of the inner band's stems. Pass up through the second A added in Row 21, down through the final ladder-stitched A just added, up through the second A added in Row 21, and down through the first A added in Row 21 *(fig. 9)*. Set the working thread aside.

Stem connection: Align the front of the inner stem so that it runs evenly along the back of the outer band. Thread a needle on the tail thread. Use your fingers to flatten the inner stem so that its edge columns touch the edge columns of the outer band. Square stitch the beads of the outer band's edge columns to the corresponding beads of the inner band *(fig. 10)*. Set the tail thread aside.

Rows 23 to 39: Using the working thread again, work herringbone stitch with two A in each stitch, keeping the beadwork behind the inner band. Set the working thread aside.

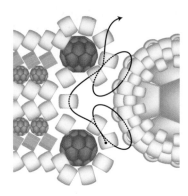

Figure 8. Attaching inner band to the bezel.

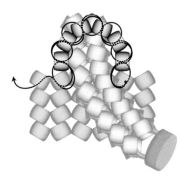

Figure 9. Outer band, Row 22.

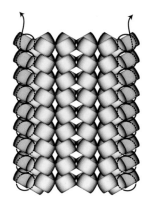

Figure 10. Stem connection.

Strap: Weave the tail thread through the beadwork to exit Row 27. Repeat Row 22, this time wrapping the ladder-stitched strip in front of the inner band. Work two rows of herringbone stitch off this band, connecting the end of each row to the nearest A of the outer band so that the strap ends are secure. Use a ladder-stitched thread path to secure the final row (*fig. 11*). Secure the tail thread and trim.

Connector: Use the working thread to pick up one 4mm crystal bead, one A, one 4mm crystal bead, and two A; pass back through the final crystal bead. Pick up one A, pass back through the next crystal bead, down through the second-to-last bead added in Row 39, and up through the final bead added in Row 39 (*fig. 12, blue thread path*).

Pick up three A and pass through the first A added in this section to outline the first 4mm crystal bead. Pick up three A and pass through the second A added in this section to outline the second 4mm crystal bead. Pick up one A; skip one right-angle weave unit from the closest connection point on the bezel, and pass through the top A of the next one, toward the strap. Pass back through the nearest A at the end of the connector. Weave through all the beads added in this section again to reinforce. Square stitch the last A exited to the nearest A on the inner strap (*fig. 12, red thread path*).

Weave through the beadwork to add a connector to the other edge of the band.

If desired, weave through the beadwork to exit the top back of the outer band and stitch it to the back center of the inner band. Secure the thread and trim.

Repeat this step for the other inner band.

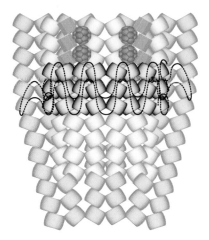

Figure 11. Outer band strap.

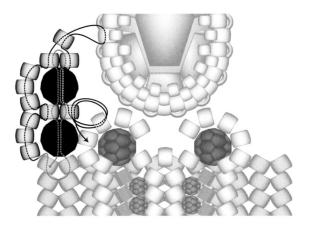

Figure 12. Connecting the outer band to the bezel.

Basics

MATERIALS

If you've picked up this book, chances are that you know your way around a bead shop, so I probably can't tell you anything new about the materials I used to design the projects in this book. But maybe you're curious about why I used these materials. Read on, and I'll tell you all my little secrets.

BEADS AND STONES

You'll be able to find most of the beads and stones in this book right at your local bead shop. If not, be sure to check the great resources listed on page 143.

CRYSTAL BEADS

Crystal beads are truly the superstars of this book. They're made of leaded glass and are made with high-tech machines that cut incredibly precise, sharp facets, adding to their dazzle. The bling factor aside, I like to use crystals because they're durable, don't fade, and come in dozens of different colors and an even wider variety of shapes. The nice thing about using crystals from Swarovski is that I can use, say, a round rose-colored crystal, and I know that a rose-colored bicone, rivoli, or margarita I might choose for the same design will be exactly (or near to exactly) the same color every time.

Swarovski Elements have polished holes and smooth edges so you don't have to worry about sharp edges. However, if you are worried about the edges fraying or cutting through the thread, use seed beads as buffers on each side of the hole and use braided beading thread when stitching crystals together.

Please see Crystal Shapes Guide (page 140), Beads and Pendants Color Chart (page 141), and Crystal Pearls Color Chart (page 142) for more information on the specific beads used in this book.

Crystal beads.

Crystal pearls.

CRYSTAL PEARLS

Crystal pearls are crystals, too! These begin with a basic round bead made of crystal glass; then they are coated with an extremely durable and lustrous finish. Because the core is crystal rather than ordinary glass or plastic like some other faux pearls, these beads have a nice weight that feels very close to natural pearls.

SEED BEADS

Next to crystals, *seed beads* are the other stars of this book. I love working with these tiny glass beads because their size makes it possible to stitch them together into flat beaded fabric, curved shapes, or long strands. They are completely versatile. I use sizes 15° (the smallest), 11°, 8°, and 6° (the largest) seed beads in this book.

As you'll see, I've used lots of *permanent galvanized* seed beads throughout. I like how the metallic look evokes the vintage, mostly metal jewelry that provided the design inspiration, but even more, I like that the finish on these beads isn't going to wear off, which is not always the case with metallic-finish seed beads. The only downside to this type of bead is that some have very thin holes, so you'll need to cull those out before you start working with them.

METAL BEADS

Metal beads are nice to use in vintage-inspired projects because much jewelry of the early twentieth century was metal centric. The most common metal beads you'll find at bead shops are pewter, brass, copper, sterling, and fine silver. Always buy high-quality metal beads—you'll be able to see and feel the difference when you hold them side by side. By paying just a little more, even if it's for better-quality base metal, you'll find that the finishes last longer and you won't run the risk of unsightly metal allergies.

STONE CABOCHONS

I've used *stone cabochons* in just one of the projects in this book, *Dinah* (page 114). I like the way the opaque stone looks so weighty against those shiny crystals, don't you? Cabochons don't have holes—they are flat on one side, domed on the other side—so they need to be bezeled or glued in place when you design with them. When buying stone cabochons, realize that they are handmade, so no two will be exactly alike. It's worth it to spend some time choosing when buying multiples of these, as is required in *Dinah*, so that you can pick out cabochons that are generally the same size.

Seed beads.

Metal beads.

Stone cabochons.

Findings

I've used all the little metal bits and pieces that hold jewelry together, or *findings*, in an understated way in this book, allowing the beads and beadwork to be the leading ladies. But it's still good to know a little bit about these jewelry-making workhorses, even to know the findings' names and what they look like, so that you'll know what to ask for when you head to the bead shop.

BEAD CAPS

As their name indicates, *bead caps* are used for decoratively finishing the ends of beads. Look at *Cleo* (page 58) to see what I'm talking about.

BEADING DOME

A *beading dome* is a finding that comes in two parts: the bottom is a flat, round, metal backing with prongs, and the top is a metal dome with a grid of holes. You'll add fringe to this type of finding for projects like *Natalie* (page 44) and *Ann* (page 22). I love these because they provide a sturdy base for fringe and can be converted into lots of different jewelry-making components, including brooches and clasps.

CHAIN

I really like mixing *chain* with beadwork; the metal provides a nice juxtaposition to the glass, and it works so well for creating strong jewelry. In this book, I've used both plated and sterling silver chain for necklace straps, for embellishment, and as length extenders.

CLASPS

The clasps I've used in this book are plain and simple because they aren't the stars of the show.

Toggle clasps are ring/bar clasps that hold together with tension.

Lobster clasps look like a lobster claw with a little spring mechanism that opens them.

Bead caps.

Beading dome.

Chain.

Toggle clasp.

Lobster clasp.

Magnetic clasps have strong magnets that hold them together. It's always good to use more than one magnetic clasp on a piece if you can, just in case your jewelry gets pulled on your ball gown or something.

Dress hooks are those little hook-and-eye wire gizmos that you find on a bra or at the top of a skirt. They work wonderfully for evasively connecting the ends of a bracelet or necklace.

Snaps, the two-part metal or plastic kind you'd find at the sewing store, work well as hidden connectors at the end of a flat bead-woven bracelet. Sew these in tightly, reinforcing the stitches several times, so as not to stress the beadwork when opening and closing the piece.

CRIMP TUBES

I like to use *crimp tubes* (rather than crimp beads) in my strung work. These tiny metal tubular beads work great to secure flexible beading wire to findings (see page 138 to find out exactly how to do this). I also heartily recommend that you purchase sterling silver or gold-filled crimp tubes instead of base metal, which I've found as temperamental as a method actress getting into character.

CRIMP COVERS

These round findings are used to cover up those sometimes ugly crimp jobs. Just open it up at the seam and close it around the crimp with your fingers, nylon-jaw pliers, or, if you're very careful and the cover is small enough, using the front notch of crimping pliers.

CUFF BLANKS

When creating an embroidered cuff, there's really nothing better to line it with than one of these *cuff blanks*. They are often made out of copper with a thin plating of brass over the top. Cuff blanks are easy to shape and bend, and they provide the structure that you need to keep your beadwork steady.

Magnetic clasp.

Dress hook.

Snap.

Crimp tubes.

Crimp covers.

Cuff blank.

EARRING FINDINGS

I like the flexibility of making my own *ear wires* (as in *Jamilla*, page 28, and *Apple Blossom Earrings*, page 39), but sometimes using commercial ear wires works just as well. Make sure to purchase high-quality base or precious metal findings to avoid not only metal allergies but also frustration. It can be quite annoying when adding a dangle to an ear wire loop and the loop snaps in two because the metal is so brittle. Too much drama, not to mention wasted time and money.

The *ear posts* that I use in several projects in this book have a round, flat metal face onto which you can glue beadwork. I highly recommend using large-size *ear nuts* for this type of finding, because the earrings tend to be large and can misshape your earlobe. Wide ear nuts are like Botox for big earrings; they help combat any sagging.

HEAD PINS

These simple findings are found in *Cleo* (page 58) and extensively in *Zsa Zsa* (page 106), providing the base to beaded dangles. *Head pins* are made up of a thin wire with a flat, perpendicular disk at one end. Again, use the highest-quality head pins that you can afford; it will make bending and wrapping loops so much easier.

JUMP RINGS

You'll mainly find *jump rings* used in this book to link components. These little circles of wire work great to make the transition from beadwork to chain or beaded link to beaded link. See page 139 for the proper technique for opening and closing these findings.

SPACER BARS

One nice way to separate multistranded pieces is with a metal *spacer bar*. In this book, I've incorporated two-hole spacer bars into the netted portion of *Marilyn* (page 40).

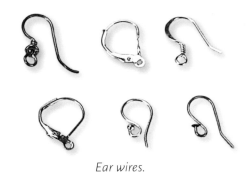

Ear wires.

Ear posts.

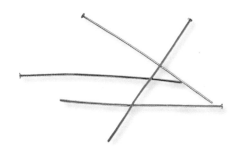

Head pins.

Jump rings.   *Spacer bars.*

Stringing Materials

You won't need to spend too much time in the stringing materials section at your local bead shop for the projects in this book because I use just these three different materials.

BRAIDED BEADING THREAD

Braided beading thread is a durable product that works great for bead weaving crystals. It's easy to thread, doesn't tangle or fray, and holds up to the weight and abrasion of crystal beads quite well. I prefer FireLine, a product of the fishing industry that's sold by the test weight. The 6-pound version is a great all-around beading thread.

Braided beading thread.

FLEXIBLE BEADING WIRE

My favorite type of stringing wire is *flexible beading wire*. It's made with an inner core of many thin cables of stainless steel that are bound together in a nylon sheath. It drapes like silk, has incredible strength, and is very durable.

METAL WIRE

Paging through the book, you'll find that I've made a few ear wires and some links using metal wire. You can buy metal wire at most bead shops—just keep in mind that the larger the gauge number, the thinner the wire. When you can, use precious metal wire, but color-coated or plated copper wire works well, too; believe me, the paparazzi won't notice when you're having your photo taken on the red carpet.

Flexible beading wire.

Metal wire.

Other Materials

There are several other supplies that you'll need to put your glamorous jewelry together.

BEESWAX

I use beeswax to stiffen my braided beading thread. Just rub the block of wax over the thread after you cut and thread the needle. This is especially helpful when you're working with doubled thread; the wax helps keep the threads stuck together.

GLUE

For tough jobs, such as heavy diva earrings that require a metal-to-beads bond, use a strong jeweler's adhesive like E-6000. Work with this glue only with good ventilation; it's much better to fry your brain cells with a well-mixed martini than with glue. For lighter jobs, use a watchmaker's glue like Hypo Cement.

Beeswax.

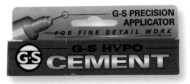

Glues.

TOOLS

These glamorous projects tend to look complicated, but in reality, they don't require many tools to construct.

BEADING NEEDLES

I use size 11 and 12 **beading needles** to stitch just about all of my beadwork. My favorite type of beading needle is a **sharp needle**. They are shorter and slightly thicker than an **English beading needle**, and I find them easier to maneuver. The type of needle you use is a personal decision, though, so try both.

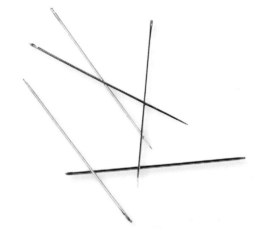

Beading needles.

SCISSORS

Scissors are obviously a necessity to cut thread, but because we're only using braided beading thread in this book, I recommend using a utility or children's craft scissors to cut the thread. Save your fine embroidery scissors for nylon thread, and use a thread burner for cutting braided beading thread close to the work.

Scissors.

THREAD BURNER

These little battery-operated machines have a pointed wire tip that reaches an intense temperature almost instantly. There's just nothing better out there than a *thread burner* to trim tails and working threads close to your beadwork.

PLIERS

Even though the majority of the pieces in this book are bead woven, you'll still need some *pliers* to pull many of the projects together. Use *chain-nose pliers*, the kind with jaws that are flat on the inside, rounded on the outside, and taper to a point, to form sharp bends. They also work well for pulling a stuck beading needle through a too-full bead.

Use *round-nose pliers*, the kind with tapered, cylindrical jaws, to form curves and loops.

Use *crimping pliers*, the specialty tool with notched jaws, to secure crimp tubes to flexible beading wire (see page 138 for a description of this technique).

WIRE CUTTERS

You'll use *wire cutters* to cut wire, of course, but also for trimming head pins. Make sure that you have a sharp pair that makes a flat, or *flush* cut, especially for when you're creating ear wires. You don't want to scratch yourself with a metal burr, do you?

EYELET SETTER

You'll need to use an eyelet setter only for one project in this book, *Natalie* (page 44). It is used primarily to set eyelets in paper or fabric, but I've found it handy for setting Swarovski rivets, too.

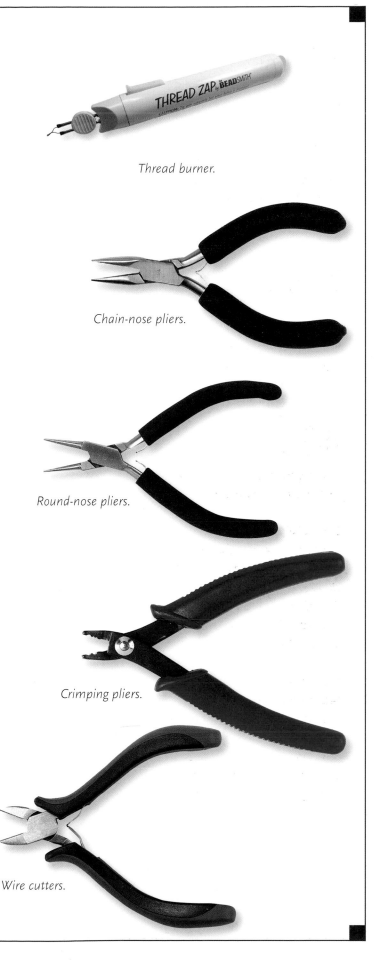

Thread burner.

Chain-nose pliers.

Round-nose pliers.

Crimping pliers.

Wire cutters.

Eyelet setter.

TECHNIQUES

Putting beads together to create jewelry can be done in myriad ways. Here is the handful of techniques you'll need to know to make all the projects in this book.

BEADWEAVING TECHNIQUES

Learn the following methods of stitching seed and other beads together to form a beaded fabric.

Fringe

Exiting from the beadworked base, pick up the number of beads desired for the fringe. Skip the last bead, pass back through the remaining beads just added, and pass into the beadworked base.

Herringbone Stitch

Use an even number of beads to ladderstitch (see below) a foundation row. With the thread exiting up through the last bead of the foundation row, pick up two beads and pass down through the next bead in the foundation (the second-to-last bead of the row) and up through the bead after that (the third-to-last bead of the row). Pick up two beads, and pass down through the next bead of the foundation row and up through the following bead; repeat to the end of the row. Loop around the thread between beads to form a turnaround, allowing you to exit up through the final bead added. Repeat to form as many rows as necessary.

Ladder Stitch

Pick up two beads and pass through both beads again. Adjust the beads so their sides touch. Pick up one bead and pass through the last bead stitched and this new bead again; repeat, adding one bead at a time, until the chain is the desired length.

Simple fringe.

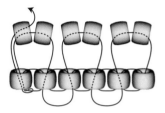

Herringbone stitch.

Ladder stitch.

General Beadweaving Know-How

THERE ARE SEVERAL TECHNIQUES you'll need to know when you pair a needle and thread with beads, no matter what stitch you're doing.

PASS THROUGH VS. PASS BACK THROUGH

When following the project instructions, keep in mind that *pass through* means to move your needle and thread through a bead in the same direction that it was added. *Pass back through* means to move through it in the opposite direction.

TAIL VS. WORKING THREAD

The length between the first bead added on a strand of beads and the thread's end is called the *tail thread*. The thread you do your stitching with is called the *working thread*.

WEAVING THROUGH BEADS

To position the needle and thread to exit a different place, you'll pass through adjacent beads, keeping the thread hidden. In the instructions this is indicated with the term *weave through the beads*.

STEPPING UP

To *step up* is to prepare the needle and thread to transition from one round to the next. In tubular peyote stitch, for example, stepping up for the next round is to pass through the first bead added in the current round.

REINFORCE

Reinforce your beadwork by passing through the beads in the same thread path that it was stitched. Doing this will strengthen the connection between beads.

ENDING AND BEGINNING THREADS

To end a thread, stop stitching when you have about 4"(10 cm) of thread left on the needle. Tie a half-hitch or an overhand knot around the thread between the beads, pass through a few beads, and pull the thread tightly to hide the knot inside a bead; repeat once or twice. Use a thread burner to trim the thread close to the beadwork.

To begin a new thread, pass through a few beads on the beadwork so that just a short tail emerges. Pass the needle around the thread between the beads, tie a half-hitch or an overhand knot, pass through a few more beads, and pull the thread taut to hide the knot inside a bead. Use a thread burner to trim the tail thread close to the beadwork.

Peyote Stitch

Flat, Even-Count

Pick up an even number of beads to the desired width (these beads will form the first two rows). Pick up one bead, skip one bead in the original row, and pass through the next bead; repeat across the row. After you have finished the third row, every other bead will stick up slightly; these are the "up" beads. On subsequent rows, pick up a bead and pass through the next up bead, working rows to the desired length.

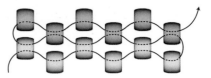

Flat, even-count peyote stitch.

Circular

Pick up five beads, tie them into a tight circle, and pass through the first bead strung. Pick up one bead, and pass through the next bead in the circle; repeat around to add a total of five beads, and then step up through the first bead added in this second round. Pick up two beads, and pass through the next bead added in the second round; repeat around to add a total of ten beads, and then step up through the first bead added in this third round. Pick up one bead, and pass through the next bead of the previous round, splitting the pair; repeat around to add a total of ten beads, and then step up through the first bead added in this round. Pick up one bead, and pass through the next bead of the previous round; repeat to add a total of ten beads. Continue working outward to the desired size, adding either one or two beads in each stitch as necessary to keep the beadwork flat.

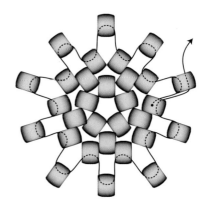

Circular peyote stitch.

Tubular

Pick up an even number of beads, tie them into a tight circle, and pass through the first bead strung. Pick up one bead, skip a bead on the initial circle, and pass through the next bead in the circle; repeat around to add half as many beads as were originally strung. Step up through the first bead added in this round. *Pick up one bead and pass through the next bead of the previous round; repeat around, pulling tightly with each stitch, then step up through the first bead added in this round. Repeat from * to form a tube to the desired length.

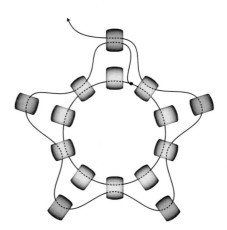

Tubular peyote stitch.

Zipping

To "zip" a piece of flat peyote-stitched beadwork means to attach the end rows of two pieces of beadwork together or to connect the first and last rows of the same piece of beadwork, forming a tube. Start by ensuring that the edge beads of the two pieces interlock like a zipper (thus the name), adding or subtracting a row as necessary. Next, weave back and forth through the up beads of each piece, lacing them together to form one continuous piece of beadwork.

Right-Angle Weave

Pick up four beads, tie them into a tight circle, and pass through the first three beads strung. Pick up three beads, and pass through the last bead exited and the first two beads just added to form another "unit"; repeat, adding three beads at a time, to reach the desired row length. Turn the row so that it sits horizontally. Exit through the nearest bead along the top edge of the strip, toward the beadwork. Pick up three beads; pass through the last bead exited and up through the first bead just added. *Pick up two beads, pass through the next edge bead along the top of the first row, up through the nearest side bead of the previous unit, through the two beads just added, and through the next edge bead at the top of the previous row. Pick up two beads, pass down through the nearest side bead of the previous unit, through the next top edge bead, and up through the first bead just added. Repeat from * across the row. Start any new rows the same way as the second one.

Square Stitch

Pick up a base row of beads to the desired width. Pick up one bead, and pass through the final base bead and the bead just added. Pick up one bead, and pass through the next bead from the previous row and the bead just added; repeat to the end of the row. Add more rows in the same manner.

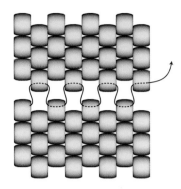

Zipping peyote-stitched edges.

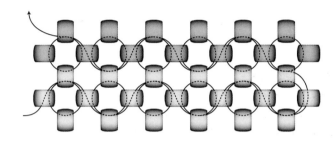

Right-angle weave.

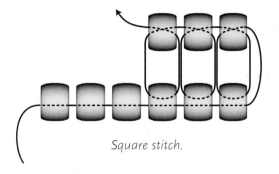

Square stitch.

OTHER TECHNIQUES

This book is beadweaving centric, but you'll need to know how to do a few other tricks as well.

Crimping

String beads onto flexible beading wire. Use the wire to string a crimp bead or tube and the ring of a clasp or other finding. Pass back through the crimp tube *(fig. 1)* and (if possible) back through a few of the last beads strung. Pull the wire to snug the beads against the clasp. Use the front notch of the crimping pliers to gently squeeze the tube into an oval shape, separating the wires *(fig. 2)*. Firmly squeeze the tube again with the back notch of the pliers, crimping the tube *(fig. 3)*. Turn the tube on its side and place it into the front notch of the pliers again. Squeeze the tube to form it into a rounded cylinder *(fig. 4)*.

Whipstitch

This method is useful for sewing two pieces of fabric together or for strengthening the edging of a piece of beadwork. For connecting fabric pieces, use a needle and knotted thread to sew into the edge of one piece of fabric and then the other. Sew into the two pieces of fabric again in the same manner, just down the edge from the last entry point. Repeat to connect the two fabric edges.

For reinforcing the sides of peyote- or brick-stitched beadwork, use a needle and thread to pass under an exposed loop of thread at the edge of the work; pass under the next exposed loop in the same direction.

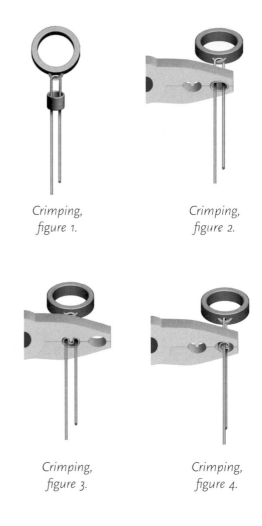

Crimping, figure 1.

Crimping, figure 2.

Crimping, figure 3.

Crimping, figure 4.

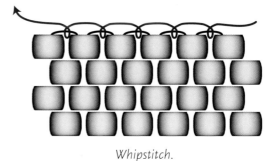

Whipstitch.

Wirework

Opening and Closing Loops and Jump Rings

Use two pairs of chain-nose pliers to grasp the ring on either side of the place where the wires meet, and gently twist one side up and one side down. Slip your connecting piece onto the loop and close with the reverse motion.

Simple Loop

Use chain-nose pliers to form a 90-degree bend in the wire $3/8$" to $1/2$" (1 to 1.3 cm) from the end (*fig. 1*). Use round-nose pliers to grasp the end of the wire. Holding firmly onto the body wire, slowly turn the pliers to form a loop in the end of the wire. Continue turning until the end of the wire meets the body wire (*fig. 2*).

Wrapped Loop

Use chain-nose pliers to form a 90-degree bend in the wire 2" (5.1 cm) from the end (*fig. 1*). With round-nose pliers, grasp the wire at the bend. Use your fingers to wrap the short end of the wire up and over the top of the pliers (*fig. 2*). Change the pliers' jaw position so that the bottom jaw is inside the loop. Swing the short wire end under the bottom jaw. Use your fingers or chain-nose pliers to grasp the short wire end. Wrap the end tightly down the neck of the wire to form several coils (*fig. 3*). Trim the excess close to the coils (*fig. 4*).

Opening and closing jump rings.

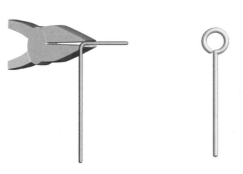

Simple loop, figure 1.   *Simple loop, figure 2.*

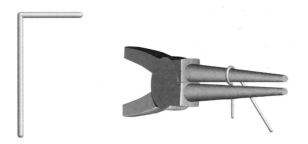

Wrapped loop, figure 1.   *Wrapped loop, figure 2.*

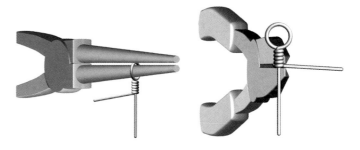

Wrapped loop, figure 3.   *Wrapped loop, figure 4.*

Crystal Shapes Guide

CREATE YOUR STYLE with SWAROVSKI ELEMENTS

Featured Swarovski Crystallized Elements

#1028
Xilion chaton

#1122
Rivoli chaton

#3200
Rivoli sew-on stone

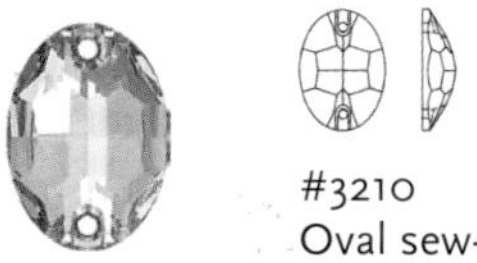

#3210
Oval sew-on stone

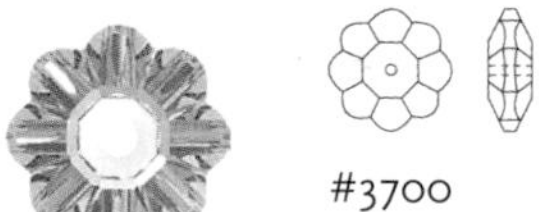

#3700
Marguerite lochrose

#4120
Oval fancy stone

#4127
Oval fancy stone

#4722
Triangular fancy stone

#5000
Round bead

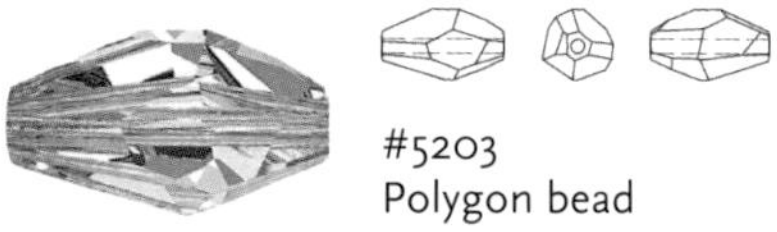

#5203
Polygon bead

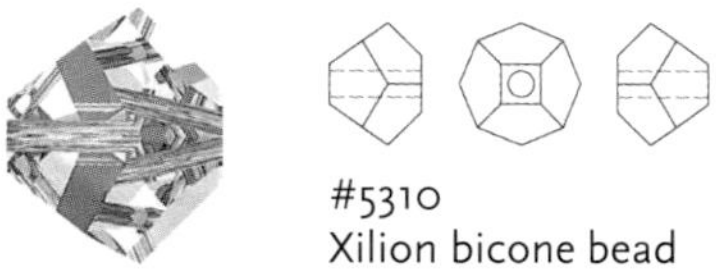

#5310
Xilion bicone bead

#5310
Simplicity bead

#5500
Teardrop bead

#5744
Flower bead

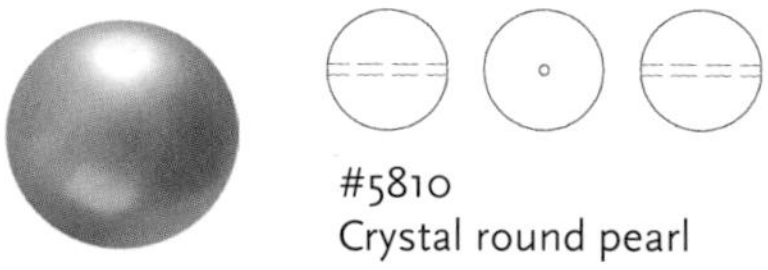

#5810
Crystal round pearl

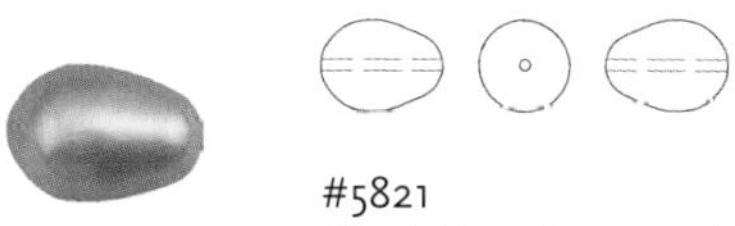

#5821
Crystal teardrop pearl

#6010
Briolette

#6090
Baroque pendant

#6714
Star pendant

#13 304
Navette (two-hole)

#17 012
Bezelled Round Stone

#60 408
Metal button (flower)

Beads and Pendants Color Chart

COLORS

 Crystal
001

 White Opal
234

 White Alabaster
281

 Rose Water Opal
395

 Rose Alabaster
293

 Vintage Rose
319

 Light Rose
223

 Rose
209

 Rosaline
508

 Indian Pink
289

 Fuchsia
502

 Ruby
501

 Padparadscha
542

 Sun
248

 Fireopal
237

 Hyacinth
236

 Indian Red
374

 Light Siam
227

 Dark Red Coral
396

Siam
208

Garnet
241

Burgundy
515

Light Amethyst
212

 Violet Opal
389

 Violet
371

 Tanzanite
539

 Amethyst
204

 Purple Velvet
277

 Dark Indigo
288

 Montana
207

 Capri Blue
243

 Sapphire
206

 Light Sapphire
211

 Aquamarine
202

 Air Blue Opal
285

 Light Azore
361

 Indian Sapphire
217

 Pacific Opal
390

 Mint Alabaster
397

 Turquoise
267

 Indicolite
379

 Caribbean Blue Opal
394

 Blue Zircon
229

 Chrysolite
238

 Peridot
214

 Erinite
360

 Emerald
205

 Palace Green Opal
393

 Olivine
228

 Khaki
550

 Lime
385

 Citrine
249

 Light Topaz
226

 Jonquil
213

 Silk
391

 Light Peach
362

 Light Colorado Topaz
246

 Topaz
203

 Light Smoked Topaz
221

 Smoked Topaz
220

 Mocca
286

 Smoky Quartz
225

Sand Opal
287

Light Grey Opal
383

Black Diamond
215

Jet
280

EFFECTS

 Crystal Aurore Boreale
001 AB

 Crystal Aurore Boreale 2x
001 AB2

 Crystal Satin
001 SAT

 Crystal Matt Finish
001 MAT

 Crystal Moonlight
001 MOL

 Crystal Silver Shade
001 SSHA

 Crystal Golden Shadow
001 GSHA

 Crystal Copper
001 COP

 Crystal Red Magma
001 REDM

 Crystal Comet Argent Light
001 CAL

 White Opal Sky Blue
234 BBL

 White Opal Star Shine
234 STS

 Crystal Bermuda Blue
001 BBL

 Crystal Heliotrope
001 HEL

 Crystal Metallic Blue 2x
001 METBL2

Crystal Vitrail Medium
001 VM

Crystal Dorado 2x
001 DOR2

Jet Nut 2x
280 NUT2

Jet Hematite
280 HEM

Jet Hematite 2x
280 HEM2

Classic Colors
Exclusive Colors

141

Crystal Pearls Color Chart

 Crystal White Pearl
001 650

 Crystal Cream Pearl
001 620

 Crystal Creamrose Light Pearl
001 618

 Crystal Creamrose Pearl
001 621

 Crystal Gold Pearl
001 296

 Crystal Bright Gold Pearl
001 306

 Crystal Copper Pearl
001 159

 Crystal Coral Pearl
001 816

 Crystal Brown Pearl
001 815

 Crystal Deep Brown Pearl
001 414

 Crystal Bronze Pearl
001 295

 Crystal Peach Pearl
001 300

 Crystal Powder Almond Pearl
001 305

 Crystal Rosaline Pearl
001 294

 Crystal Powder Rose Pearl
001 352

 Crystal Lavender Pearl
001 524

 Crystal Mauve Pearl
001 160

 Crystal Burgundy Pearl
001 301

 Crystal Bordeaux Pearl
001 538

 Crystal Maroon Pearl
001 388

 Crystal Dark Purple Pearl
001 309

 Crystal Night Blue Pearl
001 818

 Crystal Light Blue Pearl
001 302

 Crystal Tahitian-look Pearl
001 297

 Crystal Powder Green Pearl
001 393

 Crystal Light Green Pearl
001 293

 Crystal Antique Brass Pearl
001 402

 Crystal Dark Green Pearl
001 814

 Crystal Platinum Pearl
001 459

 Crystal Light Grey Pearl
001 616

 Crystal Dark Grey Pearl
001 617

 Crystal Black pearl
001 298

 Crystal Mystic Black Pearl
001 335

Sources

I SHOP AT MY LOCAL BEAD STORES as much as possible. It's important to support them so I know they'll be there when I need them! I also have some online sources I use again and again.

Artbeads.com
www.artbeads.com

The Bead Monkey
www.thebeadmonkey.com

Beyond Beadery
www.beyondbeadery.com

Bobby Bead
www.bobbybead.com

Caravan Beads, Inc.
www.caravanbeads.com

Fire Mountain Gems and Beads
www.firemountaingems.com

Fusion Beads
www.fusionbeads.com

Jean Campbell
www.jeancampbellink.com

Jo-Ann Fabrics and Crafts
www.joann.com

Michael's Art & Crafts
www.michaels.com

Mill End Textiles
www.millendtextiles.com

Nina Designs
www.ninadesigns.com

Ornamental Resources, Inc.
www.ornabead.com

Shipwreck Beads
www.shipwreckbeads.com

Soft Flex Company
www.softflexcompany.com

Tierra Cast (wholesale only)
www.tierracast.com

For more information about Swarovski Elements and the CREATE YOUR STYLE initiative, please go to www.create-your-style.com.

CREDITS

EDITOR-IN-CHIEF
Kerry I. Hoffman

TECHNICAL EDITOR
Anne Marie Soto

MANAGING EDITOR
Judy Petry

DESIGN DIRECTOR
Cheryl Stevenson

COPY EDITOR
Liz McGehee

PROOFREADER
Melissa Riesland

ILLUSTRATORS
Laurel Strand, Robin Strobel

PHOTOGRAPHER
Brent Kane

PHOTO STYLISTS
Cheryl Stevenson, Heidi Soehren

COVER DESIGNER
Cheryl Stevenson

TEXT DESIGNER
Barbara Schmitt

PRODUCTION ASSISTANT
Marijane E. Figg

Library of Congress Cataloging-in-Publication Data

Babylon, Donna.
  The total bedroom : easy-to-make quilts and
custom fabric furnishings / Donna Babylon.
     p. cm.
  ISBN 1-56477-114-8
  1. Household linens 2. Patchwork—Patterns.
3. Patchwork quilts. 4. Bedrooms. I. Title.
TT387.B33 1997
46. 9'7—dc20   96-35589
                                          CIP

MISSION STATEMENT

WE ARE DEDICATED TO PROVIDING
QUALITY PRODUCTS AND SERVICE
BY WORKING TOGETHER TO INSPIRE
CREATIVITY AND TO ENRICH
THE LIVES WE TOUCH.

The Total Bedroom: Easy-to-Make Quilts
and Custom Fabric Furnishings
© 1997 by Donna Babylon

That Patchwork Place, Inc.
PO Box 118
Bothell, WA 98041-0118 USA

Printed in the United States of America
01 00 99 98 97 96   6 5 4 3 2 1

ACKNOWLEDGMENTS

Every book is a huge undertaking. And without the support and encouragement from friends, professional associates, and family, projects like this could not be accomplished. My "support system" while writing this book was no different, and I am offering them my heartfelt gratitude.

During the initial stages and throughout the development of this book, I took several trips to Colorado, where my friend Harriet Hargrave spent countless hours with me working out the details and provided me with a good supply of the world's best burritos.

During the final push, I literally "camped" at my parents' house to get away from everyday life (and to enjoy Mom's cooking).

All the projects in this book were made by Sheila Zent and Jean Fidler. Their workmanship is exquisite and their patience never-ending.

The double-sided banding technique was used with permission from Margaret Islander of Islander Sewing Systems.

And, finally, I have to acknowledge Marti Michell, who started it all.

Fabrics for the "Traditional Room" were provided by Springmaid Fabrics.

Fabrics for the "Romantic Room" were provided by V.I.P. Fabrics.

Fabrics for the "Contemporary Room" were provided by Concord House.

Fabrics for the "Country Room" were provided by Mission Valley Textile, Inc.

Fabrics for the "Rustic Room" were provided by AE Nathan Company, Inc.

Lace for the Romantic and Rustic rooms was provided by Bonavista Fabrics (USA), Inc.

Covered button forms were provided by Prym Dritz Corporation.

That Patchwork Place would like to thank Heidi Soehren and Kerry Wenala of Woodinville, Washington, for the use of their homes for the photos in this book.

Table of Contents

Introduction

Quilting is home decorating . . . and home decorating includes quilts.

I grew up with quilts covering all the beds in the house. So, when I started writing home-decorating books, it was natural that a quilt was included somewhere. Let me tell you how it all began. . . .

When I started to make quilts, that's all I made—quilts. I only worried about the fabrics to be used in the quilt and never gave a thought to additional room accessories. I think I made some pretty great quilts. But let's face it, to actually use one of these "great quilts" in my bedroom became a challenge in itself. I couldn't find anything to match,

coordinate, or blend! That's when the idea hit to make what I call "decorator quilts." This book evolved from that initial thought. Ultimately, it grew to include ideas and instructions for the decorative components that make a room complete.

So now, when you are itchin' to make a quilt, step back and think about where you plan to use it. By including a window treatment, a bed skirt, a table covering, and a few luscious pillows in your plans, you'll be able to snuggle up in coordinated splendor. Suite dreams!

Donna

Donna Babylon has been actively involved in the home-sewing and quilting industries for most of her professional career. She owns her own publishing company, Windsor Oak Publishing, which produces home decorating how-to books. Donna is a certified window-treatment consultant and designs for The McCall Pattern Company. She is a regular guest on *Decorating with Style* and *The Carol Duval Show* on HGTV, *Our Home* on Lifetime, and *Home Matters* on Discovery. She has converted most of her home in Baltimore, Maryland, into her work space. She lives with her two cats, Ashley and Murphy, who act as her receptionist and administrative assistant respectively. In her spare time, Donna enjoys traveling, downhill skiing, and long and adventurous bike rides.

An Introduction to Home Decorating

DECORATING STYLES

Think of decorating as creating a personality for a room. The fabric you select makes a statement to whomever enters the room. And since decorating is made up of many personal choices and expressions, the ultimate outcome is a statement about its occupants. Here to inspire you are five bedroom settings: rustic, traditional, romantic, country, and contemporary. Each is highly individual—just like you!

Rustic

Sit back, relax, recharge your spirits. Pass up chairs with straight backs and go right to the comfort zone. Surround yourself with natural materials: exposed wood beams, dark paneled walls, stone or slate floorings. Hand-loomed rugs, bold plaids, and soft, cozy textures are what this room is about.

To put your room in a rustic mood:

- Recognize that comfort also means convenience. Plan for reading, casual dining, and family activities.
- Capitalize on the room's built-in amenities: a fireplace or a breathtaking view.
- Limit collectibles to a few, well-selected pieces to keep the room's casual, take-it-easy attitude intact.

Traditional

A traditional room setting can be elegant and formal, simple and lighthearted, or anywhere in between. One thing for sure—it always offers warmth, hospitality, and comfort. Fads are ignored and heritage is upheld. Rich, warm colors embrace the style of its creator.

To put your room in a traditional mood:

- Accessorize with mementos lovingly collected over the years. Display these collections proudly.
- Decorate windows with floor-length draperies, shirred valances, or fabric-covered cornices.
- Embellish table skirts and pillows with extra details, such as custom-covered cording.

Romantic

Romantic rooms allow you to indulge your passions, to surround yourself with beautiful fabrics, soft colors, and fanciful accents. The romantic room should turn your daydreams into reality. Colors should be crisp white or pastels with lavishly imposed lace. Furniture should be wicker, oak, or other light-colored pieces.

By decorating around a quilt, you can create an inviting environment to retreat to after a hectic day.

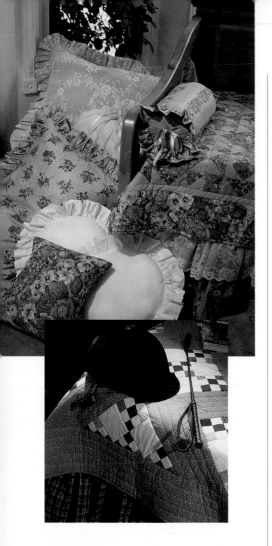

To put your room in a romantic mood:

- Arrange your collectibles in vignettes. Include dolls, Victorian bird cages, silver-framed photographs atop a lace-draped table, and—of course—fresh flowers.
- Dress the windows in balloon-type shades. Incorporate laces when possible.
- Accent with soft ruffles and fabric-covered lamp shades.

Country

Reminiscent of earlier and simpler times, today's country style focuses on handcrafted furniture, homespun textiles, and charming collectibles. Country decorating is unpretentious, friendly, and expresses a casual, uncomplicated lifestyle. Furnishings can be sparse, rustic, or refined.

To put your room in a country mood:

- Mix and match calico prints, ticking stripes, and plaids.
- Show off favorite collectibles: folk art, kitchen tools, baskets, toys, etc.
- Showcase a natural wood floor with a rustic or hooked rug. Or, stencil your own floorcloths.

Contemporary

Three words describe this decorating style: sparse, sculptured, and serene. Textures and natural colors abound with an emphasis on uncomplicated yet sophisticated furnishings. Floor plans tend to be open, giving the impression of spaciousness.

To put your room in a contemporary mood:

- Use background colors that are understated and neutral.
- Choose window treatments that are airy by design and that invite the sunshine to come inside.
- Emphasize architectural details.

SELECTING A COLOR SCHEME

You've decided to decorate your bedroom. Great! But, how do you settle on a color scheme? Good question! Start by eliminating the colors you don't like and keeping the ones you do. How do you know what colors these are? Just open your closet door. The colors you see hanging there over and over again are your favorites. If you like wearing a color, chances are you'll like living in that color too. Pictures of rooms in books and magazines will help you visualize the finished space and then analyze the mood the colors elicit. Maybe you'll be inspired by a particular food. (Who says kiwi isn't a good wall color?) Still confused? Get your color clues from a favorite painting or sculpture. The colors in any favorite object, from a vase to an area rug, can start you on your way.

Colors have an impact on emotions. It's common to hear that someone has the blues or that everything will come out rosy. Even though response to color is a personal thing, extensive studies have been conducted to learn how color affects emotions. Here are some examples:

- Red stimulates and empowers. Red increases pulse rates and raises body temperatures.
- Orange encourages conversation.
- Yellow activates, warms, and cheers. It is a great choice for rooms that lack natural light. Bright yellows stimulate; lemon yellows and golds unleash creativity.
- Pink affectionately softens a room and also flatters skin tones. It is a happy color.
- Blue suggests coolness and calmness. Pale blues bring serenity and can make a bedroom conducive to sleep; stronger blues create contentment; purple blues are meditative and encourage reflection.
- Green is restful and refreshing. Foam greens are quiet and peaceful; medium greens remind you of nature; deep greens are serious and successful; lime greens activate.
- Purple comforts and reassures.
- Violet promotes self-expression and one's artistic side.
- Neutrals (brown, taupe, gray, or white) blend, combine, and cooperate, neither activating nor pacifying space. They give us a sense of freedom.
- Pure white is optimistic, but also nostalgic (like pearls and lace).

Total Bedroom Gallery

Imagine retreating to your own homey hideaway at the end of a long day. Ahhh, the bedroom beckons. Make it the one place in your home where you can escape to relax and recharge your spirits. Surround yourself with color, charm, and comfort. Let your design fantasies take flight when creating this personal haven. Unify the room with your favorite colors and fabrics. Fashion the room with soft draping fabric, or leave it beautifully bare. Surround yourself with the things you love ... you'll find no end to the options.

Rustic

Rustic Strippy

Rustic decor picks up where country leaves off. It's a similar look, but with a less domestic touch. Its carefree, comfortable, put-your-feet-up-on-the-bed atmosphere comes across when twigs, branches, and outdoor-sports equipment are used as decorative furnishings.

A heart-shaped pillow
softens the rustic palette.

Imagine cuddling up in this room on weekend
mornings with a favorite book and a steamy
mug of hot chocolate. The multitude of pillows
in mix-and-match fabrics are main factors
in creating that cozy feeling.

Although rustic has a wild, rugged appeal, it can be
successfully paired with more civilized details.
Splashes of delicate lace are interspersed
throughout the room. The lace valance balances
the unlined panel curtains, while the layered table
skirt and bed skirt inspire romance.

Traditional

Traditional Nosegay Basket

Rich in detail, color, and design, this
traditionally styled room embraces everything
you love. It's the perfect setting to showcase
special accessories and timeless treasures.

Piping and luscious
ruffles on accessory pillows
are inviting details.

Selecting the right fabrics can
result in a bedroom that is
inherently comfortable
and exceedingly warm. Take
a simple design approach when
you create fabric accessories
such as this bed skirt.

Romantic

Romantic Pinwheel

An intimate collage of floral fabrics, pillows, and lace are the secret to creating the most romantic of rooms.

Masses of flowers in the quilt and accessory pieces are the focal points of this gardenlike bedroom. The multiflounced bed and table skirts add layers of luxury.

Pillows of all shapes and sizes are a must for true romance.

The perfect "top hat" to a wispy lace curtain is a simple, yet lavish, self-lined valance.

Country

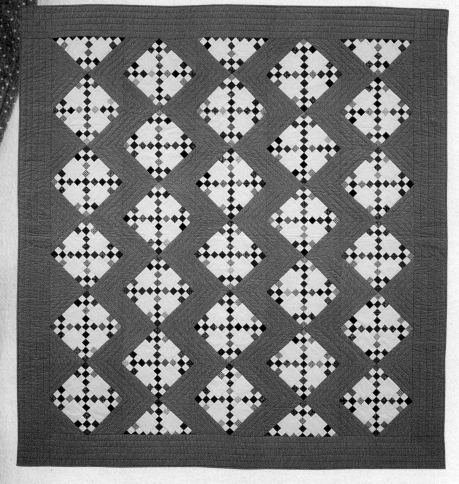

Country Nine Patch

Reminiscent of simpler times, today's country style focuses on homespun textures.

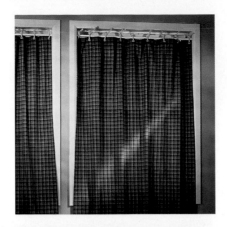

Lovingly preserved fabrics become the perfect accent pillows.

Rope-tied curtains add country flair.

Above: Imitating the resourcefulness of our ancestors, a variety of fabrics are used to create accent pillows. Even through nothing matches, the room is completely coordinated in the country spirit.
Right: Rope and grommets add bedside style to a short version of the basic table skirt.

Country decorating is unpretentious
and friendly, and expresses a casual,
uncomplicated lifestyle.

Contemporary

Contemporary Natural

Delicate light casts a gossamer glow throughout this room. Inviting vanilla whites and mellow creams combine to create a soothing and peaceful retreat.

A stack of pillows provides an appealing
contrast, adding to the room's ambience.
The clever use of button accents introduces
texture in an effective, yet inconspicuous way.

Billowy window treatments
invite the serenity of
the outdoors inside.

The subtle presence of a print in the
bed skirt is set off by the creative
placement of decorative buttons.

Quilts

Each of the five quilts in this section is at the heart of a beautiful room setting, inspiring a host of coordinated fabric furnishings. And while the quilts themselves may look complicated, they are actually quite easy to make.

RUSTIC STRIPPY

Flannel, rather than the traditional quilter's cotton, creates a cozy quilt that is soft to the touch. This quilt is featured in the "Rustic Room" (pages 8–10).

Materials

58"-wide flannel fabric
44"-wide corduroy
Batting and thread to finish

 Red-and-black plaid

 Red-and-white plaid

 Blue check

 Green plaid

Corduroy

Use the chart at right to determine how much fabric you need for your quilt size.

	TWIN	DOUBLE	QUEEN	KING
Approximate finished size (without borders)	44" x 83"	55" x 83"	65" x 83"	76" x 83"
Number of pieced panels	4	5	6	7
Combined border width	6"	6"	6"	6"
Red-and-black plaid	¾ yd.	1 yd.	1 yd.	1⅛ yds.
Red-and-white plaid	⅞ yd.	1 yd.	1¼ yds.	1⅜ yds.
Blue check	⅞ yd.	1 yd.	1¼ yds.	1⅜ yds.
Green plaid	⅞ yd.	1 yd.	1¼ yds.	1⅜ yds.
Sashing & inner border* (corduroy)	2⅜ yds.	2⅜ yds.	2⅜ yds.	2⅜ yds.
Middle border	⅜ yd.	½ yd.	½ yd.	⅝ yd.
Outer border*	2¾ yds.	2¾ yds.	2¾ yds.	2¾ yds.
Binding	½ yd.	½ yd.	½ yd.	⅝ yd.
Backing	3½ yds.	4 yds.	4½ yds.	5 yds.

*Yardage is given for cutting lengthwise border strips. Measure and cut all border strips after finishing the quilt top (see "Borders" on page 85).

Cutting

✂ *Tip:* Because flannel can be stretchier than the woven cottons that are usually used for quilts, piece a test section before cutting all the components. If the flannel stretches and is challenging to work with, fuse a very lightweight interfacing to the wrong side of the fabric before cutting. Avoid tricot-knit fusible interfacings, which can cause slippage.

	STRIP WIDTH	NUMBER OF STRIPS			
Fabric		Twin	Double	Queen	King
Red-and-black plaid	4"	5	6	7	8
Red-and-black plaid	6¼"	1	1	1	1
Red-and-white plaid	6¼"	4	5	6	7
Red-and-white plaid	3½"	1	1	1	1
Blue check	4⅜"	6	7	9	10
Green plaid	4⅜"	6	7	9	10
Sashing* (corduroy)	1½"	7	8	9	10
Binding	2½"	8	8	9	9

*Cut sashing strips along the lengthwise grain of the fabric.

1. Cut strips as indicated in the chart above for your quilt size. *Cut all strips crosswise, from selvage to selvage, unless otherwise indicated.*

2. From the 4"-wide red-and-black plaid strips, cut 4" x 4" squares:

   64 squares for a twin
   80 squares for a double
   96 squares for a queen
   112 squares for a king

3. From the 6¼"-wide red-and-black plaid strips, cut 6¼" x 6¼" squares:

   2 squares for a twin
   3 squares for a double
   3 squares for a queen
   4 squares for a king

   Cut the squares twice diagonally into quarter-square triangles (see page 80).

4. From the 6¼"-wide red-and-white plaid strips, cut 6¼" x 6¼" squares:

   32 squares for a twin
   40 squares for a double
   48 squares for a queen
   56 squares for a king

   Cut the squares twice diagonally into quarter-square triangles.

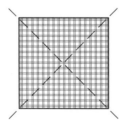

5. From the 3½"-wide red-and-white plaid strips, cut 3½" x 3½" squares:

   8 squares for a twin
   10 squares for a double
   12 squares for a queen
   14 squares for a king

   Cut the squares once diagonally into half-square triangles (see pages 79–80).

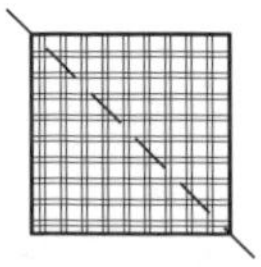

6. From both the 4⅜"-wide blue check strips and the 4⅜"-wide green plaid strips, cut 4⅜" x 4⅜" squares:

   68 squares of *each* for a twin
   85 squares of *each* for a double
   102 squares of *each* for a queen
   119 squares of *each* for a king

   Layer the blue check and the green plaid squares, right sides together, and cut once diagonally into half-square triangles.

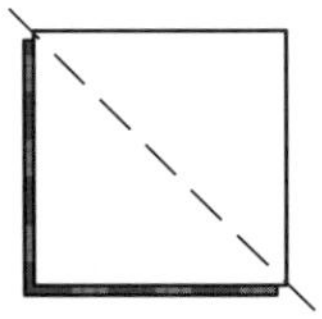

Unit Construction

Use ¼"-wide seam allowances.

1. Stitch 1 blue check and 1 green plaid half-square triangle together to form each half-square triangle unit. Make:

   136 units for a twin
   170 units for a double
   204 units for a queen
   238 units for a king

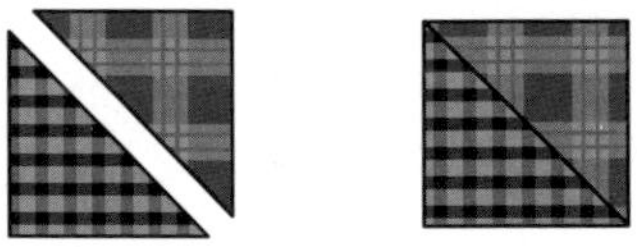

2. Stitch 2 half-square triangle units, 1 red-and-black square, and 2 red-and-white quarter-square triangles together as shown to form each Row A. Make:

   28 Row A for a twin
   35 Row A for a double
   42 Row A for a queen
   49 Row A for a king

Row A

3. Stitch 2 half-square triangle units, 1 red-and-black square, and 2 red-and-white quarter-square triangles together as shown to form each Row B. Make:

28 Row B for a twin
35 Row B for a double
42 Row B for a queen
49 Row B for a king

Row B

4. Stitch 3 half-square triangle units, 1 red-and-black square, 1 red-and-black quarter-square triangle, 2 red-and-white half-square triangles, and 2 red-and-white quarter-square triangles together as shown to form each top unit. Make:

4 top units for a twin
5 top units for a double
6 top units for a queen
7 top units for a king

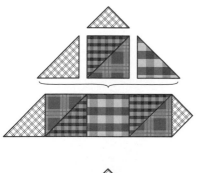

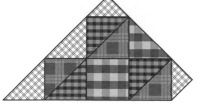

Top Unit

5. Stitch 3 half-square triangle units, 1 red-and-black square, 1 red-and-black quarter-square triangle, 2 red-and-white half-square triangles, and 2 red-and-white quarter-square triangles together as shown to form each bottom unit. Make:

4 bottom units for a twin
5 bottom units for a double
6 bottom units for a queen
7 bottom units for a king

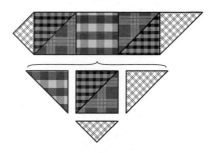

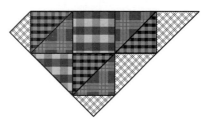

Bottom Unit

6. Stitch 14 rows together, alternating Rows A and B, to make 1 panel. Add 1 top and 1 bottom unit to complete the panel. Make:

4 panels for a twin
5 panels for a double
6 panels for a queen
7 panels for a king

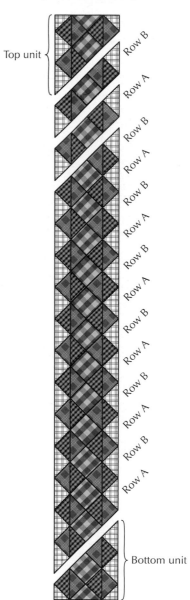

Top unit

Row B
Row A
Row B
Row A
Row A
Row A
Row B
Row A
Row B
Row A
Row B
Row A
Row B
Row A

Bottom unit

Quilt Top Assembly and Finishing

1. Arrange the panels with corduroy sashing strips in between as shown below. Assemble, following the directions for "Strippy Quilts" on page 83.

2. Measure and cut 1½"-wide inner corduroy border strips along the lengthwise grain and stitch to the quilt top. Measure and cut 2½"-wide middle border strips along the crosswise grain, and stitch to the quilt top. For both borders,

follow the directions for "Straight-Cut Borders" on page 85. Measure and cut 5½"-wide outer border strips along the lengthwise grain and stitch to the quilt top, following the directions for "Mitered-Corner Borders" on pages 85–86.

3. Layer the quilt top, batting, and backing, referring to "Assembling the Layers" on page 86.

4. Hand or machine quilt, referring to "Quilting Techniques" on pages 87–88. If desired, use the quilting suggestion at right.

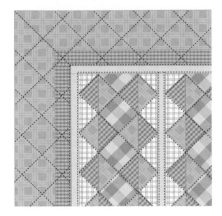

Quilting Suggestion

5. Finish the edges of the quilt, following the directions for "Binding" on page 88.

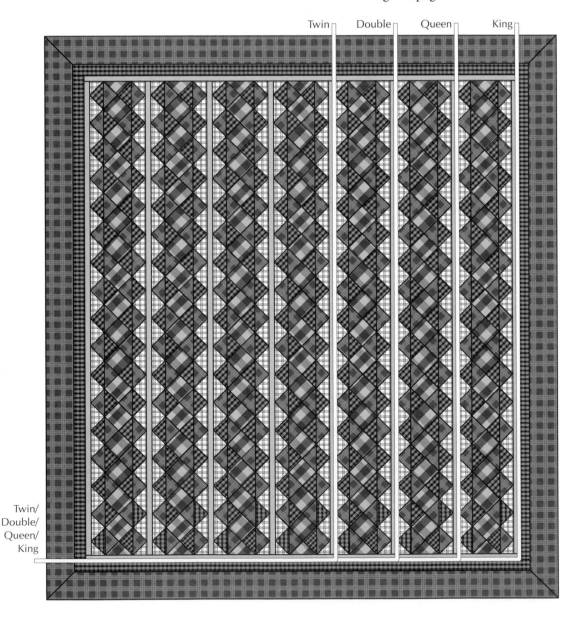

TRADITIONAL NOSEGAY BASKET

This quilt, which is featured in the "Traditional Room" (pages 11–13), effectively uses only two prints: a large floral and a medium geometric. Two coordinating solids were used to create the basket and to define the blocks. The layout is a diagonal set.

Materials

44"-wide fabric
Batting and thread to finish

 Floral print

 Geometric print

 Rust

 Green

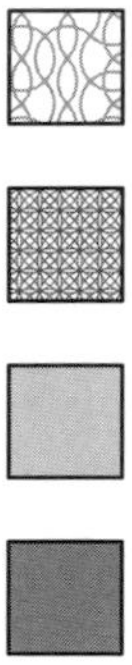

Use the chart at right (top) to determine how much fabric you need for your quilt size.

	TWIN	DOUBLE/QUEEN	KING
Approximate finished size (without borders)	45" x 74"	60" x 74"	64" x 89"
Number of blocks	15	20	30
Block layout	3 x 5	4 x 5	5 x 6
Border width	7"	7"	7"
Floral print	4 yds.	6½ yds.	7 yds.
Geometric print	1⅛ yds.	1⅛ yds.	1⅝ yds.
Rust solid (basket strips)	¾ yd.	1 yd.	1¼ yds.
Green solid (sashing & inner border)	1⅛ yds.	1⅜ yds.	1⅞ yds.
Floral border*	2½ yds.	2½ yds.	3 yds.
Floral binding	½ yd.	⅝ yd.	¾ yd.
Backing	4 yds.	4½ yds.	6 yds.

*Yardage is given for cutting lengthwise border strips. Measure and cut all border strips after finishing the quilt top (see "Borders" on page 85).

Fabric	STRIP WIDTH	NUMBER OF STRIPS		
		Twin	Double/Queen	King
Floral print	3"	2	2	3
	6¼"	2	2	3
	10"	2	3	5
	15"	2	2	5
Geometric print	3"	12	12	18
Rust solid	1½"	17	19	28
Green solid	1½"	25	31	43
Floral binding	2½"	7	8	9

Cutting

1. Cut strips as indicated in the chart above for your quilt size. *Cut all strips crosswise, from selvage to selvage, unless otherwise indicated.*

2. From the 3"-wide floral strips, cut 3" x 4" rectangles:

   15 rectangles for a twin
   20 rectangles for a double/queen
   30 rectangles for a king

3. From the 10"-wide floral strips, cut 10" x 10" squares:

   8 squares for a twin
   12 squares for a double/queen
   20 squares for a king

   These will be your alternate blocks.

4. From the 15"-wide floral strips, cut 15" x 15" squares:

   7 squares for a twin
   8 squares for a double/queen
   10 squares for a king

Cut one 15" square twice diagonally into quarter-square triangles (see page 80). These will be your corner triangles.

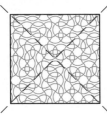

Cut the remaining squares once diagonally into half-square triangles (see pages 79–80). These will be your setting triangles.

5. From the 1½"-wide rust strips, cut 10"- and 7½"-long strips:

   15 strips of *each* for a twin
   20 strips of *each* for a double/ queen
   30 strips of *each* for a king

Unit Construction

Use ¼"-wide seam allowances.

1. Stitch two 1½"-wide rust strips and three 3"-wide geometric strips together as shown to make Strip Set #1. Press the seams to one side.

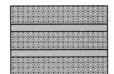

Strip Set #1

	NUMBER OF FLORAL UNITS			NUMBER OF 1½"-WIDE RUST STRIPS	
	10" Squares	Corner Triangles	Setting Triangles	7½" long	10" long
Twin	8	4	12	15	15
Double/Queen	12	4	14	20	20
King	20	4	18	30	30

2. Stitch two 3"-wide geometric strips and two 1½"-wide rust strips together as shown to make Strip Set #2. Press the seams to one side.

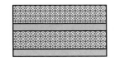

Strip Set #2

3. Stitch one 3"-wide geometric strip, one 1½"-wide rust strip, and one 6¼"-wide floral strip together as shown to make Strip Set #3. Press the seams to one side.

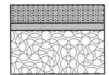

Strip Set #3

4. Cut Strip Sets #1, #2, and #3 into 3"-wide units. Cut:

   15 units of *each* for a twin
   20 units of *each* for a double/ queen
   30 units of *each* for a king

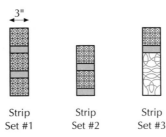

Strip Set #1   Strip Set #2   Strip Set #3

5. Stitch 1 Strip Set #1 unit to one 10"-long rust strip. This is Row #1. Make:

   15 Row #1 for a twin
   20 Row #1 for a double/queen
   30 Row #1 for a king

Row #1

6. Stitch 1 Strip Set #2 unit to one 7½"-long rust strip; stitch to one 3" x 4" floral rectangle. This is Row #2. Make:

   15 Row #2 for a twin
   20 Row #2 for a double/queen
   30 Row #2 for a king

Row #2

7. Stitch 1 Row #1, 1 Row #2, and 1 Strip Set #3 together as shown to complete the Basket block. Make:

15 blocks for a twin
20 blocks for a double/queen
30 blocks for a king

Basket Block

Quilt Top Assembly and Finishing

1. Arrange the basket blocks, 10" alternate blocks, setting triangles, sashing, and corner triangles into rows for the size you are making as shown on page 30. Assemble, following the directions for "Diagonal-Set Quilts with Sashing" on page 83.

2. Measure and cut 1½"-wide inner border strips and stitch to the quilt top, following the directions for "Straight-Cut Borders" on page 85. Measure and cut 7½"-wide floral border strips along the lengthwise grain, following the directions for "Mitered-Corner Borders" on pages 85–86.

Row A   Row B   Row C

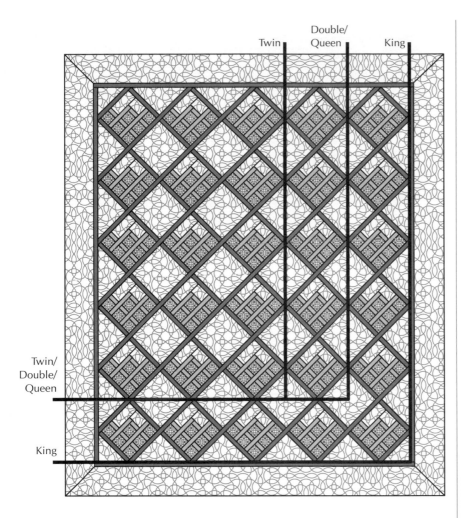

Twin

Double/Queen

King

Twin/Double/Queen

King

3. Layer the quilt top, batting, and backing, referring to "Assembling the Layers" on page 86.

4. Hand or machine quilt, referring to "Quilting Techniques" on pages 87–88. If desired, use the quilting suggestion below.

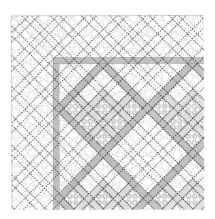

Quilting Suggestion

5. Finish the edges of the quilt, following the directions for "Binding" on page 88.

ROMANTIC PINWHEEL

This easy quilt, featured in the "Romantic Room" (pages 14–16), is composed of two blocks that use the same four fabrics in different combinations. By using a simple layout of alternating blocks, a secondary design (the pinwheel) appears.

Materials

44"-wide fabric
Batting and thread to finish

 Large floral

 Small floral

 Pink

 Lilac

 Green

Use the chart at right (top) to determine how much fabric you need for your quilt size.

	TWIN	DOUBLE	QUEEN/KING
Approximate finished size (without borders)	40" x 80"	60" x 80"	80" x 80"
Number of A blocks	16	24	32
Number of B blocks	16	24	32
Block layout	4 x 8	6 x 8	8 x 8
Border width	6"	6"	6"
Large floral	1⅛ yds.	1½ yds.	2 yds.
Small floral	1⅝ yds.	2¼ yds.	3 yds.
Pink accent	¾ yd.	⅞ yd.	1¼ yds.
Lilac accent	¾ yd.	⅞ yd.	1¼ yds.
Green accent	1⅝ yds.	2⅜ yds.	3⅛ yds.
Inner border	⅜ yd.	⅜ yd.	⅜ yd.
Outer border*	2¾ yds.	2¾ yds.	2¾ yds.
Binding	½ yd.	⅝ yd.	¾ yd.
Backing	5 yds.	5 yds.	8 yds.

*Yardage is given for cutting lengthwise border strips. Measure and cut all border strips after finishing the quilt top (see "Borders" on page 85).

Fabric	STRIP WIDTH	NUMBER OF STRIPS		
		Twin	Double	Queen/King
Large floral	4⅛"	4	5	7
	3⅜"	6	8	11
Small floral	5½"	10	14	19
Pink accent	3⅜"	6	8	11
Lilac accent	3⅜"	6	8	11
Green accent	3"	19	28	37
Binding	2½"	7	8	9

Cutting

1. Cut strips as indicated in the chart above for your quilt size. *Cut all strips crosswise, from selvage to selvage, unless otherwise indicated.*

2. From the 4⅛"-wide large floral strips, cut 4⅛" x 4⅛" squares:

   32 squares for a twin
   48 squares for a double
   64 squares for a queen/king

3. From the 3⅜"-wide large floral strips, cut 3⅜" x 3⅜" squares:

64 squares for a twin
96 squares for a double
128 squares for a queen/king

Cut the squares once diagonally into half-square triangles (see pages 79–80).

4. From the 5½"-wide small floral strips, cut 3" x 5½" rectangles:

128 rectangles for a twin
192 rectangles for a double
256 rectangles for a queen/king

5. From the 3⅜"-wide pink strips, cut 3⅜" x 3⅜" squares:

64 squares for a twin
96 squares for a double
128 squares for a queen/king

Cut the squares once diagonally into half-square triangles.

6. From the 3⅜"-wide lilac strips, cut 3⅜" x 3⅜" squares:

64 squares for a twin
96 squares for a double
128 squares for a queen/king

Cut the squares once diagonally into half-square triangles.

7. From the 3"-wide green strips, cut 3" x 3" squares:

256 squares for a twin
384 squares for a double
512 squares for a queen/king

Unit Construction

Use ¼"-wide seam allowances.

1. Stitch 1 large floral and 1 pink half-square triangle together to make half-square triangle Unit #1. Make:

64 Unit #1 for a twin
96 Unit #1 for a double
128 Unit #1 for a queen/king

Unit #1

2. Stitch 1 large floral and 1 lilac half-square triangle together to make half-square triangle Unit #2. Make:

64 Unit #2 for a twin
96 Unit #2 for a double
128 Unit #2 for a queen/king

Unit #2

3. Stitch 1 small floral rectangle and 2 green squares together to make a flying-geese unit (see page 82). Make:

128 flying-geese units for a twin
192 flying-geese units for a double
256 flying-geese units for a queen/king

Flying-Geese Unit

4. Stitch 4 lilac triangles to 1 large floral 4⅛" square as shown to make Unit #3. Press the seams toward the corner triangles. Make:

16 Unit #3 for a twin
24 Unit #3 for a double
32 Unit #3 for a queen/king

Unit #3

5. Stitch 4 pink triangles to 1 large floral 4⅛" square as shown to make Unit #4. Press the seams toward the corner triangles. Make:

16 Unit #4 for a twin
24 Unit #4 for a double
32 Unit #4 for a queen/king

Unit #4

6. Stitch 2 Unit #1 and 1 flying-geese unit together as shown to make Row #1. Make:

32 Row #1 for a twin
48 Row #1 for a double
64 Row #1 for a queen/king

Row #1

7. Stitch 2 flying-geese units and 1 Unit #3 together as shown to make Row #2. Make:

16 Row #2 for a twin
24 Row #2 for a double
32 Row #2 for a queen/king

Row #2

8. Assemble Block A, stitching 2 Row #1 and 1 Row #2 together as shown. Make:

16 Block A for a twin
24 Block A for a double
32 Block A for a queen/king

Block A

9. Stitch 2 Unit #2 and 1 flying-geese unit together as shown to make Row #3. Make:

32 Row #3 for a twin
48 Row #3 for a double
64 Row #3 for a queen/king

Row #3

10. Stitch 2 flying-geese units and 1 Unit #4 together as shown to make Row #4. Make:

16 Row #4 for a twin
24 Row #4 for a double
32 Row #4 for a queen/king

Row #4

11. Assemble Block B by stitching 2 Row #3 and 1 Row #4 together as shown. Make:

16 Block B for a twin
24 Block B for a double
32 Block B for a queen/king

Block B

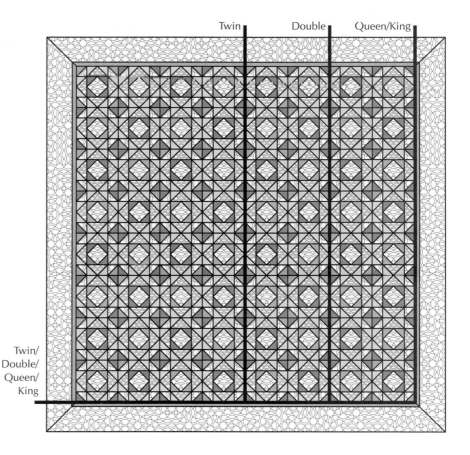

Quilt Top Assembly and Finishing

1. Arrange the blocks as shown above. Assemble, following the directions for "Straight-Set Quilts" on page 83.
2. Measure and cut 1½"-wide inner border strips along the crosswise grain. Measure and cut 6½"-wide outer border strips along the lengthwise grain. For both borders, follow the directions for "Mitered-Corner Borders" on pages 85–86.
3. Layer the quilt top, batting, and backing, referring to "Assembling the Layers" on page 86.

4. Hand or machine quilt, referring to "Quilting Techniques" on pages 87–88. If desired, use the quilting suggestion below.

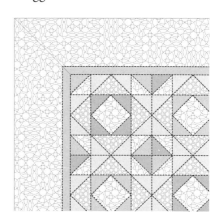

Quilting Suggestion

5. Finish the edges of the quilt, following the directions for "Binding" on page 88.

COUNTRY NINE PATCH

This super-easy quilt, featured in the "Country Room" (pages 17–19), is set in a zigzag pattern that produces a secondary design when completed. Create a scrap quilt by using assorted dark fabrics for the Double Nine Patch squares. Single out one fabric (in this case, a deep red) to be used for the center squares only. For all the alternate squares, choose a light-colored fabric (in this case, a cream print).

For the corner triangles and setting triangles, choose a coordinating accent color (in this case, a medium blue).

Materials

44"-wide fabric
Batting and thread to finish

 Cream print

 Dark fabrics

 Dark red

 Medium blue

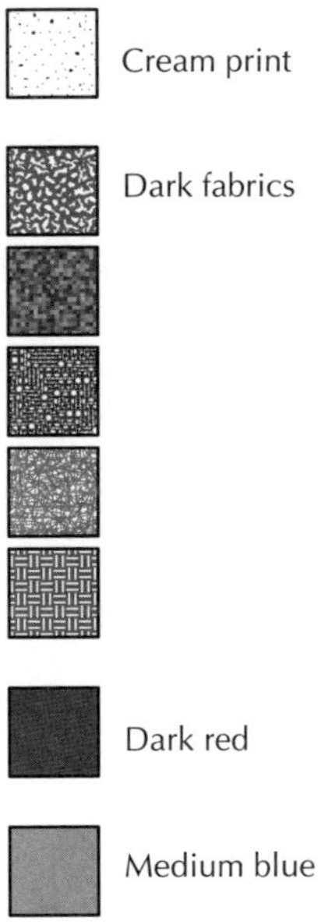

Use the chart at right (top) to determine how much fabric you need for your quilt size.

	TWIN	DOUBLE	QUEEN	KING
Approximate finished size (without borders)	38" x 76"	51" x 76"	64" x 76"	76" x 89"
Number of blocks	20	26	33	45
Border width	7"	7"	7"	7"
Light (cream print)	1½ yds.	1¾ yds.	2⅛ yds.	3 yds.
Darks*	17 strips	21 strips	25 strips	35 strips
Center square	¼ yd.	¼ yd.	⅜ yd.	½ yd.
Accent (medium blue)	1½ yds.	2⅛ yds.	2⅝ yds.	3⅜ yds.
Border**	3 yds.	3 yds.	3 yds.	3½ yds.
Binding	⅝ yd.	⅝ yd.	¾ yd.	¾ yd.
Backing	3 yds.	4 yds.	4½ yds.	6½ yds.

*Cut each strip 1½" x 44". Select a variety of colors (12 to 15 different fabrics), including blue, green, brown, tan, and burgundy.

**Yardage is given for cutting lengthwise border strips. Measure and cut all border strips after finishing the quilt top (see "Borders" on page 85).

Fabric	STRIP WIDTH	NUMBER OF STRIPS			
		Twin	Double	Queen	King
Light	1½"	16	20	24	35
	3½"	7	9	11	15
Darks	1½"	16	21	25	35
Center	1½"	4	5	6	9
Binding	2½"	8	8	9	10

Cutting

1. Cut strips as indicated in the chart above for your quilt size. *Cut all strips crosswise, from selvage to selvage, unless otherwise indicated.*

2. From the accent (medium blue) fabric, cut 14" x 14" squares:

   9 squares for a twin
   11 squares for a double
   14 squares for a queen
   20 squares for a king

Cut the squares twice diagonally into quarter-square triangles (see page 80). These will be your setting triangles.

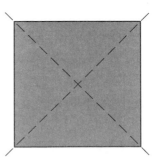

3. From the accent (medium blue) fabric, cut 10" x 10" squares:

4 squares for a twin
4 squares for a double
6 squares for a queen
6 squares for a king

Cut the squares once diagonally into half-square triangles (see pages 79–80). These will be your corner triangles.

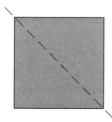

4. From the 3½"-wide strips of light (cream print) fabric, cut 3½" x 3½" squares:

80 squares for a twin
104 squares for a double
132 squares for a queen
180 squares for a king

Unit Construction

Use ¼"-wide seam allowances.

1. Recut all the dark fabric strips into assorted lengths (no shorter than 3"). Stitch them together randomly into 44"-long pieced strips. Make:

16 strips for a twin
20 strips for a double
24 strips for a queen
34 strips for a king

2. Stitch 1 light (cream print) 1½"-wide strip and 2 pieced strips together as shown to make Strip Set #1. Press the seams toward the darker fabric. Make:

8 Strip Set #1 for a twin
10 Strip Set #1 for a double
12 Strip Set #1 for a queen
17 Strip Set #1 for a king

Strip Set #1
Stagger fabric for scrappy look.

3. Stitch 2 light (cream print) 1½"-wide strips and 1 dark red 1½"-wide center strip together as shown to make Strip Set #2. Press the seams toward the darker fabric. Make:

4 Strip Set #2 for a twin
5 Strip Set #2 for a double
6 Strip Set #2 for a queen
9 Strip Set #2 for a king

Strip Set #2

4. Cut all the strip sets into 1½" units. When cutting Strip Set #1, discard the sections that do not make a complete unit. Cut:

200 Strip Set #1 units and 100 Strip Set #2 units for a twin
260 Strip Set #1 units and 130 Strip Set #2 units for a double
330 Strip Set #1 units and 165 Strip Set #2 units for a queen
450 Strip Set #1 units and 225 Strip Set #2 units for a king

Discard.

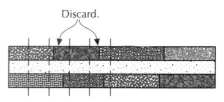

Cut Strip Set #1 into 1½" units.

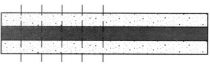

Cut Strip Set #2 into 1½" units.

5. Toss all the Strip Set #1 units into a sack. Randomly pull out and stitch 2 Strip Set #1 units to 1 Strip Set #2 unit as shown to make a Nine Patch block. Press the seams away from the center. Make sure the Strip Set #1 units in each patch contain different dark fabrics. Make:

100 Nine Patch blocks for a twin
130 Nine Patch blocks for a double
165 Nine Patch blocks for a queen
225 Nine Patch blocks for a king

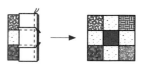

6. Assemble a Double Nine Patch block by stitching 5 Nine Patch blocks and 4 light (cream print) 3½" squares together in an alternating pattern as shown. Make:

20 Double Nine Patch blocks for a twin

26 Double Nine Patch blocks for a double

33 Double Nine Patch blocks for a queen

45 Double Nine Patch blocks for a king

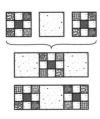

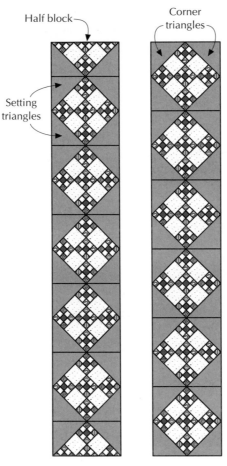

Double Nine Patch Block

7. Working on the wrong side of 1 Double Nine Patch block, place the ¼" mark of a ruler diagonally over the seam intersections as shown; cut, making a half block. Save the smaller triangle for another project. Make:

2 half blocks for a twin
4 half blocks for a double
4 half blocks for a queen
6 half blocks for a king

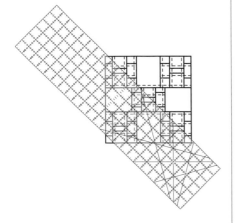

8. Stitch the Double Nine Patch blocks, the half blocks, the setting triangles, and the corner triangles together as shown, making the number of panels indicated for your quilt size.

Half block—

Corner triangles

Setting triangles

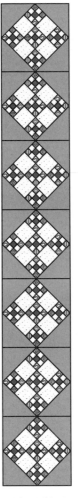

Make:
1 (twin)
2 (double)
2 (queen)

Make:
2 (twin)
2 (double)
3 (queen)

Make 3 (king).

Make 3 (king).

Quilt Top Assembly and Finishing

1. Arrange the panels as shown at right. Assemble, following the directions for "Diagonal Strippy Quilts" on page 84.

2. Measure and cut 7½"-wide border strips along the lengthwise grain and stitch to the quilt top, following the directions for "Mitered-Corner Borders" on pages 85–86.

3. Layer the quilt top, batting, and backing, referring to "Assembling the Layers" on page 86.

4. Hand or machine quilt, referring to "Quilting Techniques" on pages 87–88. If desired, use the quilting suggestion below.

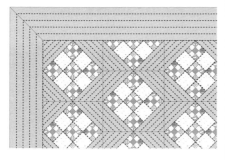

Quilting Suggestion

5. Finish the edges of the quilt, following the directions for "Binding" on page 88.

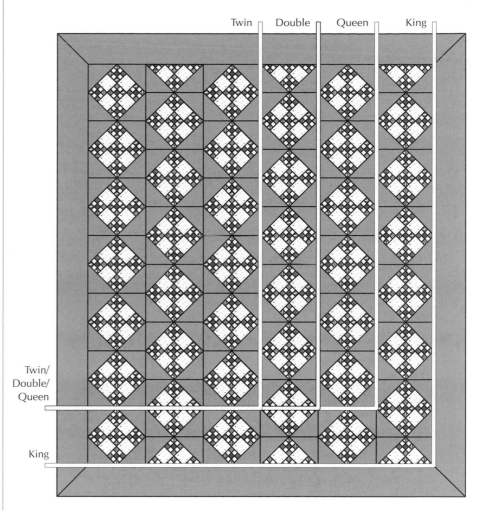

CONTEMPORARY NATURAL

This quilt, featured in the "Contemporary Room" (pages 20–22), is the perfect showcase for an abundance of fabrics in the tan and natural color family. For interest and texture, choose prints that vary in motif, scale, and value. To make the quilt as shown, select one fabric and use it for the accent fabric, outer border, and binding, as well as for some of the half-square triangles. This quilt is a great way to use fat quarters!

✂ *Tip:* For those who are new to quilting, the term "fat quarter" refers to the way the fabric is cut. A fat quarter measures 18" x 22", which is more usable than the standard quarter yard that measures 9" x 44". Fat quarters are often sold in coordinated bundles in quilt shops.

Materials

44"-wide fabric
Batting and thread to finish

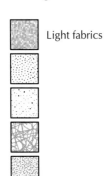

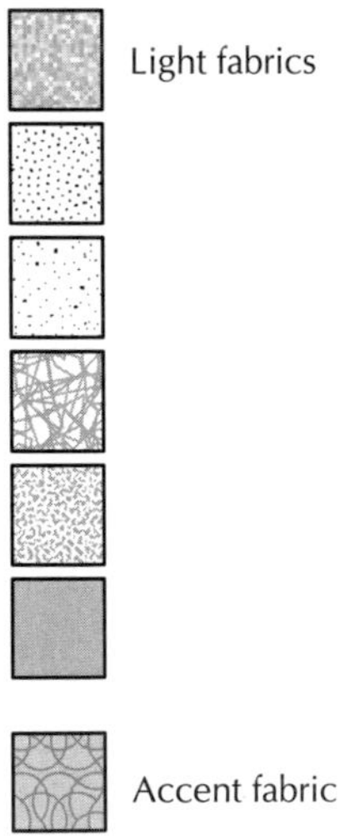

Light fabrics

Accent fabric

	TWIN	DOUBLE	QUEEN	KING
Approximate finished size (without borders)	36" x 72"	54" x 72"	72" x 72"	72" x 90"
Number of blocks	32	48	64	80
Block layout	4 x 8	6 x 8	8 x 8	8 x 10
Combined border width	7½"	7½"	7½"	7½"
Lights	9 fat qtrs.	13 fat qtrs.	17 fat qtrs.	20 fat qtrs.
Accent	1½ yds.	1¾ yds.	2⅜ yds.	2⅞ yds.
Inner border	⅜ yd	½ yd.	½ yd.	½ yd.
Outer border*	2½ yds.	2½ yds.	2½ yds.	3 yds.
Binding	⅝ yd.	⅝ yd.	¾ yd.	¾ yd.
Backing	3½ yds.	4 yds.	5 yds.	6 yds.

Yardage is given for cutting lengthwise border strips. Measure and cut all border strips after finishing the quilt top (see "Borders" on page 85).

Use the chart above to determine how much fabric you need for your quilt size.

✏ *Note:* The number of fat quarters listed above will yield the appropriate number of triangles and squares to complete the quilt top. If you select a greater variety of fabrics, this quilt will become even more interesting!

Cutting

Cut all strips crosswise, from selvage to selvage, unless otherwise indicated.

1. From a variety of fat quarters, cut 3½" x 3½" squares:

    96 squares for a twin
    144 squares for a double
    192 squares for a queen
    240 squares for a king

2. From the accent fabric, cut 10" x 10" squares:

    18 squares for a twin
    24 squares for a double
    32 squares for a queen
    40 squares for a king

    Cut the squares once diagonally into half-square triangles (see pages 79–80).

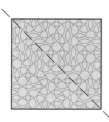

3. From the accent fabric, cut 2½"-wide binding strips:

    7 strips for a twin
    8 strips for a double
    9 strips for a queen
    9 strips for a king

Unit Construction

Use ¼"-wide seam allowances.

1. Pair the accent fabric and the fat quarters together in as many combinations as possible. Using a 3⅞" grid, construct half-square triangle units (see page 81). Make:

    96 half-square triangle units for a twin
    144 half-square triangle units for a double
    192 half-square triangle units for a queen
    240 half-square triangle units for a king

2. Assemble 3 half-square triangle units and three 3½" squares as shown to form 1 stair-step unit. Press the seams in one direction. Make:

    32 stair-step units for a twin
    48 stair-step units for a double
    64 stair-step units for a queen
    80 stair-step units for a king

    Vary the fabrics, if possible, so no two units are alike.

Stair-Step Unit

3. Working on the wrong side of a stair-step unit, place the ¼" mark of a ruler diagonally over the seam intersections as shown. Cut, making a triangle. Discard the small triangles. Repeat for all stair-step units.

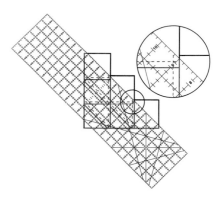

4. Assemble a block by stitching 1 stair-step triangle to 1 accent triangle. Press the seams toward the accent triangle. Make:

    32 blocks for a twin
    42 blocks for a double
    64 blocks for a queen
    80 blocks for a king

Quilt Top Assembly and Finishing

1. Arrange the blocks as shown at right. Assemble, following the directions for "Straight-Set Quilts" on page 83.

2. Measure and cut 2"-wide inner border strips along the crosswise grain and stitch to the quilt top, following the directions for "Straight-Cut Borders" on page 85. Measure and cut 7"-wide strips along the lengthwise grain and stitch to the quilt top, following the directions for "Mitered-Corner Borders" on pages 85–86.

3. Layer the quilt top, batting, and backing, referring to "Assembling the Layers" on page 86.

4. Hand or machine quilt, referring to "Quilting Techniques" on pages 87–88. If desired, use the quilting suggestion below.

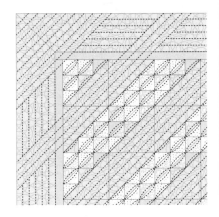

Quilting Suggestion

5. Finish the edges of the quilt, following the directions for "Binding" on page 88.

Bed Skirts

A bed skirt is not only decorative, but practical too. In the functional mode, it covers the box spring, mattress, and bed frame—as well as items stored under the bed. The decorative part comes from the creative use of fabrics and embellishments. For example, the "Rustic Room's" bed skirt unexpectedly incorporates lace as one of its three layers, while the button accents on the "Contemporary Room's" bed skirt echoes a similar detail on the pillows.

DECKS

All skirts are attached to a platform of fabric called the "deck." The deck lies between the mattress and the box spring. It is traditionally made from medium-weight fabric, such as muslin or sheeting. Sometimes, it is more economical to use the extra-wide fabric that is widely available for the deck. However, if you're on a budget, the deck is the perfect place to use unwanted or unloved fabric from your stash. After all, no one but you will see the deck.

✂ *Tip:* Decks can be made from fitted sheets. Simply cover the box spring with the sheet, then mark along the top edge with a fabric marker. Use this line as your seam line when attaching the skirt to the deck.

DECK SIZE	FABRIC	
(including seam & hem allowances)	44"-wide	90"-wide
Twin (39" x 77½")	2¼ yds.	1¼ yds.
Double (55" x 77½")	3⅛ yds.	1⅝ yds.
Queen (61" x 82½")	3½ yds.	1¾ yds.
King (77" x 82½")	4½ yds.	2¼ yds.

Materials
44"- or 90"-wide fabric

Use the chart above to determine how much fabric you need for your bed size.

Cutting

For a twin-size deck, cut 1 panel, 39" x 77½".

For a double-size deck:
From 44"-wide fabric, cut 2 panels, each 39¼" x 55". Stitch together as shown at right, using ½"-wide seam allowances.
From 90"-wide fabric, cut 1 panel, 55" x 77½".

For a queen-size deck:
From 44"-wide fabric, cut 2 panels, each 41¾" x 61". Stitch together as shown at right, using ½"-wide seam allowances.
From 90"-wide fabric, cut 1 panel, 61" x 82½".

For a king-size deck:
From 44"-wide fabric, cut 2 panels, each 41¾" x 77". Stitch together as shown below, using ½"-wide seam allowances.
From 90"-wide fabric, cut 1 panel, 77" x 82½".

Piecing Diagram (Deck)
for 44"-wide fabric

GATHERED BED SKIRT

The following instructions are for a basic gathered bed skirt, such as the one in the "Traditional Room" (page 13) and the "Country Room" (page 17). With a few minor changes, these basic instructions can be used to create a layered bed skirt, such as the ones in the "Rustic Room" (page 9) and the "Romantic Room" (page 15). In the "Rustic Room," the bed skirt has three layers: lace on top, red plaid fabric on the bottom, and green plaid in between. In the "Romantic Room," the bed skirt consists of two layers: a floor-length ruffle fashioned from a coordinating fabric and a shorter layer of lace on top.

Materials

44"-, 58"-, or 90"-wide fabric

Use the chart at right (top) to determine how much fabric you need for your bed size.

For a basic gathered bed skirt, an 18" finished length is standard. For a layered bed skirt, the finished length of each layer is up to you. However, a pleasing proportion is 18" for the bottom layer and 12" and/or 14" for the additional layer(s). Remember to determine how much fabric you need for each layer.

Cutting

Use the chart at right to determine how many crosswise panels to cut for your bed size and fabric width. Cut all panels using the full width of the fabric (from selvage to selvage).

BED SIZE	RUFFLE	FABRIC		
	Finished Length	44"-wide	58"-wide	90"-wide
Twin	12"	5¼ yds.	4¼ yds.	2⅞ yds.
	14"	5¾ yds.	4¾ yds.	3¼ yds.
	18"	7 yds.	5¾ yds.	3⅞ yds.
Double	12"	4½ yds.	4¼ yds.	2⅞ yds.
	14"	6¼ yds.	4¾ yds.	3¼ yds.
	18"	7¾ yds.	5¾ yds.	3⅞ yds.
Queen	12"	4 yds.	4¾ yds.	3¼ yds.
	14"	6¾ yds.	5¼ yds.	3¾ yds.
	18"	8¼ yds.	6⅜ yds.	4½ yds.
King	12"	6½ yds.	5⅛ yds.	3¾ yds.
	14"	7¼ yds.	5¾ yds.	4¼ yds.
	18"	8⅞ yds.	7 yds.	5 yds.

BED SIZE	RUFFLE		NUMBER OF PANELS		
			Fabric		
	Finished Length	Cutting Length	44"-wide	58"-wide	90"-wide
Twin	12"	16½"	11	9	6
	14"	18½"	11	9	6
	18"	22½"	11	9	6
Double	12"	16½"	12	9	6
	14"	18½"	12	9	6
	18"	22½"	12	9	6
Queen	12"	16½"	13	10	7
	14"	18½"	13	10	7
	18"	22½"	13	10	7
King	12"	16½"	14	11	8
	14"	18½"	14	11	8
	18"	22½"	14	11	8

The length of the skirt or the ruffle layers can vary according to the height of your bed. Yardages have been provided for 12", 14", and 18" finished lengths. If your bed requires a different finished length, follow this formula:

1. Determine the cut length by measuring from the top of the box spring to the floor or to the bottom of ruffle layer. Add 4½" for seam and hem allowances.

2. Determine the fullness by adding the side measurements and the foot measurement. Multiply this total by 2.5.

3. Divide the fullness by the width of your fabric. This tells you how many crosswise panels to cut.

4. Multiply the number of panels by the cut length (see step 1). Divide by 36". This is the amount of yardage you need.

BED SIZE	FABRIC	NUMBER OF PANELS		
		Side 1	Side 2	Foot
Twin	44"-wide	4¼	4¼	2¼
	58"-wide	3¼	3¼	1¾
	90"-wide	2¼	2¼	1¼
Double	44"-wide	4¼	4¼	3
	58"-wide	3¼	3¼	2½
	90"-wide	2¼	2¼	1½
Queen	44"-wide	4½	4½	3½
	58"-wide	3½	3½	2¾
	90"-wide	2¼	3½	1¾
King	44"-wide	4½	4½	4¼
	58"-wide	3½	3½	3¾
	90"-wide	2¼	3½	2¼

Sewing

METHOD #1

Use ½"-wide seam allowances.

Use this construction technique For a layered bed skirt, assemble and gather each layer individually, then stitch them together as they are applied to the deck.

1. Cut and assemble the deck (see page 41). At one end of the deck, mark 2" in from the edge. This is the head. At the other end, mark ½" in at each corner. This is the foot.

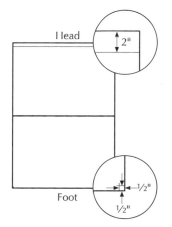

2. For the ruffle, stitch the fabric panels together as indicated in the chart above for your bed size and fabric width to make 2 side skirt sections and 1 foot skirt section.

3. To hem the lower edge of each skirt section, fold the long raw edge under 4" to the wrong side; press. Tuck the raw edge in to meet the fold; press again, creating a 2" double hem. Stitch or fuse in place.

✄ *Tip:* For a professional finish, blindstitch the hems.

4. To hem the side edges of each skirt section, fold one short raw edge under 2" to the wrong side; press. Tuck the raw edge in to meet the fold; press again, creating a 1" double hem. Stitch or fuse in place. Repeat, hemming both short edges of each skirt section.

5. Gather the long, unfinished edge of each skirt section to fit the corresponding edge of the deck.

6. With right sides together, pin 1 side skirt to the deck between the markings. Adjust the gathers to fit. Stitch. Repeat for the other side skirt and the foot skirt. For a layered bed skirt, pin or baste the ruffles to the deck, starting with the shortest and ending with the longest. Stitch through the deck and all the ruffles.

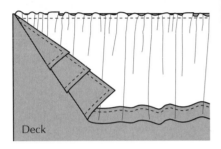

Layered Bed Skirt

7. Press the seam allowances toward the deck. (*Optional:* Zigzag, overcast, or serge the seam allowances together.) Topstitch around the sides and lower edge of the deck through all layers.

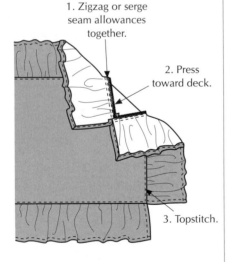

1. Zigzag or serge seam allowances together.

2. Press toward deck.

3. Topstitch.

8. Press and stitch a 1" double hem at the head of the deck.

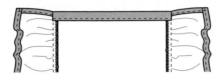

METHOD #2

Use ½"-wide seam allowances.

Use this construction technique for beds that do not have any detail at the foot to interfere with the skirt.

For a layered bed skirt, assemble and gather each layer individually, then stitch them together as they are applied to the deck.

1. Cut and assemble the deck (see page 41). At one end of the deck, mark 2" in from the edge for the head. At the other end, round off the corners in a gentle curve for the foot.

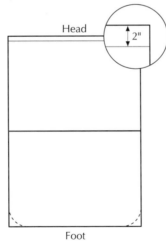

Head

2"

Foot

2. For the ruffle, stitch the fabric panels together into one continuous strip.

3. To hem the lower edge, make a 2" double hem as in Method #1, step 3, on page 43.

4. To hem the two side edges, make a 1" double hem as in Method #1, step 4, on page 43.

5. Gather the long, unfinished edge of the skirt.

6. With right sides together, pin the skirt to the sides and foot of the deck starting and stopping at the 2" mark at the head. Adjust the gathers to fit; stitch.

7. Press the seam allowances toward the deck. (*Optional:* Zigzag, overcast, or serge the seam allowances together.) Topstitch around the sides and lower edge of the deck through all layers.

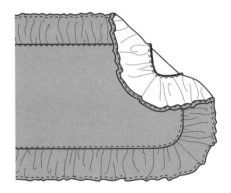

8. Press and stitch a 1" double hem at the head of the deck.

TAILORED BED SKIRT

This bed skirt is featured in the "Contemporary Room" (page 22).

A series of separate panels, in different combinations of lining and fabric, are arranged in an alternating pattern to make this bed skirt. These panels will be referred to in the following directions as right end, left end, center, right foot, left foot, and center foot.

Materials
44"-wide fabric

Contrasting fabric for buttons
1⅛"-diameter covered button forms:
- 10 for twin or double bed
- 16 for queen or king bed
- Point turner

Use the chart at right to determine how much fabric you need for your bed size.

Cutting

Directions are for a bed skirt with a 14" finished length. Adjustments for an 18" finished length are in parentheses. Cut all pieces so the cutting length (15" or 19") follows the lengthwise grain of the fabric.

TWIN

From the striped fabric, cut:
    4 pieces, each 35½" x 15" (19")
    2 pieces, each 44" x 15" (19")
    2 pieces, each 29½" x 15" (19")

From the large floral fabric, cut:
    5 pieces, each 19" x 15" (19")

DOUBLE

From the striped fabric, cut:
    4 pieces, each 35½" x 15" (19")
    2 pieces, each 44" x 15" (19")
    2 pieces, each 37½" x 15" (19")

Bed Size		Fabric		
	Finished Length	Striped	Large Floral	Lining
Twin	14"	3½ yds.	1⅜ yds.	2¼ yds.
	18"	4¼ yds.	1⅝ yds.	2¾ yds.
Double	14"	3½ yds.	1⅜ yds.	2¼ yds.
	18"	4¼ yds.	1⅝ yds.	2¾ yds.
Queen	14"	4¾ yds.	1¾ yds.	2⅝ yds.
	18"	6 yds.	2¼ yds.	3¼ yds.
King	14"	4¾ yds.	1¾ yds.	3 yds.
	18"	6 yds.	2¼ yds.	3¾ yds.

From the lining fabric and using the diagram below, cut:
    5 pieces, each 19" x 15" (19")
    4 pieces, each 16½" x 15" (19")
    2 pieces, each 7" x 15" (19")
    2 pieces, each 10½" x 15" (19")

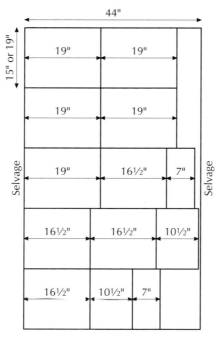

Cutting Diagram:
Lining Pieces for Twin Bed

From the large floral fabric, cut:
    5 pieces, each 19" x 15" (19")

From the lining fabric and using the diagram below, cut:
    5 pieces, each 19" x 15" (19")
    2 pieces, each 18½" x 15" (19")
    4 pieces, each 16½" x 15" (19")
    2 pieces, each 7" x 15" (19")

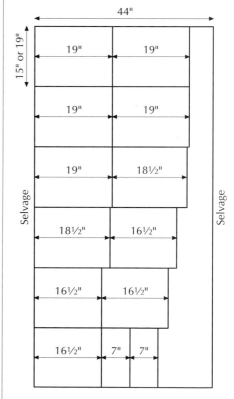

Cutting Diagram:
Lining Pieces for Double Bed

QUEEN

From the striped fabric, cut:
  6 pieces, each 30½" x 15" (19")
  5 pieces, each 41" x 15" (19")

From the large floral fabric, cut:
  8 pieces, each 19" x 15" (19")

From the lining fabric and using the diagram below, cut:
  8 pieces, each 19" x 15" (19")
  6 pieces, each 11½" x 15" (19")

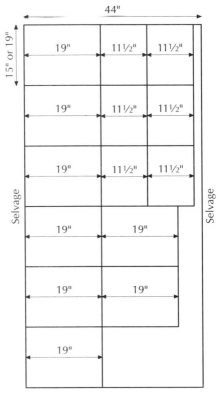

Cutting Diagram:
Lining Pieces for Queen Bed

KING

From the striped fabric, cut:
  4 pieces, each 30½" x 15" (19")
  5 pieces, each 41" x 15" (19")
  2 pieces, each 36½" x 15" (19")

From the large floral fabric and using the diagram below, cut:
  8 pieces, each 19" x 15" (19")

From the lining fabric and using the diagram below, cut:
  2 pieces, each 16½" x 15" (19")
  8 pieces, each 19" x 15" (19")
  4 pieces, cach 11½" x 15" (19")
  1 piece, 15" x 15" (19")

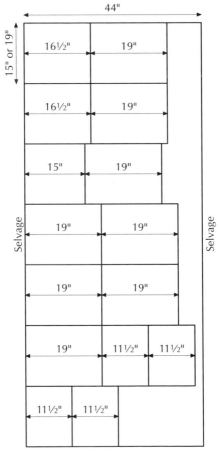

Cutting Diagram:
Lining Pieces for King Bed

Sewing

Use ½"-wide seam allowances.

LEFT ENDS (ALL SIZES)

1. Stitch lining and striped pieces together as shown. Press the seam allowances to one side. Repeat, making 2 left end panels.

   Twin or Double: Use two 35½"-wide striped and two 16½"-wide lining pieces.
   Queen or King: Use two 30½"-wide striped and two 11½"-wide lining pieces.

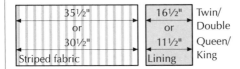

Left End Panel

2. Fold each panel right sides together with the 15" (19") side edges matching. Stitch along the side and lower edges as shown. Trim the corner seam allowances diagonally.

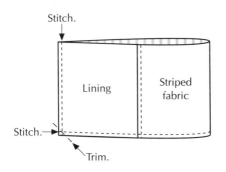

3. Turn each panel right side out. Using a point turner, gently push out the corners. Press each panel flat.

RIGHT ENDS (ALL SIZES)

Following the directions for the left end panels, assemble 2 mirror-image right end panels.

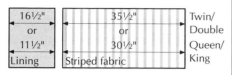

Right End Panel

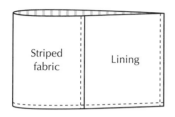

CENTER (TWIN AND DOUBLE)

1. Stitch lining and striped pieces together as shown, using one 44"-wide striped and one 7"-wide lining piece. Press the seam allowances to one side. Repeat, making 2 center panels.

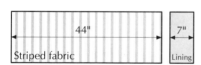

Center (Twin/Double)

---

2. Fold each panel right sides together with the 15" (19") side edges matching. Stitch along the side edge.

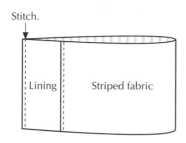

3. Lay each panel on a large, flat surface; adjust it so the lining section is centered. Pin along the lower edge; stitch. Trim the corner seam allowances diagonally.

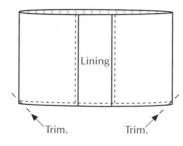

4. Turn each panel right side out. Using a point turner, gently push out the corners. Press each panel flat.

CENTER (QUEEN AND KING)

1. Fold one 41"-wide striped piece in half, right sides together. Stitch along the 15" (19") edge. Press the seam allowances open. Repeat, making 5 center panels for a queen-size bed or 4 center panels for a king-size bed.

✏ *Note:* The extra queen-size panel will be used as the center foot panel.

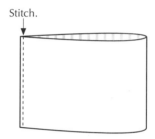

2. Lay each panel on a large, flat surface; adjust it so the seam is centered. Pin along the lower edge; stitch. Trim the corner seam allowances diagonally.

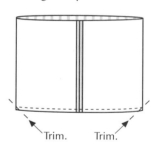

3. Turn each panel right side out. Using a point turner, gently push out the corners. Press each panel flat.

LEFT FOOT (ALL SIZES)

1. Stitch lining and striped pieces together as shown. Press the seams to one side.

   Twin: Use one 29½"-wide striped and one 10½"-wide lining piece.
   Double: Use one 37½"-wide striped and one 18½"-wide lining piece.
   Queen: Use one 30½"-wide striped and one 11½"-wide lining piece.
   King: Use one 36½"-wide striped and one 16½"-wide lining piece.

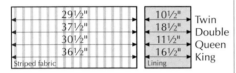

Left Foot

2. Fold the panel right sides together with 15" (19") edges matching. Stitch along the side and lower edges. Trim the corner seam allowances diagonally.

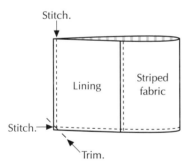

3. Turn the panel right side out. Using a point turner, gently push out the corners. Press it flat.

RIGHT FOOT (ALL SIZES)

Following the directions for the left foot panel, assemble 1 mirror-image right foot panel.

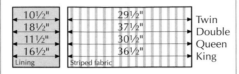

Right Foot

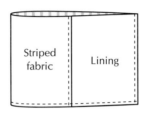

CENTER FOOT (KING SIZE)

1. Stitch the remaining 41"-wide striped and the 15" lining piece together as shown. Press the seam allowances to one side.

Center Foot

2. Fold the panel right sides together with the 15" (19") side edges matching. Stitch along the side edge.

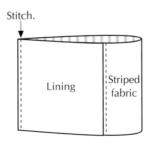

3. Lay the panel on a large, flat surface; adjust it so the lining section is centered. Pin along the lower edge; stitch. Trim the corner seam allowances diagonally.

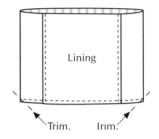

4. Turn the panel right side out. Using a point turner, gently push out the corners. Press the panel flat.

UNDERFLAPS (ALL SIZES)

1. Place one 19" x 15" (19") lining and one 19" x 15" (19") floral piece right sides together. Stitch around the sides and lower edge. Trim the corner seam allowances diagonally. Repeat, making 5 underflap panels for a twin-size or double bed or 8 underflap panels for a queen- or king-size bed.

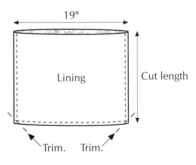

2. Turn each panel right side out. Using a point turner, gently push out the corners. Press each panel flat.

DECK

Cut and assemble the deck (see page 41). At one end of the deck, mark 2" from the edge. This is the head. At the other end, mark ½" from the corners. This is the foot.

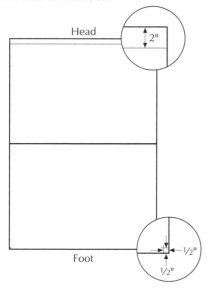

Head

2"

Foot

½"

½"

FINAL ASSEMBLY

1. Check the chart above to make sure you have the required number of panels for your bed size.
2. Arrange the end, center, and foot panels around the deck between the markings as shown.

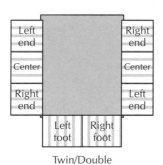

Left end		Right end
Center		Center
Right end		Left end
	Left foot / Right foot	

Twin/Double

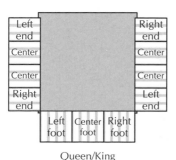

Left end		Right end
Center		Center
Center		Center
Right end		Left end
	Left foot / Center foot / Right foot	

Queen/King

Panel Type	Number of Finished Panels			
	Twin	Double	Queen	King
Right end	2	2	2	2
Left end	2	2	2	2
Center	2	2	4	4
Right foot	1	1	1	1
Left foot	1	1	1	1
Center foot	—	—	1	1
Underflap	5	5	8	8

3. Flip the panels over so the deck and panels are right sides together and the raw edges are even; pin.
4. On one side of the deck, center the underflap panels over the openings between the striped panels as shown. Adjust the panels, if necessary, so the lower edges are aligned; pin. Stitch the panels to the deck. Repeat for the other side and foot of the deck.

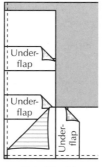

Under-flap

Under-flap

Under-flap

Twin/Double

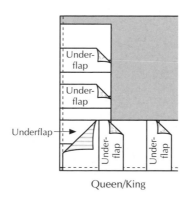

Underflap

Under-flap

Under-flap

Under-flap

Under-flap

Queen/King

5. Zigzag, overcast, or serge the seam allowances together. Press the seam allowances toward the deck. Topstitch around the sides and lower edge of the deck through all layers.
6. Press and stitch a 1" double hem at the head of the deck.
7. Cover the button forms with the contrasting fabric. Turn back the striped panels at the desired angle, exposing the floral panels. Press, making sharp creases. Position the covered buttons as desired and sew them in place.

Pillows

A bedroom doesn't seem complete without a profusion of pillows. Decorative pillows and pillow shams can enhance your decor. Use them to:

- Soften the abundance of color in a quilt. Add pillows in coordinating solids as in the "Romantic Room" (page 15).
- Unify a room. Use pillows to repeat a detail found elsewhere as with the button accents in the "Contemporary Room" (page 22).
- Create a focal point where no two pillows are the same as in the "Country Room" (page 18).
- Emphasize the colors and patterns of your quilt as in the "Rustic Room" (page 10) and the "Traditional Room" (page 12).

PILLOW SHAMS

Pillow shams are decorative covers for bed-size pillows. These covers can be removed nightly. However, you may prefer to keep them on at all times. This will certainly save time when making the bed in the morning!

The pillow shams in this book are based on the following pillow sizes:

Standard	20" x 26"
Queen	20" x 30"
King	20" x 38"

Use the accompanying charts to determine how much fabric and batting you need. Before cutting, measure your pillow to see if it corresponds to the typical pillow sizes. If not, adjust your cutting measurements accordingly. As a general rule, for the pillow front, add 1" to your pillow's width and length measurements; for the pillow back, add 1" to your pillow's width and 15" to your pillow's length measurements.

✂ *Tip:* All the pillow shams in this book have a professional appearance because I used a fleece-type batting to add body and create a smooth surface.

RUFFLED SHAMS

These shams are featured in the "Rustic Room" (page 9) and the "Romantic Room" (page 15).

Materials *(for 2 shams)*

44"-wide fabric
45"-wide fleece-type batting
10 yds. of buttonhole twist, pearl cotton, or lightweight cord

Cutting

For each standard-size sham, cut:
1 front, 21" x 27"
1 back, 21" x 42"
6 ruffle strips, each 7" x 44"

For each queen-size sham, cut:
1 front, 21" x 31"
1 back, 21" x 46"
7 ruffle strips, each 7" x 44"

YARDAGE (FOR 2 SHAMS)		
	Fabric	Batting
Standard	4⅜ yds.	¾ yd.
Queen	5 yds.	1 yd.
King	5¾ yds.	1⅛ yds.

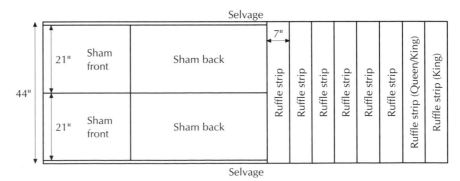

Cutting Diagram for 1 Ruffled Sham

For each king-size sham, cut:
  1 front, 21" x 39"
  1 back, 21" x 54"
  8 ruffle strips, each 7" x 44"

Fold the back piece in half, 21" edges matching; cut along the fold, creating 2 backs.

Cut the batting to match the sham front.

Sewing

Use ½"-wide seam allowances.

1. Pin the batting to the wrong side of the sham front. Machine baste around the edges to hold the layers together. Divide each edge in half and mark the centers.

2. To assemble the ruffle, place 2 ruffle strips right sides together at a 90° angle. Offset the ends to create 2 same-size tabs. Draw a diagonal line as shown. Stitch directly over this line, being careful not to stretch the strips. Trim the excess fabric and press the seam allowances to one side. Repeat for all strips, forming a circle by stitching the last strip to the first.

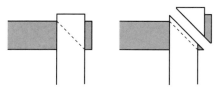

Trim excess.

✂ *Tip:* On a pillow sham, the most attractive finished width for a ruffle is 3". A narrower ruffle tends to look skimpy, whereas a wider ruffle is usually too floppy.

3. Fold the ruffle wrong sides together with raw edges even; press. Divide the ruffle into quarters; mark with pins or a fabric marker.

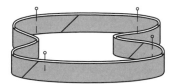

4. To gather the ruffle, set your machine for a long, wide zigzag stitch. Place buttonhole twist, pearl cotton, or lightweight cord ⅜" from the raw edge of the ruffle. Zigzag over the cord, being careful not to catch it in the stitching. Gather the ruffle to fit the pillow by pulling on the cord.

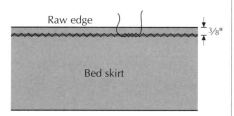

Raw edge

⅜"

Bed skirt

5. With right sides together, pin the ruffle to the sham front, matching the markings. Adjust the gathers to fit. Stitch. If you are pleased with the distribution of the gathers, pull out the cording. If not, remove the stitches from the section that needs to be adjusted, redistribute the gathers, and restitch the seam.

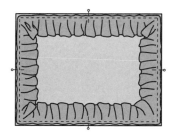

✂ *Tip:* For a professional-looking pillow, do not stretch the gathers around the corner; instead, fill the area with gathers. When the pillow cover is turned right side out, the ruffle will be full at each corner, rather than skimpy.

6. To hem the back openings, fold 2" to the wrong side along one 21" edge of one sham back; press. Tuck the raw edge under to meet the fold; press again, creating a 1" double hem. Stitch or fuse in place. Repeat for the other sham back.

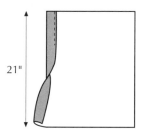

21"

7. With right sides together, pin the sham backs to the sham front so the finished edges of the backs overlap as shown. Stitch directly over the ruffle stitching line, then turn right side out. Check to make sure you didn't catch the loose edge of the ruffle in the seam. If everything is satisfactory, turn the sham wrong side out again. To eliminate bulk, trim the corner seam allowances diagonally. Trim the remaining seam allowances to ¼". Zigzag, overcast, or serge the seam allowances together. Turn the sham right side out and insert the pillow through the opening.

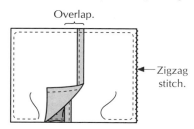

Overlap.

Zigzag stitch.

LACE-COVERED RUFFLED SHAMS

These very feminine pillow shams, featured in the "Romantic Room" (page 15), combine two fabrics: a solid and a delicate lace. The lace is layered over the solid to create a peek-a-boo effect.

To create these shams, follow the previous directions for the ruffled shams with the following adjustments:

1. From the lace, cut a second front and second set of ruffle strips for each sham. Because lace is available in various widths, it is difficult to provide exact yardages here. The lace used in the pillow in the "Romantic Room" was 60" wide and lent itself nicely to this treatment. Refer to the cutting directions for the ruffled shams to help you calculate the lace yardage and to determine the length of the ruffle strips.
2. Baste the lace front and fabric front together, right sides up with lace on top; handle as one.
3. Join the fabric ruffle strips and the lace ruffle strips separately, then baste the strips together, right sides up with lace on top. Handle as one, starting with step 3 on page 51.

FLANGED SHAMS

These attractive tailored shams are featured in the "Rustic Room" (page 9) and the "Contemporary Room" (page 22).

Materials (for 2 shams)

44"-wide fabric
45"-wide fleece-type batting

YARDAGE (FOR 2 SHAMS)		
	Fabric	Batting
Standard	4⅝ yds.	1½ yds.
Queen	5 yds.	1½ yds.
King	6 yds.	1½ yds.

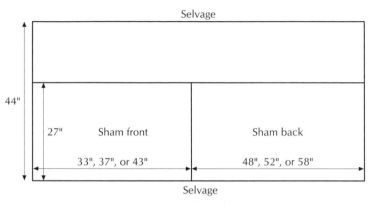

Cutting Diagram for 1 Flanged Sham

Cutting

For each standard-size sham, cut:
  1 front, 27" x 33"
  1 back, 27" x 48"

For each queen-size sham, cut:
  1 front, 27" x 37"
  1 back, 27" x 52"

For each king-size sham, cut:
  1 front, 27" x 43"
  1 back, 27" x 58"

Fold the back piece in half, 27" edges matching; cut along the fold, creating 2 backs.

Cut the batting to match the sham front.

Sewing

Use ½"-wide seam allowances.

1. Pin the batting to the wrong side of the sham front. Machine baste around the edges to hold the layers together.

2. To hem the back openings, fold 2" to the wrong side on one 27" edge of one sham back; press. Tuck the raw edge under to meet the fold; press again, creating a 1" double hem. Stitch or fuse in place. Repeat for the other sham back.

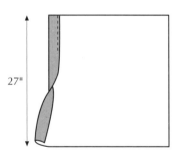

3. With right sides together, pin the sham backs to the sham front so the finished edges of the back overlap as shown on the next page; stitch. To eliminate bulk, trim the corner seam allowances diagonally. Trim the other seam allowances to ¼".

Zigzag, overcast, or serge the seam allowances together. Turn the sham right side out; press.

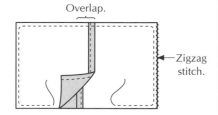

Overlap.

Zigzag stitch.

✂ *Tip:* When stitching corners, leave the needle in the down position, lift the presser foot, pivot the fabric, lower the presser foot, and continue stitching. For added reinforcement, stitch directly over the first stitching at each corner.

4. To form the flange, topstitch all around the sham, 3" from the edge.

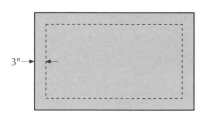

3"

5. Insert the pillow through the back opening.

STRIPED FLANGED SHAMS

These shams are featured in the "Traditional Room" (page 12).

Materials (for 2 shams)
44"-wide fabric
45"-wide fleece-type batting

YARDAGE (FOR 2 SHAMS)		
	Fabric	Batting
Standard	4½ yds	1½ yds.
Queen	4¾ yds.	1½ yds.
King	5¼ yds.	1½ yds.

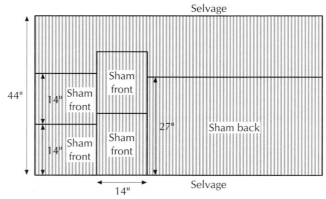

Cutting Diagram for 1 Striped Flanged Sham

Cutting

For each standard-size sham, cut:
    4 rectangles, each 14" x 17"
    1 back, 27" x 48"

For each queen-size sham, cut:
    4 rectangles, each 14" x 19"
    1 back, 27" x 52"

For each king-size sham, cut:
    4 rectangles, each 14" x 22"
    1 back, 27" x 58"

Fold the back piece in half, 27" edges matching; cut along the fold, creating 2 backs.

From the batting, cut:
    1 rectangle, 21" x 27", for each standard-size sham
    1 rectangle, 21" x 31", for each queen-size sham
    1 rectangle, 21" x 39", for each king-size sham

Sewing

Use ½"-wide seam allowances.

1. Stitch the 4 rectangles together, positioning the stripes as shown to form the sham front.

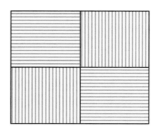

2. To assemble the sham, follow the directions for the flanged shams, "Sewing," steps 1–5, on pages 52–53.

Flanged Shams with Button Trim

These shams, featured in the "Contemporary Room" (page 22), duplicate the button details on the curtains and bed skirt.

Materials (for 2 shams)

44"-wide fabric
45"-wide fleece-type batting
Contrasting fabric for buttons
5 covered button forms, 1⅛"
    diameter

YARDAGE (FOR 2 SHAMS)		
	Fabric	Batting
Standard	5 yds.	1½ yds.
Queen	5½yds.	1½ yds.
King	6 yds.	1½ yds.

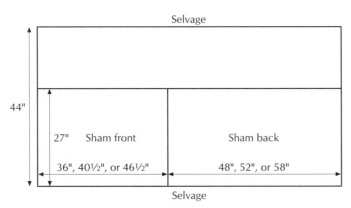

Cutting Diagram for 1 Flanged Sham

Cutting

For each standard-size sham, cut:
    1 front, 27" x 36½"
    1 back, 27" x 48" rectangle

For each queen-size sham, cut:
    1 front, 27" x 40½"
    1 back, 27" x 52"

For each king-size sham, cut:
    1 front, 27" x 46½"
    1 back, 27" x 58"

Fold the back piece in half, 27" edges matching; cut along the fold, creating 2 backs.

Cut the batting to match the sham front.

Sewing

Use ½"-wide seam allowances.

1. Fold the sham front in half, wrong sides together and 27" edges matching. Stitch 1¾" from the fold.

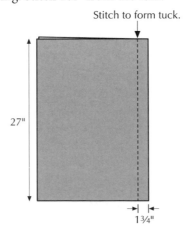

Stitch to form tuck.

27"

1¾"

2. Open out the front and press the tuck to one side.
3. To assemble the sham, follow the directions for the flanged shams, "Sewing," steps 1–4, on pages 52–53.
4. Cover the button forms with the contrasting fabric. Sew the buttons in place, spacing them evenly down the middle of the tuck and positioning the first and last buttons 1½" in from the edge of the flange.

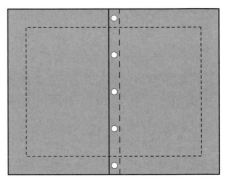

Center buttons on tuck; hand sew in place.

5. Insert the pillow form through the opening.

FLANGED SHAMS WITH PIPING

Contrasting piping adds a dash of color on these pillow shams, featured in the "Traditional Room" (page 13). To create your own covered piping, see page 56.

Materials (for 2 shams)

- 44"-wide fabric
- 45"-wide fleece-type batting
- Contrasting piping

Cutting

1. Follow the directions for the flanged shams, "Cutting," on page 52.
2. Using a saucer as a template, gently curve all 4 corners of the sham front. Cut the batting to match the sham front.

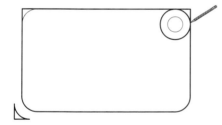

	YARDAGE (FOR 2 SHAMS)		
	Fabric	Batting	Piping
Standard	4⅝ yds.	1½ yds.	7 yds.
Queen	5 yds.	1½ yds.	7 yds.
King	6 yds.	1½ yds.	8 yds.

Sewing

Use ½"-wide seam allowances.

1. Pin the batting to the wrong side of the sham front. Machine baste around the edges to hold the layers together.
2. On the right side of the sham front, pin and baste the piping in place around the edges, following the directions for applying piping on page 57.
3. To hem the back openings, fold 2" to the wrong side along one 27" edge of one sham back; press. Tuck the raw edge under to meet the fold; press again, creating a 1" double hem. Stitch or fuse in place. Repeat for the other sham back.
4. With right sides together, pin the sham backs to the sham front so the finished edges of the back overlap and the raw edges match as shown. Trim the corners on the sham backs to match the sham front.

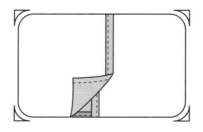

Using a zipper foot, stitch as close as possible to the piping. Trim the seam allowances to ¼". Zigzag, overcast, or serge the seam allowances together.

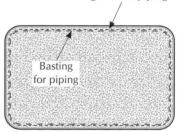

Stitch sham front to sham back, stitching close to piping.

Basting for piping

5. Turn the sham right side out; press. Remove any visible basting stitches. To form the flange, topstitch all around the sham, 3" from the edge.

3" — Piping

6. Insert the pillow through the back opening.

Although it is possible to use purchased piping, custom-covered piping adds a special decorator touch to your projects. For custom piping, the filler is usually a 100% cotton cording called "cable cord." If the filler is a very thick cable cord, the finished piping is sometimes referred to as "welting."

Continuous Bias Strips

For smooth piping, the fabric strips that cover the cording must be cut on the bias. The strips should be equal to the diameter of the cording plus at least 1" for seam allowances.

One fat quarter (18" x 22") yields approximately 4 yards of 2"-wide bias strips—enough to add piping to any of the pillow shams in this book.

1. To establish a true bias line on the fat quarter, fold down the upper left corner until edges A and B match. To mark the bias line, finger-press at each end of this diagonal fold; unfold the fabric and draw a line connecting these marks. Carefully cut along the drawn line.

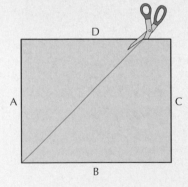

2. Pin the two shapes right sides together with edges A and C matching as shown. Stitch, using a ¼"-wide seam allowance. Press the seam allowances to one side.

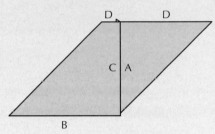

3. On the wrong side of the fabric, draw lines parallel to the bias edge. The distance between these lines should equal the width needed to cover your cording.

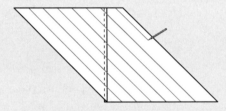

4. Arrange the fabric right sides together with edges B and D matching. Match the drawn lines, offsetting them 1 strip width as shown. Stitch, using a ¼"-wide seam allowance. Press the seam allowances to one side.

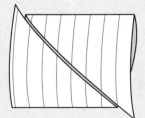

5. Cut along the drawn lines until the entire tube is transformed into one long bias strip.

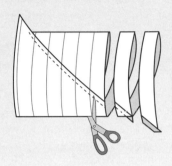

Covering the Cording

Place the bias strip wrong side up with the cording in the center. Fold the strip around the cording so the raw edges are even. Attach the zipper foot to your sewing machine. Stitch close to the cording.

✏ **Note:** This stitching line should not be extremely tight against the cording. The looseness will be eliminated when the piping is applied to the project.

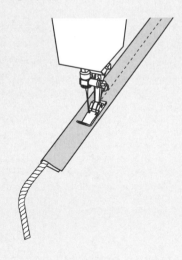

Applying Piping

1. Pin the piping to the right side of the project, raw edges even. Using a zipper foot, machine baste, starting approximately 2" from the first end of the piping and stitching as close as possible to the cording. Stop stitching approximately 3" from the first end of the piping; leave the needle in the fabric. Trim the excess piping, leaving a 1" overlap.

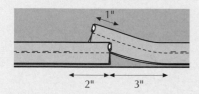

2. Starting 2" in from the end of the overlap, remove the cover stitches to expose the cording. Trim 1" from the cording so the two ends butt together.

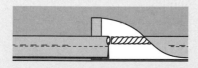

3. On the overlap, fold the end of the cover under ½". Butt the ends of the cording together; lap the folded cover over and around the cording. Finish stitching the piping to the project.

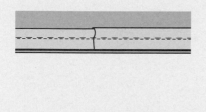

DOUBLE-FLAP SHAMS

These shams, featured in the "Contemporary Room" (page 22), use a bit of machine quilting to add depth and definition to the flaps.

Materials (for 2 shams)

44"-wide fabric
45"-wide fleece-type batting
2 large grommets
1¾ yds. of hemp-type rope
Hot glue and glue gun
Point turner

YARDAGE (FOR 2 SHAMS)		
	Fabric	Batting
Standard	3½ yds.	1½ yds.
Queen	4 yds.	3⅝ yds.
King	5 yds.	4½ yds.

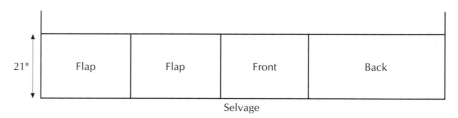

Cutting Diagram for 1 Double-Flap Sham

Cutting

For each standard-size sham, cut:
    1 front, 21" x 27"
    1 back, 21" x 42"
    2 flaps, each 21" x 28"

For each queen-size sham, cut:
    1 front, 21" x 31"
    1 back, 21" x 46"
    2 flaps, each 21" x 33"

For each king-size sham, cut:
    1 front, 21" x 39"
    1 back, 21" x 54"
    2 flaps, each 21" x 41"

Fold the back piece in half, 21" edges matching; cut along the fold, creating 2 backs.

Pin the flaps right sides together and cut edges even. Draw diagonal lines as shown, dividing the flaps into 4 triangles. Cut along the diagonal lines. Save the side triangles for another

project. You now have 2 flap fronts and 2 flap facings.

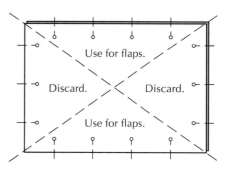

Cut the batting to match the sham front and the flaps.

Sewing

Use ½"-wide seam allowances.

1. Pin the front batting to the wrong side of the sham front. Machine baste around the edges to hold the layers together. Repeat for the flap fronts. Mark the center on each long edge of the sham front.

2. With right sides together, stitch 1 flap front to 1 flap facing, leaving the longest edge open for turning. Repeat for the other flap front and flap facing. Mark the center at the open edge of each flap.

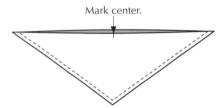

Mark center.

To eliminate bulk, trim the corner seam allowances diagonally. Trim the remaining seam allowances to ¼".

3. Turn the flaps right side out. Using a point turner, gently push the fabric to create a sharp point at each corner. Press the flap flat. Machine quilt each flap as shown, spacing the quilting lines 1½" apart.

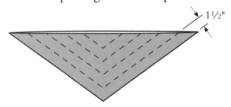

1½"

4. With right sides up, pin 1 flap to each long edge of the sham front as shown, matching the cut edges and center marks. Note that the ends of the flap will extend beyond the edge of the sham front. This is necessary for the flap to fit correctly when the sham is completed. Machine baste ½" from the edge through all layers. Repeat for the other flap.

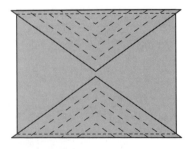

5. Hem the sham backs. Join the front and backs, following the directions for the ruffled shams, "Sewing," steps 6 and 7, on page 51, but disregarding the ruffle references.

6. Attach a grommet approximately 1" in from the tip of each flap, following the manufacturer's instructions. Insert the pillow through the back opening. Insert a 30" piece of rope through the grommets and tie the ends in a square knot. To secure, place a small dab of hot glue inside the knot. Fray the ends of the rope if desired.

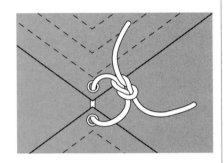

ACCENT PILLOWS

Small pillows in assorted sizes and shapes add a layer of luxury to the bedroom. Although they may look expensive, they can often be made from scraps left over from other projects.

Accent pillows can:
- Add a splash of color
- Introduce new colors, shapes, and textures
- Unify the other elements in the room
- Provide seasonal changes

Individual pillows should have their own personality, but when viewed as a group, a common thread should be obvious (no pun intended).

SQUARE RUFFLED PILLOW

This pillow is featured in the "Traditional Room" (page 12).

Materials

1⅝ yds. of 44"-wide fabric
15" square of fleece-type batting
1⅝ yds. of contrasting piping
14"-square pillow form

Cutting

From the fabric, cut:
1 front, 15" x 15"
1 back, 15" x 44"
4 ruffle strips, each 7" x 44"

Fold the back piece in half, 15" edges matching; cut along the fold, creating 2 backs.

Sewing

Use ½"-wide seam allowances.
1. Pin the batting to the wrong side of the front. Machine baste around the edges. Divide each edge in half and mark.
2. Machine baste the piping to the front, following the directions for applying piping on page 57.
3. Follow the directions for the ruffled shams, "Sewing," steps 2–5, on page 51.
4. Fold each back in half, wrong sides together, with 15" edges matching; press.
5. Finish the pillow cover, following the directions for the ruffled shams, "Sewing," step 7, on page 51.

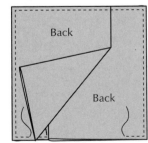

Back

Back

Ruffled Heart Pillow

This pillow is featured in the "Rustic Room" (page 10).

Materials

1¼ yds. of 44"-wide fabric
18" square of fleece-type batting
14" heart-shaped pillow form or fiberfill stuffing

Cutting

Use the heart-shaped pattern printed on the pillow-form package or the pattern at right to cut the front and back.

From the fabric, cut:
   1 front
   1 back
   4 ruffle strips, each 6" x 44"

Cut the batting to match the front.

Sewing

Use ½"-wide seam allowances.

1. Pin the batting to the wrong side of the front. Machine baste around the edges to hold the layers together. Divide the edge into quarters by marking the 2 points and along the sides as indicated on the diagram.

2. Follow the directions for the ruffled shams, "Sewing," steps 2–5, on page 51.

3. With right sides together, pin the front to the back. Stitch directly over the ruffle stitching line. Backstitch at the beginning and end, leaving a 6" opening for turning. Turn the cover right side out. Check to make sure you didn't catch the loose edge of the ruffle in the seam. If everything is satisfactory, turn the cover wrong side out again. To eliminate bulk, trim the seam allowance at the point diagonally. Trim the remaining seam allowance to ¼". Clip or notch the curves to ensure a smooth line.

4. Turn the cover right side out. Insert the pillow form or stuff the pillow with the fiberfill. Hand sew the opening closed.

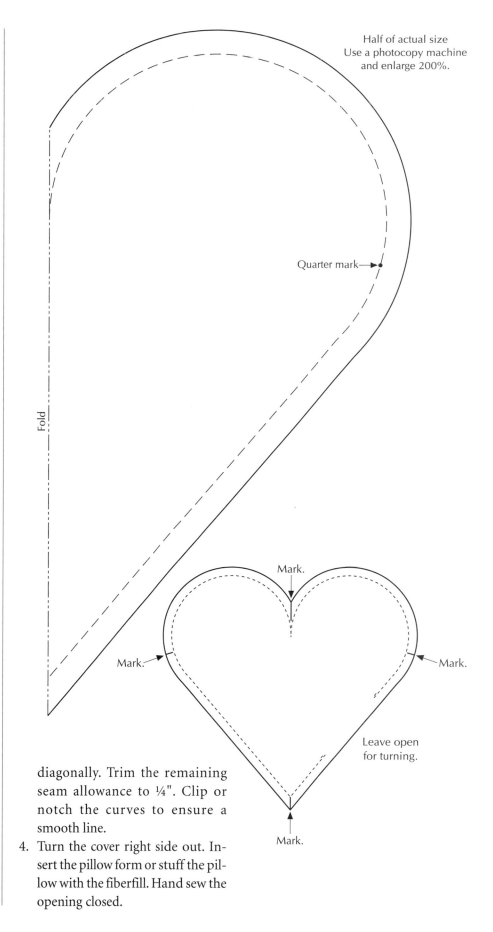

Half of actual size
Use a photocopy machine and enlarge 200%.

Fold

Quarter mark →

Mark.

Mark.

Mark.

Mark.

Leave open for turning.

NECKROLL PILLOW

This pillow is featured in the "Romantic Room" (page 15).

Materials

1¼ yds. of 44"-wide fabric
17" x 21" piece of fleece-type batting
2 yds. of ½"-wide ribbon
6" x 16" neckroll pillow form

Cutting

From the fabric, cut:
    1 pillow cover, 17" x 21"
    2 ends, each 4½" x 30"
    2 ruffle strips, each 6" x 44"

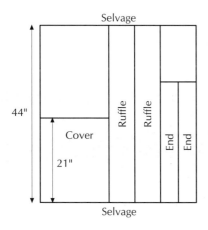

Sewing

Use ½"-wide seam allowances.

1. Pin the batting to the wrong side of the pillow cover. Machine baste around the edges to hold the layers together.

2. Fold the cover in half, right sides together. Stitch along the long edge.

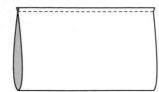

Press the seam open. Turn the cover right side out.

3. Prepare 2 ruffles, following the directions for the ruffled shams, "Sewing," steps 2–4, on page 51, and gathering each ruffle to fit the cover ends.

4. With right sides together, pin a ruffle to each end of the cover. Adjust the gathers to fit. Stitch.

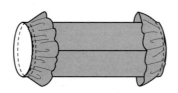

5. With right sides together, match and pin the 4½" edges of one end section. Stitch the seam, leaving a ½" opening 1" from one edge as shown. Backstitch at the beginning and end of the opening.

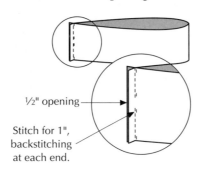

½" opening

Stitch for 1", backstitching at each end.

On the long edge closest to the opening, press under ¼". Fold the pressed edge under ¾"; press again. Stitch close to the first fold, creating a casing. Using a long machine basting stitch, gather the other long edge slightly to fit the cover opening.

Casing

Gather this edge slightly.

With right sides together and raw edges even, pin the end to the cover opening; stitch.

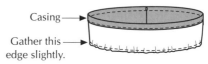

Repeat for the other cover end.

6. Cut the ribbon into 2 equal pieces. Insert a piece into 1 casing; pull the ribbon taut to close the opening and tie the ends in a bow. Insert the pillow form. Insert the remaining ribbon into the other casing, pull the ribbon taut, and tie the ends in a bow.

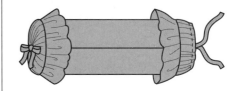

ROUND RUFFLED PILLOW

This pillow is featured in the "Romantic Room" (page 15).

Materials

1 yd. of 44"-wide fabric
13" x 13" square of fleece-type batting
Fiberfill stuffing
14" x 14" square of tissue paper or brown paper
Ruler

Cutting

1. Draft the pattern for the pillow by folding the tissue or brown paper into quarters. Using a ruler as a compass, measure out 6½" from the folded corner and draw a curved edge. Cut along the curved line and open up the pattern.

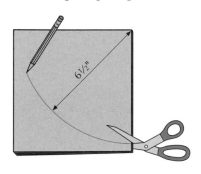

2. Using the paper pattern, cut 1 pillow front and 1 pillow back from the fabric. From the remaining fabric, cut 3 ruffle strips, each 7" x 44".
3. Cut the batting to match the pillow front.

Sewing

Use ½"-wide seam allowances.
1. Divide and mark the edge of the pillow front into quarters.
2. Follow the directions for the ruffled shams, "Sewing," steps 1–5, on page 51.

3. Follow the directions for the ruffled heart pillow, "Sewing," steps 3 and 4, on page 59, disregarding references to trimming the point.

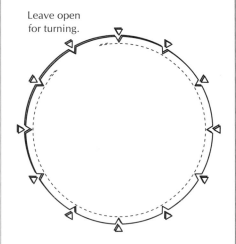

Leave open for turning.

ALLOVER PATCHWORK PILLOW

This pillow, featured in the "Country Room" (page 18), is the perfect way to put your fabric scraps to beautiful use!

Materials

Fabric scraps (assorted light, medium, and dark solids and prints)
14½" x 14½" square of fabric for pillow back
14½" x 14½" square of fleece-type batting
14"-square pillow form

Cutting

From the fabric scraps, cut:
196 squares, each 1½" x 1½".

Sewing

Use ¼"-wide seam allowances.
1. Toss all the 1½" squares into a sack. Randomly pull out and join the squares until you've completed 5 or 6 rows of 14 squares each; lay them out and construct the remaining

rows to balance the lights and darks. Assemble a total of 14 rows of 14 squares each.
2. Stitch the rows together. Press the pillow front.
3. Pin the batting to the wrong side of the patchwork front. Quilt in-the-ditch at each seam line.

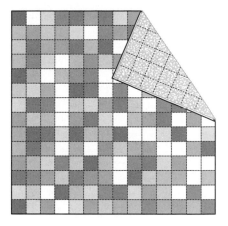

4. Pin the pillow back to the patchwork front, right sides together. Stitch, leaving a 4" opening along one side for turning. To eliminate bulk, trim the corner seam allowance diagonally.
5. Turn the cover right side out and insert the pillow form. Hand sew the opening closed.

PILLOWCASE PILLOW

This pillow is featured in the "Country Room" (page 19).

Materials

1 yd. of 44"-wide fabric
16"-square pillow form
Rubber band
1 yd. of rope
Hot glue and glue gun

Cutting

From the fabric, cut:
1 rectangle, 28" x 32"

Sewing

Use ½"-wide seam allowances.

1. Fold the rectangle right sides together with 28" edges matching. Stitch together along the side and lower edges. Backstitch at the beginning and end of the stitching to secure the seam. To eliminate bulk, trim the corner seam allowances diagonally.

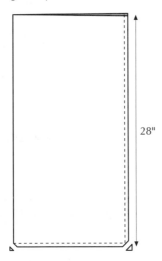

2. Clean-finish the upper edge, using a zigzag, overcast, or overlock stitch. Fold the finished edge down 6" to the wrong side; press. Stitch along the finished edge through all layers.

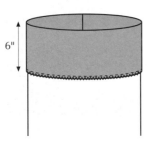

3. Turn the pillow cover right side out. Insert the pillow form through the opening. Use the rubber band to secure the opening approximately 4" down from the top. Tie the rope in a knot, covering the rubber band. Tie half knots at the ends of the rope. Secure all knots with hot glue.

SQUARE FLANGED PILLOW

This pillow is featured in the "Country Room" (page 18).

Materials

1⅛ yds. of 44"-wide fabric
20" x 20" square of fleece-type batting
14"-square pillow form

Cutting

From the fabric, cut:
1 front, 20" x 20"
1 back, 20" x 44"

Fold the back piece in half, 20" edges matching; cut along the fold, creating 2 backs.

Sewing

Use ½"-wide seam allowances.

1. Fold each back in half, wrong sides together and 20" edges matching; press.
2. Pin the batting to the wrong side of the front. Machine baste around the edges to hold layers together.
3. Finish the pillow cover, following the directions for the flanged shams, "Sewing," steps 2–5, on pages 52–53. Topstitch 2½" from the finished edge of the cover.

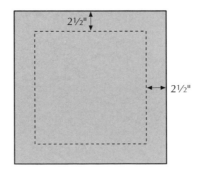

CINCHED PILLOW

This pillow is featured in the "Country Room" (page 18).

Materials

½ yd. of 44"-wide fabric
½ yd. of 45"-wide fleece-type batting
16"-square pillow form
2¼ yds. of rope
Hot glue and glue gun

Cutting

From the fabric, cut:
1 front, 17" x 17"
1 back, 17" x 17"

Cut 2 pieces of batting to match the front and back.

Sewing

Use ½"-wide seam allowances.

1. Pin the batting front to the wrong side of the cover front. Machine baste around the edges to hold the layers together. Repeat for the cover back.
2. Pin the cover front to the cover back, right sides together. Stitch, leaving a 4" opening along one edge for turning. To eliminate bulk, trim the corner seam allowances diagonally. Trim the remaining seam allowances to ¼".

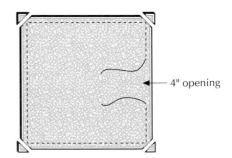

3. Turn the cover right side out and insert the pillow form. Hand sew the opening closed.

4. Cut the rope into 2 equal lengths. Tie the ropes together with a square knot as shown, keeping the cut ends even.

5. Center the pillow back over the knot, bring the ends of the rope up and around the pillow front, and tie them snugly in a square knot, cinching the pillow. Tie half knots at the ends of the ropes. Secure all knots with hot glue.

BUTTON FLANGED PILLOW

This pillow is featured in the "Contemporary Room" (page 22).

Materials

1 yd. of 44"-wide fabric
15" x 16½" piece of fleece-type batting
Contrasting fabric for buttons
4 covered button forms, 1⅛" diameter
14"-square pillow form

Cutting

From the 44"-wide fabric, cut:
1 front, 15" x 16½"
1 back, 15" x 44"

Fold the back piece in half, 15" edges matching; cut along the fold, creating 2 backs.

Sewing

Use ½"-wide seam allowances.

1. Fold each back in half, wrong sides together and 15" edges matching; press.

2. Pin the batting to the wrong side of the front. Machine baste around the edges to hold layers together.

3. Finish the pillow cover, following the directions for the flanged shams, "Sewing," steps 2–5, on pages 52–53, but do not topstitch all around; instead, topstitch 1½" from one 14" edge of the cover.

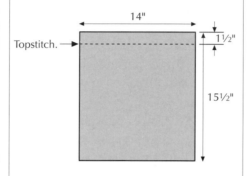

4. Cover the button forms with the contrasting fabric. Sew the buttons in place along the flange, spacing them evenly and positioning the first and last buttons 1½" from each end of the flange.

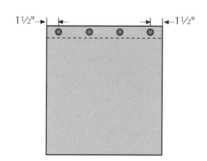

5. Insert the pillow form through the back opening.

DOUBLE-TUCKED PILLOW

This pillow is featured in the "Contemporary Room" (page 22).

Materials

½ yd. of 44"-wide striped fabric
⅝ yd. of 44"-wide floral fabric
15" x 15" square of fleece-type batting
Contrasting fabric for buttons
8 covered button forms, 1⅛" diameter
14"-square pillow form

Cutting

From the striped fabric, cut:
1 center panel, 10" x 15"
1 back, 15" x 44"

Fold the back in half, 15" edges matching; cut along the fold, creating 2 backs.

From the floral fabric, cut:
2 side panels, each 6" x 15"

Sewing

Use ½"-wide seam allowances.

1. Fold each back in half, wrong sides together and 15" edges matching; press.

2. Press under 2" along 1 long edge of a floral side panel.

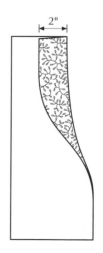

3. To assemble the front, pin the side panel with the pressed edge to the center panel so the folded edge overlaps 2".

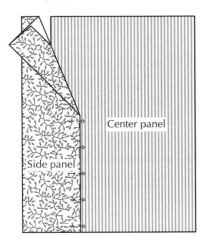

Turn the panels over and stitch through all layers, ½" from the inner raw edges. Repeat with the other side panel.

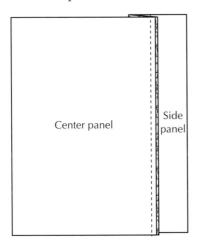

4. Pin the batting to the wrong side of the front. Machine baste around the edges to hold layers together.

Batting

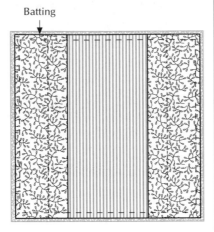

5. Finish the pillow cover, following the directions for the flanged shams, "Sewing," steps 2–5, on pages 52–53, but disregarding the references to topstitching.

6. Cover the button forms with the contrasting fabric. Sew the buttons in place, spacing them evenly down the middle of each tuck and positioning the first and last buttons 1½" from each end of the tucks.

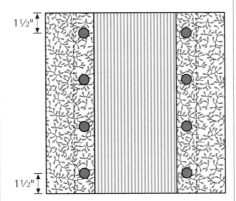

7. Insert the pillow form through the opening.

Window Treatments

Believe it or not, window treatments—especially the ones featured in this book—are among the easiest home-decorating projects you can make. These window treatments were selected because they can be easily adapted to most window sizes and styles. The simplest window treatment may be all that's needed to complete a room.

WINDOW TREATMENT BASICS

- Avoid installing the rods directly onto the wooden frame. Instead, position the rods outside the frame or opening. The studs that are usually around the frame edge will provide the support that's needed to withstand the weight of the window treatments. To ensure hitting the center of a stud, place the brackets approximately 2" above and 1" out from the side of the frame.

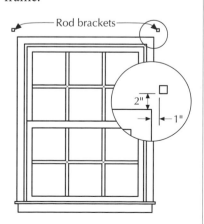

- Select and install the hardware before measuring for your window treatment.
- When making rod pocket–style window treatments, you need the finished width and the finished length.
- Valances need to be in pleasing proportion to the window height. A good finished length for a valance is between 16" and 18" (including the heading). This length may or may not be suitable for your window. If you're not good at visualizing, cut a large piece of paper the length you are considering and tape it to the rod. Step back and observe the effect.
- To achieve the desired fullness, you may need to cut and piece fabric panels. For curtains, plan your piecing so a full panel is at the center of the window and a partial panel is toward the frame. For a valance, use one full-width center panel and two narrower side panels.

Piecing for Curtains

Piecing for Valances

- If your fabric has a repeating design, measure the vertical distance between the repeat. Multiply the repeat distance by the number of fabric panels needed (this number will be determined in your curtain or valance directions). Add this amount to the cut length (which is also determined in the directions). The extra fabric allows you to match the motifs.

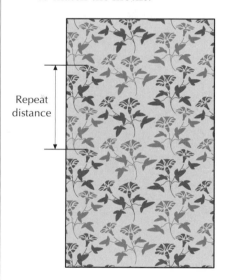

- For accurate cutting and measuring, straighten the fabric so the crosswise cut edge is perpendicular to the selvage edge.

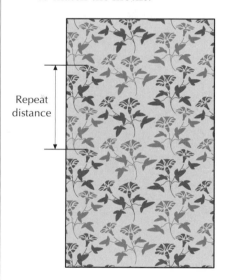

To straighten folded fabric from a bolt:

Place the fabric on a large, flat surface, and smooth it out so there are no bumps or creases. If necessary, adjust the fold so the selvage edges match exactly. Place a wide quilter's ruler against the selvage edge, aligning the horizontal line on the ruler with the folded edge of the fabric. Using a rotary cutter, cut across the fabric, along the edge of the ruler.

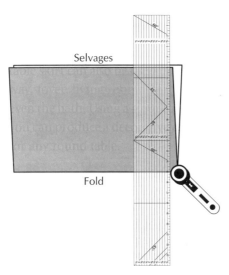

Selvages

Fold

To straighten fabric from a tube:

Smooth out the fabric on a large, flat surface. Position a piece of notebook paper at a 90° angle to the selvage. Place a yardstick or quilter's ruler along the long edge of the paper. Using chalk, draw a line along the edge of the ruler, extending it across the width of the fabric. Cut along the chalk line.

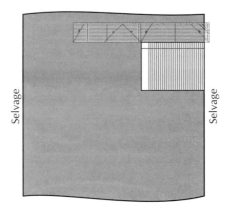

Selvage

Selvage

- Double hems are often used at the edges of curtains and valances because they add just a bit of extra weight to help the window treatment hang properly. To make a double hem, fold the raw edge of the fabric over to the wrong side in an amount equal to twice the depth of the finished hem. (For example, for a double 2" hem, fold over 4".) Press. Tuck the raw edge in to meet the fold; press again. Stitch or fuse in place.

GLOSSARY

Refer to the following definitions when making your window treatment.

Cut length: the total length measurement, including allowances for the heading and hem. This is the measurement to use when cutting fabric lengths for your treatments.

Fabric width: the width of the fabric as it is sold from the bolt.

Finished length: the measurement from the top of the rod to the spot where you want your treatment to end.

Finished width: the width of the window treatment, including the bracket-to-bracket rod measurement plus any returns.

Fullness: the allowance for gathers; usually 2½ to 3 times the width of the window. Use the higher number for lightweight and sheer fabrics.

Heading: the top of the window treatment that extends above the rod.

Pattern repeat: the vertical distance between the same design or motif in the fabric.

Return: the distance the rod extends from the wall.

Rod pocket: a fabric casing where the curtain rod is inserted for hanging.

UNLINED PANEL CURTAINS

These curtains are featured in the "Rustic Room" (page 9). To complement them, add the lace valance (page 72).

Materials

44"- or 58"-wide fabric
Standard flat curtain rod

Yardage Calculations
(for 1 pair of curtains)

1. Install the rod. Measure the length of the rod plus returns (if any). Write this measurement here:___.
2. Multiply the rod length by 2.5 or 3, depending on the fullness desired. Write this measurement here:___. Add 12" to this measurement for the side hems. Write this measurement here:___.
3. To determine the number of fabric panels needed, divide the final measurement in step 2 by the width of the fabric; round up to the nearest whole number. Write this number here:___.
4. Measure from the top of the rod to where you want the curtains to end. Add 19" for the rod pocket, heading, and hem allowance. Write this measurement here:___. This is your cut length.

☞ **Note:** If your fabric has a repeat, follow the directions in "Window Treatment Basics" on page 65.

5. Multiply the cut length (step 4) by the number of panels needed (step 3). Divide this number by 36 to convert the total into yardage; round up to the nearest ¼ yard. This is the amount of fabric you need.

✂ **Tip:** If you are measuring for floor-length curtains in a carpeted area, cover the carpet with a thin piece of cardboard to get a more accurate measurement.

Cutting

1. Divide the number of panels needed for a pair of curtains (determined in "Yardage Calculations," step 3) by 2. This is how many panels are needed for each curtain.
2. Straighten one end of the fabric (see page 66).
3. Cut 1 fabric panel equal to your cut length. This panel will be your guide for cutting the remaining panels. Place it directly on top of the remaining fabric, matching the motifs, and cut the next panel. Repeat until all panels are cut.

Sewing

Use ½"-wide seam allowances.

1. Piece the panels, if necessary, adding partial panels at the outside edges.

✂ **Tip:** Always stitch from the bottom edge to the top. This way, if the fabric shifts and the match of the motifs is slightly off, any problem will fall into the heading where it will not be as noticeable.

2. Finish the lower edge with a 4" double hem.

✂ **Tip:** For a professional finish, blindstitch the hem.

3. Finish each side edge with a 1½" double hem.
4. To create the heading, fold the upper edge down 8" to the wrong side; press. Tuck the raw edge under to meet the fold; press again. Stitch along the second fold through all layers. To create the rod pocket, measure down 2" from the upper edge and mark with a fabric marker. Stitch along the marked line.

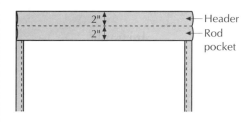

LACE PANEL CURTAINS

These curtains, featured in the "Romantic Room" (page 15), are a simpler variation of the unlined panel curtains (page 67).

Materials

Lace fabric*
Standard flat curtain rod

Select a lace that is attractively finished along the selvages.

Yardage Calculations

Install the rod. Measure from the top of the rod to where you want the curtains to end. Add 8" for the bottom hem. How much you add for the top depends on whether or not you want a header. For a rod pocket only, add 4". For a rod pocket and header, add 8". Write the total here: ___. This is your cut length. For a pair of curtains, double the cut length.

Divide the total cut length of the curtains by 36 to convert the total into yardage; round up to the nearest ¼ yard. This is the amount of lace fabric you need.

Cutting and Sewing

1. Cut the lace fabric crosswise into 2 panels.
2. Finish the lower edge of each panel with a 4" double hem.
3. For a header and rod pocket, finish the upper edge, following the directions for the unlined panel curtains, "Sewing," step 4, on page 67. For a rod pocket only, finish the upper edge with a 2" double hem.

✂ *Tip:* For an inconspicuous hemline on lace fabric, use a zigzag stitch instead of a straight stitch.

ROPE-TIED CURTAINS

These curtains are featured in the "Country Room" (page 18).

Materials

44"-wide fabric
16 large grommets
5½ yds. of hemp-type rope
Decorative rod and finials
Hot glue gun and glue

Yardage Calculations
(for 1 pair of curtains to fit a window 36" to 60" wide)

1. Install the brackets so the rod is 2" above the upper edge of the window frame and the ends are even with the outside edge of the frame. (The finials will extend beyond the frame.)

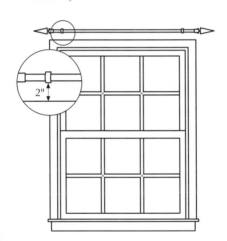

2. Measure from the upper edge of the window frame to the floor. To this measurement, add 12" for top and bottom hem allowances. Write this measurement here:___. This is the cut length.
3. Multiply the cut length by 2. Write this measurement here:___. Divide this measurement by 36 to convert the total to yardage; round up to the nearest ¼ yard.

Cutting and Sewing

1. Straighten one end of the fabric (see page 66).
2. Cut the fabric into 2 panels, each equal to the cut length.
3. Finish the lower edge of each panel with a 4" double hem.
4. Finish each side edge with a 2" double hem.
5. To finish the upper edge, fold the raw edge down 4" to the wrong side; press. Tuck the raw edge under to meet the fold, creating a 2" double hem. Open the hem allowance. Remove the side hem stitches above the fold lines. Trim the side hem allowances above the fold lines as shown to eliminate bulk when applying the grommets.

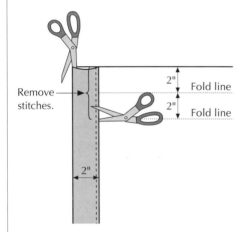

Fold the corner over at a 45° angle to meet the bottom fold line. Refold the hem allowance. Stitch or fuse in place.

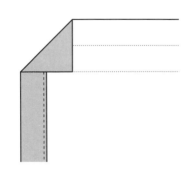

6. Determine the placement of the grommets across the upper edge of each curtain. The first and last grommets should be at the corners, approximately ½" from the upper edge and ½" from the side edge (see illustration below). Space the remaining grommets approximately 6" to 8" apart. Mark the grommet positions on the wrong side of the curtain by tracing around the inside opening of each eyelet. Attach the grommets where marked, following the manufacturer's instructions.

7. Cut the rope into 16 pieces, each 12" long. Insert 1 piece through each grommet and knot the ends together. Install the curtain on the rod. Adjust the knots so the upper edges of the curtain and the window frame are aligned. To secure, place a small dab of hot glue inside each knot. Fray the ends of the rope if desired.

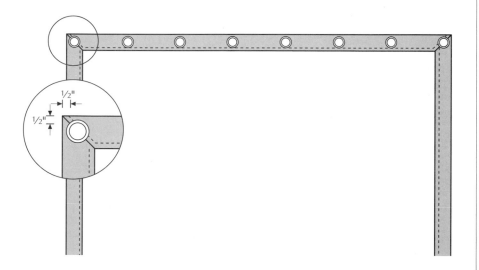

BANDED AND BUTTONED CURTAINS

These curtains are featured in the "Contemporary Room" (page 22).

Materials
44"-, 58"-, or 90"-wide fabric

Batiste or other lightweight or sheer fabric for curtains
Contrasting fabric for bands
Contrasting fabric for buttons
10 covered button forms, 1⅛" diameter
Decorative rod and finials

Yardage Calculations
CURTAIN FABRIC

1. Install the rod. Measure the length of the rod. Write this measurement here:___.
2. Multiply the rod length by 3. Write this measurement here:___.
3. To determine the number of fabric panels needed, divide the measurement in step 1 by the width of the fabric; round up to the nearest whole number. Write this number here:___.
4. Measure from the top of the rod to where you want the curtains to end. Add 4" for the rod pocket. Write this measurement here:___. This is your cut length.
5. Multiply the cut length by the number of panels needed (step 3). Divide this number by 36 to convert the total into yardage; round up to the nearest ¼ yard. This is the amount of curtain fabric you need.

BAND FABRIC

Each band goes around the two sides and the lower edge of each curtain. The bands are cut 4½" wide. For a pleasing appearance, cut each band from one length of fabric so it doesn't have to be pieced. Here's how to calculate the yardage for the band fabric, using your own curtain measurements.

1. Multiply the number of panels (see "Curtain Fabric," step 2) by the fabric width. Divide this measurement by 2. Write this measurement here:___. This is the cut width of each curtain.
2. Add 1 curtain cut width plus 2 curtain cut lengths plus 8". Write this measurement here:___. This is the band cut length. Divide the band cut length by 36 to convert the total into yardage; round up to the nearest ¼ yard. This is the amount of contrasting fabric you need for the bands.

Cutting

1. Divide the number of panels needed for a pair of curtains (determined in step 3 of "Curtain Fabric") by 2. This is how many panels you need for each curtain.
2. Straighten one end of the curtain fabric (see page 66).
3. From the curtain fabric, cut the required number of fabric panels, each equal to the cut length.
4. From the band fabric, cut 2 bands, each 4½" wide by the cut length.

Sewing

Use ½"-wide seam allowances.

1. Piece the curtain panels, if necessary, by adding the partial panels at the outside edges. Clean-finish the seam with a zigzag or overcast stitch; a French seam is also nice.

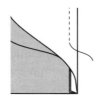

For piecing, clean-finish with a zigzag or overcast stitch, or make a French seam.

2. On the wrong side of the curtain fabric, press or use a chalk marker to draw a line 2" in from each side and the lower edge.

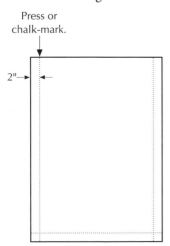

Press or chalk-mark.

2"→ ←

3. Fold the band in half lengthwise, wrong sides together; press.
4. Open the band. Starting at the upper edge, place the right side of the band against the wrong side of the curtain so the band edge is 1¾" from the curtain edge as shown. Stitch ¼" from the band edge over the marked line. Stop stitching about 10" from the marked bottom line. Cut the thread.

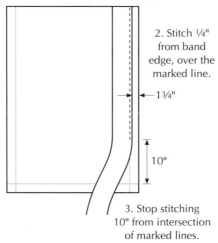

1. Place right side of band against wrong side of curtain; mark.

2. Stitch ¼" from band edge, over the marked line.

←1¾"

10"

3. Stop stitching 10" from intersection of marked lines.

5. Refold the band. At the intersecting marked line, make a ¼"-deep clip in the band's raw edges. (If necessary, mark the band first so the clip is exactly ¼" deep.) Measure down 4" from the clip and clip the band again.

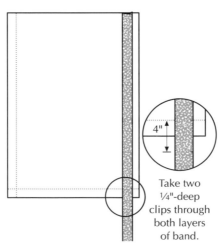

4"

Take two ¼"-deep clips through both layers of band.

6. Open the band again. Note that there are 2 sets of clips on each edge of the band. Fold the band under between the clips so the right sides are together and the clips match at both edges. Mark the center of the band at the fold.

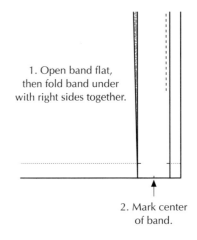

1. Open band flat, then fold band under with right sides together.

2. Mark center of band.

7. Keeping the curtain fabric out of the way, miter the band. To do this, start at the inner point of one set of clips and stitch diagonally to the center mark, pivot, and stitch diagonally to the inner point of the other set of clips. Backstitch at the beginning and end of the stitching.

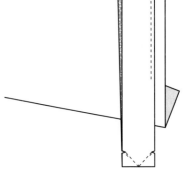

Stitch a point into band; begin stitching ¼" from cut edge.

8. Fold the band back down. Continue stitching the band to the curtain. Stitch down to the clip; stitch 1 stitch past the clip line. Leave the needle in the fabric, lift the presser foot, pivot the fabric, and rearrange the band so it is parallel to and 1¾" from the lower edge of the curtain. Continue stitching until 10" from the next corner. Cut the thread. To miter the next corner, repeat, starting with step 4. Finish stitching the band to the curtain.

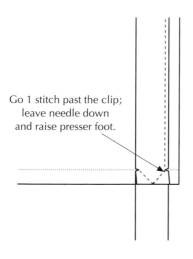

Go 1 stitch past the clip; leave needle down and raise presser foot.

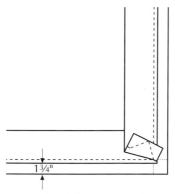

1¾"

Pivot band, lower presser foot, and continue stitching.

9. Trim the bulk from inside the band at each corner. Fold the band over the edge and to the right side of the curtain, making sharp corners.

Adjust the curtain fabric so it is smooth inside the band. Press the band's raw edge under ¼"; pin, matching the pressed edge to the stitching line. Stitch close to the pressed edge through all layers.

10. To create the heading, press the upper edge down 4" to the wrong side. Tuck the raw edge under to meet the fold. Stitch close to the second fold through all layers.

11. Cover the button forms with contrasting fabric. To mark the button placement on the band, measure down 3" from the curtain's top edge and center the mark on the band. Make 4 more marks, spaced 4" apart. Sew a button at each mark. Do this on the outside edge of each curtain.

12. At the inner corner of each curtain, make a 1⅛"-long machine buttonhole. Position the buttonhole so it is centered on the band and parallel to the side edge of the curtain.

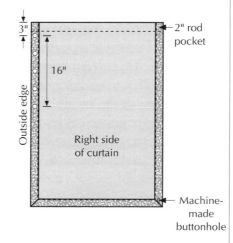

3"

16"

Outside edge

Right side of curtain

2" rod pocket

Machine-made buttonhole

13. Install the curtain on the rod. Bring each inside corner up to the corresponding lowest button and pull the button through the buttonhole. Adjust the curtains to evenly distribute the fullness.

LACE VALANCE

This valance is featured in the "Rustic Room" (page 10) and is paired with the unlined panel curtains (page 67).

This type of valance comes with most of the work done for you. All you have to do is hem the sides and weave the decorative rod through the ready-made openings. Lace valance panels are available in 12", 18", and 24" lengths.

Materials

Lace valance panel
Decorative curtain rod

Yardage Calculations

1. Install the decorative rod over the panel curtains so it is slightly above the upper edge of the curtains.

2. Measure across the rod from bracket to bracket. Multiply this measurement by 1.5. Add 3" for side hems. Divide this number by 36 to convert the total into yardage; round up to the nearest ¼ yard. This is the amount of fabric you need.

Sewing

1. To hem each side, fold the raw edge over 1½" to the wrong side; stitch. To camouflage the stitching, use a medium-width zigzag.

2. Weave the rod through the openings in the top of the valance. Install the rod at the window.

SELF-LINED VALANCE

This valance is featured in the "Romantic Room" (page 16).

Materials (per valance)

For a window up to 40" wide, use 1 valance.

For a window 40" to 115" wide, use 2 valances.

2⅜ yds. of 44"-wide fabric*
2½"-wide curtain rod
Optional: Nylon netting

If the fabric has a repeat, add twice the distance between the repeat to this amount.

Cutting and Sewing

Use ½"-wide seam allowances.

1. Cut 2 fabric panels, each 41" long by the width of the fabric.
2. Cut 1 panel in half lengthwise. Stitch the half widths to the outside edges of the full width. Press the seams open.
3. Fold the fabric in half, right sides together and long edges matching. Stitch ½" from the long cut edges to form a tube. Press the seam open.

4. Finish each side edge with a 1½" double hem.
5. Turn the tube right side out and arrange it so the crosswise seam is at the upper edge. Press along the upper edge only, making a sharp crease. Measure and mark 2" and 5" down from the pressed edge. Stitch along both marked lines to create the rod pocket and heading.

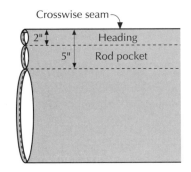

6. Install the valance on the rod. Distribute the gathers evenly.

✂ *Tip:* This valance can take on a whole new personality by inserting nylon netting in the tube to create the desired amount of pouf.

LINED VALANCE

This valance is featured in the "Traditional Room" (page 12).

Materials

44"-, 58"-, or 90"-wide fabric

Striped fabric
Lining fabric
Standard flat curtain rod

Yardage Calculations

1. Install the rod. Measure the length of the rod plus returns (if any). Write this measurement here:___.
2. Multiply the rod length by 2.5 or 3, depending on the fullness desired. Write this measurement here:___. Add 4" to this measurement for the side hems. Write this number here:___.
3. To determine the number of fabric panels needed, divide the final measurement in step 2 by the width of the fabric; round up to the nearest whole number. Write this number here:___.
4. Measure from the top of the rod to where you want the valance to end. Add 14" for the rod pocket, heading, and hem allowances. Write this measurement here:___. This is your cut length.

✏ *Note:* If your fabric has a repeat, follow the directions in "Window Treatment Basics" on page 65.

5. Multiply the cut length by the number of panels needed. Divide this number by 36 to convert the total into yardage; round up to the nearest ¼ yard. This is the amount of fabric and the amount of lining you need. However, if you are using a different width lining, repeat steps 3–5 to calculate the yardage.

Cutting and Sewing

Use ½"-wide seam allowances.

1. Cut panels from the striped fabric and the lining fabric, following the directions for the unlined panel curtains on page 67.

2. Piece the striped panels if necessary. If 2 panels are needed, cut 1 panel in half lengthwise. Stitch 1 half width to each outside edge of a full width of fabric, matching the design motifs. If 3 panels are needed, stitch them together side by side.

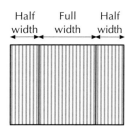

Valance with 2 Panels

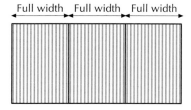

Valance with 3 Panels

3. Piece the lining fabric if necessary. Trim 2" from each side of the lining and 1" from the lower edge.

4. Finish the lower edge of the valance with a 3" double hem.

5. Finish the lower edge of the lining with a 3" double hem.

6. Place the lining over the valance, right sides together; match and pin them together along one side edge.

Note that the lining is 1" shorter and 4" narrower than the valance. Stitch the side seam.

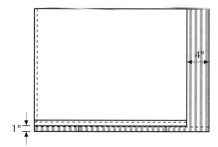

7. Gently pull the lining to meet the opposite edge of the valance; pin, then stitch. Press the seams toward the lining.

8. Turn the valance right side out. Adjust it so the lining is centered from side to side and the striped fabric wraps around to the lining side equally on each side; press. Fold the bottom corners diagonally as shown and hand sew in place.

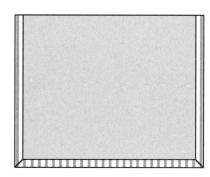

9. Finish the heading, following the directions for the unlined panel curtains, "Sewing," step 4, on page 67.

Table Skirts

Want to start decorating your room and don't know quite where to begin? A floor-length table skirt is one of the most economical solutions for many decorating dilemmas. Although it's shown here in bedrooms, a round table skirt can also be used in the hallway, foyer, living room, den, kitchen, even the bath. Using a simple formula, you can produce a decorative covering for any round table.

BASIC ROUND SKIRT

This table covering is featured in the "Country Room" (page 18).

Materials

44"-wide fabric

Yardage Calculations

1. Measure the diameter of the table-top. Write this measurement here:___.
2. Measure the drop (the distance from the top to the floor or other point where you want the skirt to end). Multiply the drop by 2. Add 2" for hem allowances. Write this total here:___.
3. Add the final measurements in steps 1 and 2. Write this total here:___. This is the cutting diameter of the table skirt.

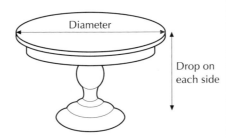

4. To determine the number of fabric panels needed, divide the cutting diameter by the width of the fabric; round up to the nearest whole number. Write this number here:___.
5. Multiply the cutting diameter by the number of panels needed; divide by 36 to convert the total into yardage and round up to the nearest ¼ yard. This is the amount of fabric you need.

Cutting and Sewing

Use ½"-wide seam allowances.

1. Cut the number of panels required for your table skirt. Piece if necessary. If 2 panels are required, use 1 full panel in the center and equal-width panels on either side.

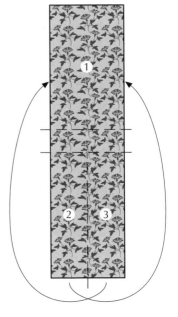

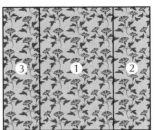

Match the pattern repeat.

SECRET STORAGE

The only drawback to a round table skirt is the empty space it occupies. However, you can turn that empty space into instant storage by making your own table. Go to the hardware store and purchase a large, round plastic garbage can. Cut a plywood circle at least 3" larger than the diameter of the garbage can. (Pre-cut wood circles are available at some hardware stores.) Use the garbage can as the base. Remove the lid and use the plywood circle as the tabletop. Fill this storage area with out-of-season clothing, magazines, etc., or use it as a place to stash fabric.

2. Fold the pieced panels into quarters, right sides together. Make sure the edges are even, the fabric is smooth, and the piecing seams are aligned. Pin randomly to secure the layers.

3. From the inner folded corner or "pivot point," measure a distance equal to ½ the cutting diameter; using a fabric pencil, mark a smooth curve. Cut along the marked line.

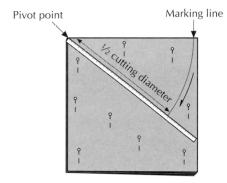

Pivot point   Marking line

½ cutting diameter

4. Unfold the panels. Fold the raw edge of the fabric up 1" to the wrong side; press. Working in small sections, tuck the raw edge under to meet the fold; press again. You have formed a ½" double hem. Stitch or fuse in place.

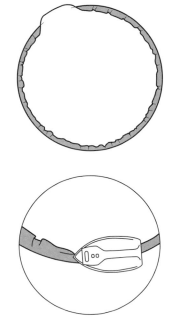

RUFFLED SKIRT

This table covering is featured in the "Romantic Room" (page 15). Two coordinating fabrics were used: one for the skirt and the other for the ruffle.

Materials

44"-wide fabric
Fabric for table skirt
Coordinating fabric for ruffle

Yardage Calculations

THE SKIRT

To determine the yardage for the skirt, refer to the basic round skirt yardage calculations on page 74. In step 3, add the final measurements from steps 1 and 2, then subtract 18". Use this measurement as the cutting diameter in steps 4 and 5.

THE RUFFLE

1. Multiply the cutting diameter of the table skirt by 3 to determine the approximate circumference. Write this measurement here:___.

2. Multiply the circumference by 3 (to add ruffle fullness). Write this measurement here:___. This is your ruffle width.

3. Divide the ruffle width by the fabric width. This will give you the number of crosswise fabric strips needed to make the ruffle. Write the number of strips here:___.

4. The cut length of the ruffle is 11½". Multiply the number of strips by 11½". Divide this number by 36 to convert the total into yardage; round up to the nearest ¼ yard.

CUTTING AND SEWING

Use ½"-wide seam allowances.

1. Follow the directions for the basic round skirt, "Cutting and Sewing," steps 1–3, on pages 74–75.

2. Cut the required number of fabric strips for the ruffle.

3. Stitch the ruffle strips together, end to end, to form a circle.

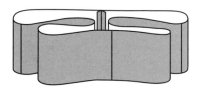

4. Fold the lower edge of the ruffle up 2" to the wrong side; press. Tuck the raw edge in to meet the fold; press again. You have formed a 1" double hem. Stitch or fuse in place.

5. Divide and mark the edge of the table skirt and the upper edge of the ruffle into quarters. Gather the upper edge of the ruffle to fit the lower edge of the table skirt. With right sides together, pin the ruffle to the table skirt, matching the markings. Adjust the gathers to fit. Stitch. Zigzag, overcast, or serge the seam allowances. Press the seam toward the table skirt.

CORDED SKIRT

This table covering is featured in the "Traditional Room" (page 12).

Materials

44"-wide fabric
Fabric for table skirt
Coordinating fabric for welting
¾"-diameter cording for welting

Yardage Calculations

SKIRT FABRIC

To determine the yardage for the skirt, refer to the basic round skirt yardage calculations on page 74. In step 2, add 1" for hem allowances.

To determine the amount of cording, multiply the diameter of the table skirt by 3.25. Divide by 36" to convert the total into yardage.

WELTING FABRIC

Approximately 10 yds. or 360" of 3¾"-wide bias strips can be cut from 1 yard of 44"-wide coordinating fabric. This will provide enough strips to cover cording for a 105"-diameter table skirt.

Cutting and Sewing

1. Follow the directions for the basic round skirt, "Cutting and Sewing," steps 1–3, on pages 74–75.
2. Cut 3¾"-wide bias strips from the coordinating fabric, following the directions for continuous bias strips on page 56.
3. Cover the cording, following the directions on page 56.
4. Working on the right side of the skirt, pin the welting to the lower edge with raw edges even. Stitch, following the directions for applying piping on page 57.
5. Turn the welting down and the seam allowances up to the wrong side of the table skirt. Steam the welting in place. Topstitch the table skirt close to the welting through all layers.

THREE-TIERED SKIRT

This table covering is featured in the "Rustic Room" (page 10), where the unusual combination of flannels and lace coexist in happy harmony. For a more conventional look, choose three coordinated prints or solids that echo the accent colors in your quilt.

Materials

58"-wide flannel fabric for
tabletop and ruffle
44"-wide coordinating fabric for
ruffle
Lace fabric with one decorative
edge for top ruffle
Optional: Fusible interfacing

Yardage Calculations

TABLETOP

1. Measure the diameter of the tabletop; add 1". You will need enough fabric to cut this size circle.
2. If you are using a soft fabric, fusible interfacing will add body. Purchase enough interfacing to reinforce the tabletop fabric.

RUFFLE

Determine the finished length of each ruffle. The lengths are up to you. If you are using lace, the design of the lace may dictate the ruffle proportions. For the 27"-tall table in the "Rustic Room," the top (lace) ruffle is 17" long, the middle ruffle is 19" long, and the bottom ruffle is 27" long. Write your finished length measurements here: top ruffle __"; middle ruffle __"; bottom ruffle __".

To determine the circumference of the tabletop, multiply the diameter by 3.14 or measure around the rim of the tabletop.

For each ruffle:

1. Multiply the tabletop circumference by 2.5 (to add ruffle fullness). Write this measurement here: ____. This is your ruffle width.
2. Divide the ruffle width by the width of the fabric. Write this number here:____. This is the number of crosswise fabric strips needed to make the ruffle.
3. If your lace has a finished edge, add ½" for a seam allowance to the ruffle length to determine the cut length. For all other fabrics, add 2½" seam and hem allowances to the ruffle length to determine the cut length. Write this number here: ____.
4. Multiply the cut length (step 3) by the number of fabric strips. Divide this number by 36 to convert the total into yardage; round up to the nearest ¼ yard.

Cutting

1. Cut a circle of fabric equal to the diameter of the tabletop plus 1". If desired, apply fusible interfacing to the wrong side of this circle.
2. Cut the required number of fabric strips for each ruffle from the appropriate fabric.

Sewing

Use ½"-wide seam allowances.

1. Stitch each set of ruffle strips together, end to end, to form a circle.
2. Fold the lower edge of the ruffle up 2" to the wrong side; press. Tuck the raw edge under to meet the fold; press again. You have formed a 1" double hem. Stitch or fuse in place.

3. Divide and mark the edge of the top and the upper edge of each ruffle into quarters. Gather the upper edge of each ruffle to fit the edge of the tabletop.

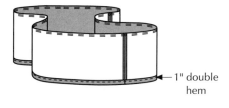

1" double hem

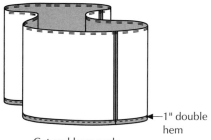

1" double hem

Cut and hem each
ruffle layer individually.

4. With right sides together, pin the top ruffle to the tabletop, matching the markings. Adjust the gathers to fit. Machine baste. Repeat for the middle ruffle, then for the bottom ruffle. Stitch the ruffles to the tabletop. Zigzag, overcast, or serge the seam allowances. Press the seam toward the tabletop.

5. Topstitch around the edge of the tabletop through all layers.

LACE TOPPER

A simple square of lace adds old-world charm to a modern room setting as illustrated in the "Romantic Room" (page 15).

Materials
Lace with 2 decorative (selvage) edges*

*The width of the lace determines the size of the square. The lace used for the topper in the "Romantic Room" is 54" wide, and the finished cloth is 54" square.

Yardage Calculations

Multiply the width of the lace (from selvage to selvage) by 2. Divide this number by 36 to convert the total into yardage; round up to the nearest ¼ yard. This is the amount you need.

Cutting

1. From the lace, cut 2 squares, using the full width of the fabric for the size of the square. For example, from 54"-wide fabric, cut 2 squares, each 54" x 54".
2. Cut each square twice diagonally into quarter-square triangles. Save the 4 triangles that do not have decorative edges for another project.

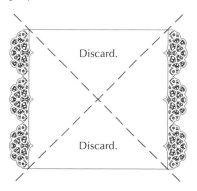

Discard.

Discard.

Sewing

Use ¼"-wide seam allowances.

1. Place 2 quarter-square triangles right sides together with raw edges even. Serge or stitch and overcast together along one raw edge, forming 1 half-square triangle unit. Press the seam to one side. Repeat for the remaining 2 quarter-square triangles.

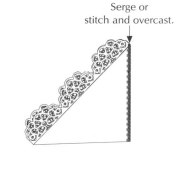

Serge or
stitch and overcast.

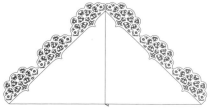

2. Place the 2 half-square triangle units right sides together with center seams aligned. Serge or stitch and overcast along the raw edge. Press the seam to one side. Press the topper flat.

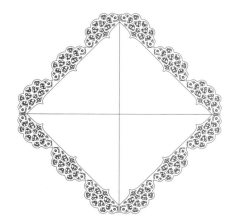

Quiltmaking Basics

FABRIC

Select high-quality, 100% cotton fabrics. They hold their shape well and are easy to handle. Cotton blends can be more difficult to stitch and press. Sometimes, however, the right color or design outweighs the extra attention that may be necessary to control the cotton blend.

Yardage requirements are provided for all the projects in this book. Except for the Rustic Strippy quilt, which uses 58"-wide flannel, they are based on 44"-wide fabric with 42 usable inches after preshrinking. Some quilts call for an assortment of scraps. If you have access to scraps, feel free to use them, then supplement with purchased fabrics in colors that complete your desired quilt project.

To test for colorfastness and to remove excess dye, preshrink all fabrics. Wash dark and light colors separately; otherwise, dark colors may run onto light fabrics. Some fabrics require several rinses to eliminate the excess dyes. Press fabrics so that when the pieces are cut out, they will be accurate.

GENERAL SUPPLIES

Marking tools: A variety of tools are available to mark fabrics when tracing around templates or marking quilting lines. You can also mark fabric with a regular pencil or fine-lead mechanical pencil. Use a silver or yellow marking pencil on darker

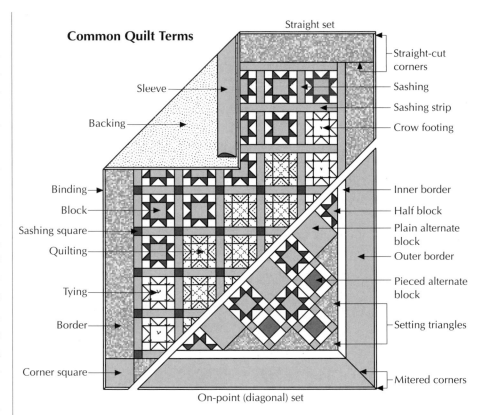

Common Quilt Terms

Straight set
Straight-cut corners
Sashing
Sashing strip
Crow footing
Sleeve
Backing
Inner border
Half block
Plain alternate block
Outer border
Binding
Block
Sashing square
Pieced alternate block
Quilting
Tying
Setting triangles
Border
Corner square
Mitered corners
On-point (diagonal) set

fabrics. Chalk pencils or chalk-wheel markers also make clear marks. Be sure to test whatever tool you decide to use on your fabric first to make sure the marks can be easily removed.

Needles: For machine piecing, a fine needle (size 10/70) works well for most lightweight cottons. For heavier fabrics, use size 12/80.

Rotary-cutting tools: You will need a rotary cutter, cutting mat, and clear acrylic rulers. These tools will speed you on your way to finishing the projects quickly and easily. The mat is specially designed for the rotary cutter; it is self-healing and can withstand

the extremely sharp blade of the cutter. The ruler is used as a guide when measuring and cutting your fabric.

Safety pins: Use No. 2 brass, rust-proof safety pins as an alternative to hand basting the quilt layers.

Scissors: Use your best scissors to cut fabric only. Use an older pair of scissors to cut paper, cardboard, and template plastic. Small, 4" scissors with sharp points are handy for clipping thread.

Seam ripper: Use this tool to remove stitches from incorrectly sewn seams.

Sewing machine. To machine piece, you'll need a sewing machine in top-notch working order and with a good straight stitch. A simple tune-up is strongly recommended, especially if you are cleaning the dust balls off your machine. Nothing is more frustrating than having a machine go haywire after you've started a project.

Special feet: A walking foot and a darning foot are recommended for machine quilting. A walking foot prevents tucks from forming as you machine quilt. A darning foot is required for freehand quilting.

Straight pins: Long, fine quilter's pins, with glass or plastic heads, are easy to handle.

Thread: Use a good-quality, strong, all-purpose cotton or cotton-covered polyester thread. For machine piecing, use a light neutral, such as beige or tan, for light-colored fabrics, and a dark neutral, such as dark gray, for darker fabrics. Use white or light-colored thread for basting. (Dye from dark thread can leave small dots of color on light fabrics.)

ROTARY CUTTING

Instructions for quick and easy rotary cutting are provided wherever possible. All measurements include standard ¼"-wide seam allowances. If you are unfamiliar with rotary cutting, read the brief introduction that follows. For more detailed information, see Donna Thomas's *Shortcuts: A Concise Guide to Rotary Cutting* (published by That Patchwork Place).

Strips and Squares

1. Fold the fabric and match the selvages; align the crosswise and lengthwise grains as much as possible. Place the folded edge closest to you on the cutting mat. To make a cut at a right angle to the fold, align a square ruler along the folded edge of the fabric. Then place a long, straight ruler to the left of the square ruler, just covering the uneven raw edges of the left side of the fabric. Reverse this procedure if you are left-handed.

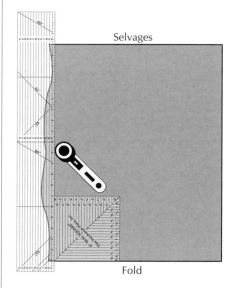

Selvages

Fold

2. Remove the square ruler and cut along the right edge of the ruler, rolling the rotary cutter away from you. Discard this strip.
3. To cut strips, align the required measurement on the ruler with the newly cut edge of the fabric. For example, to cut a 3"-wide strip, place the ruler's 3" mark along the edge of the fabric. All the measurements for cut strips include ¼"-wide seam allowances. Therefore, a 3"-wide strip with a

¼"-wide seam allowance on each long edge will finish to 2½".

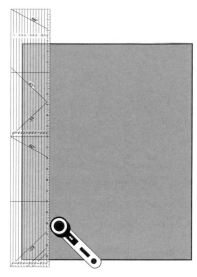

4. To cut squares, cut strips in the required widths. Trim away the selvage ends. Align the required measurement on the ruler with the left edge of the strip, and cut a square. Continue cutting until you have the number of squares needed.

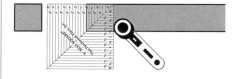

Half-Square Triangles

To make half-square triangles, you will cut a square in half on the diagonal. The short sides of the triangle will be on the straight grain of the fabric. The square's cut size should be ⅞" longer than one short side of the finished triangle to allow for seam allowances.

1. Cut squares the required size as directed in your project.

2. Stack the squares. Align the ruler with 2 diagonally opposite corners; cut the squares in half. Each square yields 2 triangles.

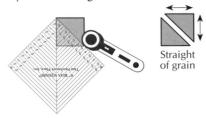

Straight of grain

Quarter-Square Triangles

To make quarter-square triangles, you will cut a square in quarters on the diagonal. The long side of the triangle will be on the straight grain of the fabric. The square's cut size should be 1¼" longer than the long side of the finished triangle to allow for seam allowances.

1. Cut squares the required size as directed in your project.
2. Stack the squares. Align the ruler with 2 diagonally opposite corners; cut the squares in half. Repeat, using the other 2 diagonally opposite corners. Each square yields 4 triangles.

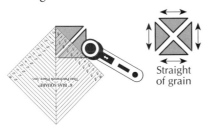

Straight of grain

BASIC MACHINE PIECING

Stitching Basics

Measurements for all components of each quilt are based on blocks that finish accurately to the desired size plus ¼" on each edge for seam allowances. To achieve this, you must maintain a consistent ¼"-wide seam allowance throughout your piecing.

Otherwise, the quilt blocks will not be the desired finished size. If this happens, the size of everything else in the quilt is affected, including alternate blocks, sashings, and borders.

Establishing an Accurate Seam Guide

Take the time to establish an exact ¼"-wide seam guide on your machine. Some machines have a special quilting foot designed so the right-hand and left-hand edges of the foot measure exactly ¼" from the center needle position. This feature allows you to match the edge of the presser foot with the edge of the fabric for a perfect ¼"-wide seam allowance.

If your machine doesn't have a special quilting foot, you can create a seam guide so it will be easy to stitch an accurate ¼"-wide seam allowance.

1. Place a ruler or piece of graph paper with 4 squares to the inch under your presser foot.
2. Gently lower the needle onto the first line, ¼" from the right edge of the ruler or paper. Place several layers of masking tape or a piece of moleskin (available in drugstores) along the right edge of the ruler or paper, making sure it does not interfere with the feed dogs. Test the guide to see if your seams are ¼" wide; if not, reposition the tape or moleskin.

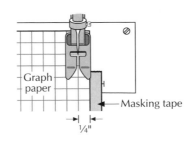

Graph paper

Masking tape

¼"

Chain Piecing

Chain piecing is an efficient system that saves time and thread.

1. Start by joining the first pair of units. Stitch from cut edge to cut edge; use 12 to 15 stitches per inch. At the end of the seam, stop sewing, but do not cut the thread.
2. Feed the next pair of units under the presser foot, as close as possible to the first pair.
3. Continue feeding pieces through the machine without cutting the threads in between.
4. When all the units have been joined, remove the chain from the machine and clip the threads between the units.

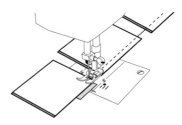

Chain Piecing

Be consistent when you chain-piece. To avoid confusion, start with the same edge on each pair and the same color on top. There is no need to backstitch; each seam will be crossed and held by another seam in the assembly process.

Easing

When joining two units that are slightly different in size (less than ⅛"), pin the places where the two pieces should match and in the middle, if necessary, to distribute the excess fabric evenly. Stitch the seam with the longer piece on the bottom. The feed dogs will ease the two pieces together.

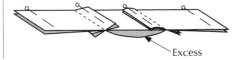

Excess

Pressing

When piecing a quilt, always press; never iron. Pressing is done by lifting the iron up and putting it back down in another spot. Ironing is done with a sweeping, side-to-side motion. Ironing can stretch the fabric and distort the shape of your units.

The traditional rule in quiltmaking is to press seams to one side, toward the darker color whenever possible. After stitching, press the seam flat to "set" the stitches; then open up the seamed unit, place it right side up, and press the seam in the desired direction.

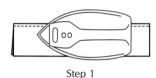

Step 1

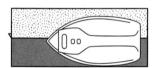

Step 2

When joining two seamed units, plan ahead so you can press the seam allowances in opposite directions as shown. This reduces bulk and makes it easier to match seam lines. Where two seams meet, the seam allowances will butt up against each other, making it easier to join units with perfectly matched seam intersections. Press carefully to avoid distorting the shapes.

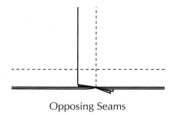

Opposing Seams

SPECIALTY MACHINE PIECING

Half-Square Triangle Units

Half-square triangle units are used in many quilt designs. They are made by sewing two half-square triangles together to make a square. There are several different methods for making these units. Instructions are provided for cut-and-pieced squares and for gridded piecing.

PAIRS OF HALF-SQUARE TRIANGLE UNITS

Using this method, each pair of squares yields two half-square triangle units. To avoid distortion, press the units carefully.

1. Cut squares the required size as directed in your project.
2. Draw a diagonal line from corner to corner on the back of the lightest fabric.

3. Place the square with the drawn line on top of another square, right sides together. Stitch ¼" from the drawn line on both sides. Cut along the drawn line.

4. Press the unit flat, then press the seam allowances toward the darker fabric; trim the points that extend beyond the triangles as shown.

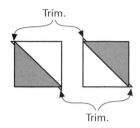

Trim.

Trim.

MULTIPLE HALF-SQUARE TRIANGLE UNITS

Use this method to create multiple half-square triangle units.

1. Cut 2 fabrics into same-size rectangles (no larger than 18" x 22"). Place the fabric rectangles right sides together. On the lighter fabric, draw a border all around, ½" from the edge of the fabric. Then, using the size specified in your project, draw a grid.

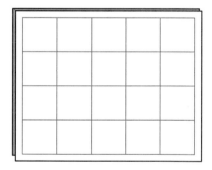

2. Draw a diagonal line through every other row of squares.

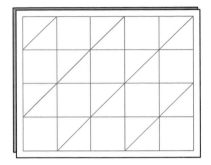

3. Draw diagonal lines in the opposite direction, through the "empty" squares.

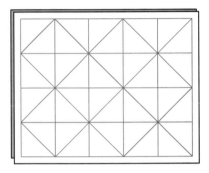

4. Stitch ¼" from and on both sides of the drawn diagonal lines. If you begin at one corner and follow the arrows as indicated, you can stitch in one continuous line.

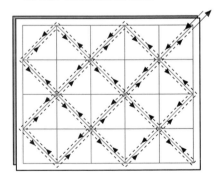

5. After the stitching is completed, cut along the drawn lines.

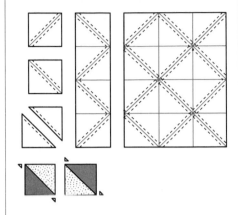

6. Press the seam allowances toward the darker fabric. Trim the points that extend beyond the triangles.

Strip-Pieced Units

Traditionally, individual squares were cut, then sewn together to form a block design. Although there is still a place for this method, strip piecing is usually much faster and just as accurate.

1. Cut the required size and number of strips as directed in your project.
2. Place the strips right sides together. Stitch along one edge, using a ¼"-wide seam allowance and 8 to 10 stitches per inch. Be very careful not to pull on the strips while sewing, as this may cause distortion. Add as many strips as the pattern requires. Press the seam allowances toward the darkest fabric so no shadowing occurs.

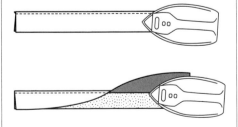

3. With the right side of the fabrics facing up, cut the strips into rows, cutting perpendicular to the seam lines. After several cuts, check the edge; straighten it if necessary.

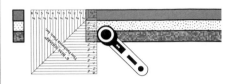

Flying-Geese Units

1. Cut the required number of squares and rectangles as directed in your project.
2. On the wrong side of each square, draw a diagonal line from corner to corner.

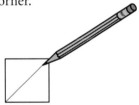

3. With right sides together, match a square to one end of a rectangle. Stitch along the diagonal line. Trim ¼" from the stitching line as shown. Press the seam allowances toward the triangle.

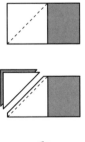

4. With right sides together, match another square to the other end of the rectangle. Stitch along the diagonal line. Trim ¼" from the stitching line as shown. Press the seam allowances toward the triangle.

ASSEMBLING THE QUILT TOP

Squaring the Blocks

When your blocks are complete, take the time to square them up. Using a Bias Square® or a large square ruler, measure your blocks to make sure they are the desired size plus an extra ¼" on each edge for seam allowances. For example, if you are making 6" x 6" blocks, they should all measure 6½" x 6½" before you sew them together. If the sizes of the completed blocks vary greatly, trim the larger ones to match the size of the smallest one. Be sure to evenly trim all four sides; otherwise, your block will be lopsided.

If your finished blocks do not match the finished size as stated in your project, you will have to adjust all the other components (setting triangles, sashing, borders, etc.) accordingly.

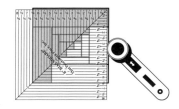

Straight-Set Quilts

1. Arrange the blocks as shown in your project.
2. Stitch the blocks together in horizontal rows. Press the seam allowances in opposite directions from row to row.

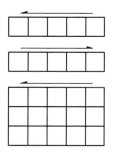

3. Stitch the rows together, aligning the seams between the blocks. Press the seam allowances to one side.

Diagonal-Set Quilts with Sashing

1. Arrange the blocks, side triangles, and corner triangles as shown in your project. Stitch a short sashing strip to the right edge of each block, each left side triangle, and the lower left corner triangle.

2. Stitch the blocks and triangles together in diagonal rows. Press the seam allowances in opposite directions from row to row. Stitch a long sashing strip to the bottom edge of each row and to the top corner triangle as shown.

3. Stitch the rows together, aligning the seams between the blocks. Add the bottom corner triangle last.

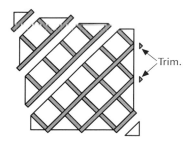

Strippy Quilts

1. Stitch the blocks together in diagonal rows as shown in your project. Press the seam allowances in opposite directions from row to row.
2. Join the diagonal rows into vertical strips. Press the seam allowances in one direction.
3. Stitch a sashing strip to the right and left edge of the first vertical strip. Stitch a sashing strip to the right edge of the remaining vertical strips.
4. Stitch the vertical strips together. Press the seam allowances open.

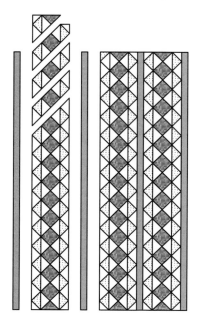

Diagonal Strippy Quilts

This setting is sometimes called a zigzag setting. The setting triangles form a secondary design on the quilt top. *Hint:* Use a print for the setting triangles to disguise the vertical seams that join the strips.

1. Cut the setting triangles so the longest edge is on the straight grain of the fabric.
2. Cut the corner triangles so the right angles are on the straight grain of the fabric.
3. Arrange the blocks and setting triangles as shown in your project. Some blocks will have to be cut into half blocks to finish the alternating strips. To cut these blocks, establish the center line diagonally from corner to corner. Measure ¼" from the center line and cut.

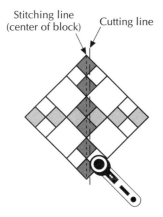

Stitching line (center of block)   Cutting line

4. Stitch the blocks and setting triangles together to form diagonal rows. Press the seam allowances in opposite directions from row to row. Stitch the diagonal rows together to form the vertical strips.

5. Add the corner triangles to the top and bottom edges of the strips that end with a full block.

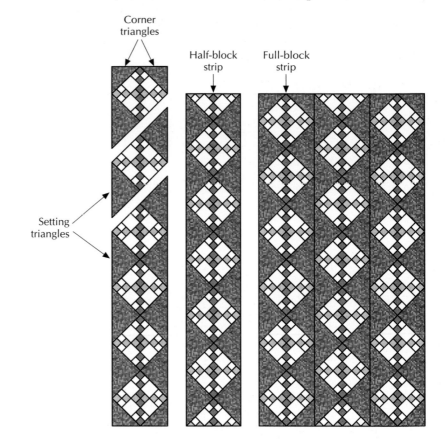

Corner triangles

Half-block strip

Full-block strip

Setting triangles

6. Stitch the vertical strips together, alternating full-block and half-block strips.

BORDERS

For best results, measure and cut borders to the correct size first, then stitch them to the quilt top. Do not cut and stitch border strips to the quilt, then trim them to fit. Doing this usually results in a quilt with wavy borders. This is because the edges of a quilt often stretch during construction. Sometimes, each edge stretches to a different length.

To determine how long to cut the border strips, measure the quilt top through the center in both directions. This method results in a finished quilt that is as straight and as square as possible, without wavy edges.

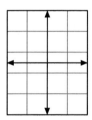

Plain border strips are commonly cut along the crosswise grain and pieced when extra length is needed. Borders can also be cut along the lengthwise grain. This requires extra yardage, but eliminates the need for piecing. *The yardages for the quilts in this book allow for the narrow borders to be cut along the crosswise grain of the fabric, and the wide borders to be cut along the lengthwise grain.*

Borders can be applied with straight-cut or mitered corners. The choice is up to you.

Straight-Cut Borders

1. Measure the length of the quilt top through the center. Cut the side border strips equal to that measurement, piecing if necessary. Mark the center at the side edges of the quilt top and the border strips. With right sides together, pin the borders to the sides of the quilt top, matching the center marks and the ends. Stitch, easing to fit if necessary. Press the seam allowances toward the border.

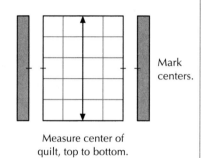

Measure center of quilt, top to bottom.

2. Measure the width of the quilt (including side borders) across the center. Cut the top and bottom border strips equal to that measurement, piecing if necessary. Mark the center at the top and bottom edges of the quilt top and at the edges of each border strip. With right sides together, pin the borders to the top and bottom edges of the quilt top, matching the center marks and ends. Stitch, easing to fit if necessary. Press seam allowances toward the border.

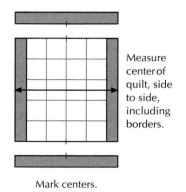

Measure center of quilt, side to side, including borders.

Mark centers.

Mitered-Corner Borders

1. Before you begin, decide how wide you want your border to be. Then, estimate the finished outside dimensions (length and width) of your quilt, including borders. Cut 4 border strips (top, bottom, and sides) equal to the corresponding measurements plus at least ½" for seam allowances. If possible, add 5" to 6" to the cut length to give yourself some leeway. Mark the centers of the quilt edges and the border strips.

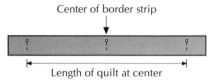

Center of border strip

Length of quilt at center

☞ *Note:* If your quilt will have multiple borders, stitch the individual border strips together to create four border sections (top, bottom, and sides). Treat each section as a single border strip. This will make mitering the corners easier and more accurate.

2. With right sides together, pin 1 border strip to the quilt top, matching the centers. The strip should extend the same distance at each end of the quilt top. Stitch, using a ¼"-wide seam allowance. Begin and end stitching ¼" from the corners of the quilt top. Press the seam allowances toward the borders. Repeat for the other 3 border strips.

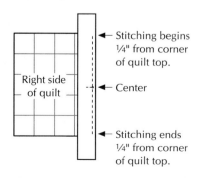

Right side of quilt

Stitching begins ¼" from corner of quilt top.

Center

Stitching ends ¼" from corner of quilt top.

3. Place the first corner to be mitered on the ironing board. Fold one strip under at a 45° angle. Adjust, if necessary, until the seam lines—or the bars in a plaid or striped fabric—match. Press and pin.

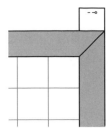

4. With right sides together, fold the upper edge of the quilt down until the edges of the top and side borders match. If necessary, use a ruler and a pencil to draw a line along the crease to make it more visible. Beginning at the inside corner, stitch along the crease line.

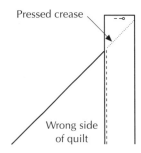

Pressed crease

Wrong side of quilt

5. Press the seam allowances open. Trim the excess border fabric, leaving a ¼"-wide seam allowance.
6. Repeat for the remaining corners.

MARKING THE QUILTING LINES

Not all quilting designs require marking. It is not necessary if you plan to quilt in-the-ditch or outline-quilt by stitching a uniform distance from the seam lines. However, most other quilting designs require marking.

Mark the quilt top *before* layering the quilt. Choose a marking tool that will be visible on your fabric. Test it on fabric scraps to make sure the marks can be removed easily. See "Marking tools" on page 78 for options. Masking tape can also be used to mark straight quilting lines. If you choose this method, work on one small section at a time and remove the tape when you stop at the end of the day. Otherwise, the sticky residue may be difficult to remove from the fabric.

ASSEMBLING THE LAYERS

Backing

Cut the quilt backing so that it extends 2" to 4" beyond the outer edges of the quilt top. For large quilts, it is usually necessary to piece two or three lengths of fabric to make a backing that is wider than the quilt top. Depending on the width of your quilt and your backing fabric, the backing can be made from two equal-width panels or from one full-width center panel and two narrower side panels. Trim the selvages before piecing the lengths. After piecing, press the seam allowances open—it will make quilting easier.

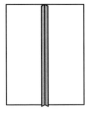

Two lengths of fabric seamed in the center

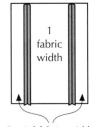

1 fabric width

Partial fabric width

Batting

Batting comes packaged in standard bed sizes, or it can be purchased by the yard. Several weights or thicknesses are available. Thick or high-loft battings are fine for tied quilts and comforters. A thin or low-loft batting is better if you intend to quilt by hand or machine.

Thin batting is available in 100% cotton, 100% polyester, and cotton-polyester blends. All-cotton batting is soft and drapeable but requires close quilting, while polyester and cotton-polyester battings require less quilting.

Unroll your batting and let it relax overnight before you layer your quilt. Some batting may need to be prewashed, while others should definitely not be prewashed; check the package for the manufacturer's instructions.

Layering

1. Press the backing to remove any wrinkles. Spread the backing, wrong side up, on a clean, flat surface. Anchor it with pins or masking tape. (Be careful not to stretch the backing out of shape.)
2. Spread the batting over the backing; smooth out any wrinkles.
3. Place the pressed quilt top on top of the batting. Working from the center to the outside edges, smooth out any wrinkles. Make sure the edges of the quilt top are parallel to the edges of the backing.
4. If machine quilting, pin-baste the layers with No. 2 rustproof safety pins. Place the pins about 6" to 8" apart and away from the area you intend to quilt. If hand quilting, hand baste the layers with needle and thread. No matter which method you choose, always start in the center and work diagonally out

to each corner. Then, when the diagonal basting is done, create a grid of horizontal and vertical basting lines, 6" to 8" apart. Finish by hand basting around the edges.

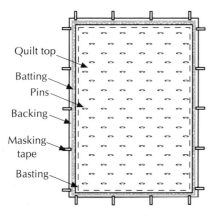

Quilt top
Batting
Pins
Backing
Masking tape
Basting

Pin-baste for machine quilting.

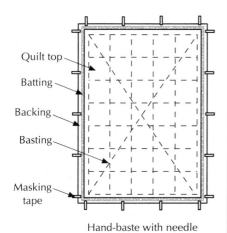

Quilt top
Batting
Backing
Basting
Masking tape

Hand-baste with needle and thread for hand quilting.

QUILTING TECHNIQUES

Traditional Hand Quilting

To quilt by hand, you will need short, sturdy needles (called "Betweens"), quilting thread, and a thimble to fit the middle finger of your sewing hand. Most quilters also use a frame or hoop to support their work. Quilting needles run from sizes 3 to 12; the higher the number, the smaller the needle. Use the smallest needle you can comfortably handle. The smaller the needle, the smaller your stitches.

1. Thread your needle with a single strand of quilting thread about 18" long, and make a small knot at one end. Insert the needle into the top layer, about 1" from the place where you want to start quilting. Push the needle out at the point where the quilting will begin. Gently pull the thread until the knot pops through the fabric and into the batting.

2. To take small, evenly spaced stitches through all three quilt layers, rock the needle up and down through all layers, until you have 3 or 4 stitches on the needle. Place your other hand underneath the quilt so you can feel the needle point with the tip of your finger when a stitch is taken.

3. To end a line of quilting, make a small knot close to the last stitch; then take a small backstitch, running the thread a needle's length through the batting. Push the needle out and gently pull the thread until the knot pops down into the batting; clip the thread at the quilt's surface.

Machine Quilting

Machine quilting is suitable for all types of quilts, from crib-size to full-size bed quilts. With machine quilting, you can quickly complete quilts that might otherwise languish on the shelf.

1. For straight-line quilting, a walking foot is extremely beneficial. It will help feed the quilt layers through the machine without shifting or puckering. Some machines have a built-in walking foot; other machines require a separate attachment. If you do not have a walking foot, make sure the layers of the quilt are well basted. Practice stitching on some layered scraps to see how your machine stitches without a walking foot. Adjust the thread tension and presser-foot pressure if necessary.

Walking Foot

Quilting in-the-Ditch

Outline Quilting

2. For free-motion quilting, you need a darning foot and the ability to drop the feed dogs on your machine. With free-motion quilting, you do not turn the fabric under

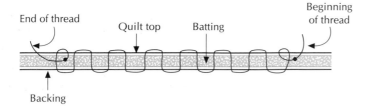

End of thread
Quilt top
Batting
Beginning of thread
Backing

the needle, but instead guide the fabric in the direction of the design. Use free-motion quilting to outline-quilt a pattern in the fabric or to create stippling and many other curved designs.

Darning Foot

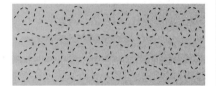
Stippling

To learn more about quilting by machine or by hand, refer to *Machine Quilting Made Easy* by Maurine Noble or *Loving Stitches: A Guide to Fine Hand Quilting* by Jeana Kimball (both published by That Patchwork Place).

BINDING

The yardages provided in this book were calculated for straight-grain binding strips.

To cut straight-grain binding strips:

Cut 2½"-wide strips across the width of the fabric. You will need enough strips to go around the perimeter of the quilt plus 10" for seams and mitered corners. To piece the strips, place the ends at right angles, right sides together, offsetting the strips ¼". Stitch diagonally from inside corner to inside corner as shown.

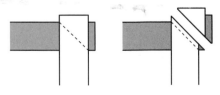
Joining Straight-Cut Strips

To attach the binding:

1. Trim the batting and backing even with the quilt-top edges.
2. Trim one end of the binding at a 45° angle. Turn under ¼" and press.

3. Fold the binding in half lengthwise, wrong sides together; press.

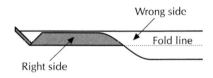
Wrong side
Fold line
Right side

4. Starting approximately 5" from the pressed end of the binding, stitch the binding to the quilt. Keep the raw edges even and use a ¼"-wide seam allowance.
5. To miter each corner, stop stitching ¼" from the corner; backstitch. Clip the thread. Fold the binding up, away from the quilt, then fold the binding back down on itself so it forms a right angle as shown. Begin stitching at the edge of the quilt; backstitch to secure.

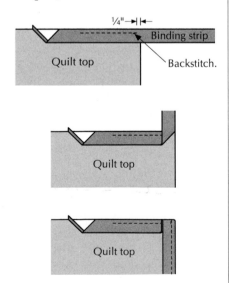
¼"
Binding strip
Quilt top
Backstitch.

Quilt top

Quilt top

6. When the last corner is mitered, stitch to within 3" of the beginning of the binding. Trim the excess binding so the ends overlap about 1". Trim at a 45° angle. Tuck the cut end of the binding into the folded end and finish stitching.

Quilt top

7. Fold the binding over the raw edges to the back of the quilt, covering the stitching and forming a miter at each corner. Blindstitch the binding in place on the quilt back and along the mitered folds.

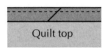
Quilt back   Quilt back

LABELS

Labels can be as elaborate or as simple as you desire. The information can be handwritten, typed, or embroidered. Be sure to sign and date your quilt; future generations will be interested to know more than just who made it and when. Include the name of the quilt, your name, your city and state, the date, the name of the recipient if it is a gift, and any other interesting or important information about the quilt.

For more information about finishing quilts, refer to *Happy Endings* by Mimi Dietrich (published by That Patchwork Place).